Studies in International Performance

Published in association with the International Federation of Theatre Research

General Editors: **Janelle Reinelt** and **Brian Singleton**

Culture and performance cross borders constantly, and not just the borders that define nations. In this new series, scholars of performance produce interactions between and among nations and cultures as well as genres, identities and imaginations.

Inter-national in the largest sense, the books collected in the *Studies in International Performance* series display a range of historical, theoretical and critical approaches to the panoply of performances that make up the global surround. The series embraces 'Culture' which is institutional as well as improvised, underground or alternate, and treats 'Performance' as either intercultural or transnational as well as intracultural within nations.

Titles include:

Patrick Anderson and Jisha Menon *(editors)*
VIOLENCE PERFORMED
Local Roots and Global Routes of Conflict

Elaine Aston and Sue-Ellen Case
STAGING INTERNATIONAL FEMINISMS

Christopher Balme
PACIFIC PERFORMANCES
Theatricality and Cross-Cultural Encounter in the South Seas

Susan Leigh Foster
WORLDING DANCE

Helen Gilbert and Jacqueline Lo
PERFORMANCE AND COSMOPOLITICS
Cross-Cultural Transactions in Australasia

Helena Grehan
PERFORMANCE, ETHICS AND SPECTATORSHIP IN A GLOBAL AGE

Judith Hamera
DANCING COMMUNITIES
Performance, Difference, and Connection in the Global City

Silvija Jestrovic and Yana Meerzon *(editors)*
PERFORMANCE, EXILE AND 'AMERICA'

Sonja Arsham Kuftinec
THEATRE, FACILITATION, AND NATION FORMATION IN THE BALKANS AND MIDDLE EAST

Alan Read
THEATRE, INTIMACY & ENGAGEMENT
The Last Human Venue

Joanne Tompkins
UNSETTLING SPACE
Contestations in Contemporary Australian Theatre

S. E. Wilmer
NATIONAL THEATRES IN A CHANGING EUROPE

Forthcoming titles:
Adrian Kear
THEATRE AND EVENT

Studies in International Performance
Series Standing Order ISBN 978–1–4039–4456–6 (hardback) 978–1–4039–4457–3
(paperback)
(*outside North America only*)

You can receive future titles in this series as they are published by placing a stand-ing order. Please contact your bookseller or, in case of difficulty, write to us at the address below with your name and address, the title of the series and the ISBN quoted above.

Customer Services Department, Macmillan Distribution Ltd, Houndmills, Basingstoke, Hampshire RG21 6XS, England

Performance, Exile and 'America'

Edited by

Silvija Jestrovic

and

Yana Meerzon

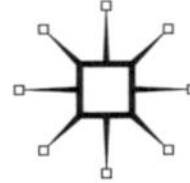

First published 2009 by
PALGRAVE MACMILLAN

Palgrave Macmillan in the UK is an imprint of Macmillan Publishers Limited,
registered in England, company number 785998, of Houndmills, Basingstoke,
Hampshire RG21 6XS.

Palgrave Macmillan in the US is a division of St Martin's Press LLC,
175 Fifth Avenue, New York, NY 10010.

Palgrave Macmillan is the global academic imprint of the above companies
and has companies and representatives throughout the world.

Palgrave® and Macmillan® are registered trademarks in the United States,
the United Kingdom, Europe and other countries.

ISBN-13: 978–0–230–57456–4   hardback

This book is printed on paper suitable for recycling and made from fully
managed and sustained forest sources. Logging, pulping and manufacturing
processes are expected to conform to the environmental regulations of the
country of origin.

A catalogue record for this book is available from the British Library.

A catalog record for this book is available from the Library of Congress.

10   9   8   7   6   5   4   3   2   1
18 17 16 15 14 13 12 11 10 09

Printed and bound in Great Britain by
CPI Antony Rowe, Chippenham and Eastbourne

Contents

List of Illustrations

Series Preface

In 2003, the current International Federation for Theatre Research President, Janelle Reinelt, pledged the organization to expand the outlets for scholarly publication available to the membership, and to make scholarly achievement one of the main goals and activities of the Federation under her leadership. In 2004, joined by Vice-President for Research and Publications Brian Singleton, they signed a contract with Palgrave Macmillan for a new book series, "Studies in International Performance".

Since the inauguration of the series, it has become increasingly urgent for performance scholars to expand their disciplinary horizons to include the comparative study of performances across national, cultural, social, and political borders. This is necessary not only in order to avoid the homogenizing tendency to limit performance paradigms to those familiar in our home countries, but also in order to be engaged in creating new performance scholarship that takes account of and embraces the complexities of transnational cultural production, the new media, and the economic and social consequences of increasingly international forms of artistic expression. Comparative studies can value both the specifically local and the broadly conceived global forms of performance practices, histories, and social formations. Comparative aesthetics can challenge the limitations of perception and current artistic knowledges. In formalizing the work of the Federation's members through rigorous and innovative scholarship, we hope to contribute to an ever-changing project of knowledge creation.

International Federation for Theatre Research
Fédération Internationale pour la Recherche Théâtrale

Acknowledgements

The appearance of the current volume *Performance, Exile and 'America'* is the final step in a long history of its co-editors' collaboration that started in 2002 when we were part of the organizing team for the international conference on theatre and exile that took place at the Graduate Centre for the Study of Drama, University of Toronto. The subject of theatre and exile has since become our major research interest, our teaching focus, and a way of understanding our own émigré experiences and realities.

The editors of the Palgrave series in "Studies in International Performance", Janelle Reinelt and Brian Singleton, have been instrumental in the process of taking our collaboration further. Their kind attention, precise feedback, ongoing support, and encouragement have been invaluable throughout this process.

Moreover, this endeavor would not be possible without the financial help of the Social Sciences and Humanities Research Council, Canada; the Faculty of Arts at the University of Ottawa; the British Council; and the Arts and Humanities Research Council, UK.

We would also like to express our gratitude to all the hard-working individuals at Palgrave, first of all to Paula Kennedy and Steven Hall, who thoroughly guided us through a difficult and meticulous process of selecting, editing, and correcting all the chapters.

This book would never have reached its audience without the intellectual support of the American Society for Theater Research, where the original seminar on Exile and America took place in November 2006, and the Canadian Association for Theatre Research (CATR), where ideas for this book were developed further. We are grateful to our families, friends, colleagues, and students at the University of Ottawa and the University of Warwick, to everyone who spent hours reading and proofing the chapters in this collection and sharing their thoughts on exile, performance, and America with us, especially Milija Gluhovic and Lisa Fitzpatrick. We would like to say a special "thank you" to Dragan Todorovic, who provided the original drawing for the cover of this volume.

Last but not least, we would like to pay special tribute to all our authors – without their patience, loyalty, enthusiasm, persistence, and belief in the project this collection would never have reached its readership.

Notes on Contributors

Alan Ackerman is an Associate Professor in the English Department of the University of Toronto. He is the author of *The Portable Theater: American Literature & the Nineteenth-Century Stage* (Johns Hopkins University Press 1999), and co-editor with Martin Puchner of *Against Theatre: Creative Destructions on the Modernist Stage* (Palgrave 2006), and editor of the journal *Modern Drama*.

Veronika Ambros is an Associate Professor at the Department of Slavic Languages and Literatures and Centre of Comparative Literatures at the University of Toronto. She is co-editor of *Structuralism(s) Today: Paris, Prague, Tartu* (Legas, 2009). Among her most recent publications are articles on the semiotics of drama and theatre: "Prague's Experimental Stage: Laboratory of Theatre and Semiotics" (in *Semiotica*, 2008, 168: 45–65); as well as articles on Czech cinema and literature such as "Daleká cesta. Sv decká výpov Alfréda Radoka" ("Distant Journey. The witness testimony of A. Radok"), in Eva Stehlíková (ed.), *Alfréd Radok Mezi Filmem a Divadlem* (*Alfréd Radok between Film and Theatre*) (AMU, 2007), "'Engaged Playwrights': Czech Drama between Enlightenment and Gentle Revolution", in J. J. King (ed.), *Western Drama through the Ages* (Greenwood Press, 2007); as well as contributions on Czech Surrealism, Jaroslav's Hašek's novel, *The Fortunes of the Good Soldier Švejk*, the work of Josef and Karel Čapek, and Golem on stage and screen to the *History of the Literary Cultures in East-Central Europe*, edited by Marcel Cornis-Pope and John Neubauer.

Dalia Basiouny is an Egyptian artist, academic, translator and newscaster. She teaches theatre at Helwen University, Egypt. Her theatre work includes directing 13 plays and curating "Playing with the Rules: Arab American Women Writers/Performers" at the Segel center. Her PhD, from the City University of New York Graduate Center, examines the political theatre of Arab-American Women Theatre after 9/11. Currently, she is developing *She and Me*, a performance piece examining the connections between women's experiences in the United States and Arab countries, and writing *Pharoes in New York* a feature film about Arab-Americans during the War on Iraq. She is the editor of the *Arab American Women Theatre Anthology* (forthcoming) and a recipient of many awards including the Fulbright Arts Grant (USA), and the British Council Chevening Scholarship (UK).

Marvin Carlson is the Sidney E. Cohn Professor of Theatre and Comparative Literature at the Graduate Center of the City University of New York. He has received an honorary doctorate from the University of Athens, the ATHE Career Achievement Award, the ASTR Distinguished Scholarship Award, the George Jean Nathan Award for Dramatic Criticism, and the Calloway Prize for writing in theatre. He is the founding editor of the journal *Western European Stages*, and the author of over one hundred scholarly articles in the areas of theatre history, theatre theory, and dramatic literature. Among his books are *The Theatre of the French Revolution* (1966), *Goethe and the Weimar Theatre* (1978), *Theories of the Theatre* (1984), *Places of Performance* (1989), *Theatre Semiotics: Signs of Life* (1990), *Performance: A Critical Introduction* (1996), *Voltaire and the Theatre of the Eighteenth Century* (1998), *The Haunted Stage* (2001) and *Speaking in Tongues* (2006). His work has been translated into 14 languages.

Lisa Fitzpatrick holds a PhD from the Graduate Centre for Study of Drama, University of Toronto, having previously studied at Trinity College, Dublin, and University College, Dublin. She now lectures in Drama at the University of Ulster in the United Kingdom. Her research and supervisory interests are in space and performance, site-specific theatre, women's writing, and the performance of violence. She has published on Martin McDonagh, contemporary theatre in Ireland, and the works of Irish women playwrights. She is currently working on an edited collection of essays on the performance of violence in contemporary Ireland.

Erith Jaffe-Berg is an Assistant Professor at the Department of Theatre at the University of California, Riverside. Her research interests include: multilingual theatre, *commedia dell'arte* and the staging of the Middle East in theatre and performance. She has published articles in *The Journal of Dramatic Theory and Criticism*, *Translation Perspectives*, *The European Studies Journal*, *il cannocchiale*, *Text and Presentation*, and *Quaderni d'Italinistica*. She has also contributed to the anthology *International Dramaturgy: Translations & Transformations in the Theatre of Timberlake Wertenbake* (PIE-Peter Lang Press, 2008) and her translation into Hebrew of *Polygraph* by the French-Canadian playwrights Robert Lepage and Marie Brassard has been published in *Canadian Plays: An Anthology* (The Hebrew University Magnes Press, 2005). Her book on multilingualism in the *commedia dell'arte, The Multilingual Art of Commedia dell'Arte,* is forthcoming from Legas Press, Ottawa. For her work, Prof. Jaffe-Berg has been awarded a National Endowment for the Humanities grant as well as a grant from the Canadian embassy. She is a member of the Son of Semele Theatre Ensemble (SOSE), an LA-based theatre company.

Diana Manole is a Doctoral Candidate at the Graduate Centre for the Study of Drama, University of Toronto, where she is completing her dissertation on post-colonial and post-communist dramas, focusing on the representation of national identity. She has presented papers at academic conferences such as ASTR 2005-08, CATR 2008, MATC 2006, FOOT 2004 and 2006, and ATHE 2003. Her article, "'What Language Shall We Pray In?' Post-Colonial Approaches to Sacred Texts and Rituals in Canadian Contemporary Drama", was published in *The Journal of Religion and Theatre*, Vol. 5, No. 2, Fall 2006. Her main research and teaching interests are: world theatre history; theory of drama and performance; exilic drama and theatre; theatre directing and playwriting. In addition to her academic work, Manole is a professional director, writer, and journalist. Her literary work has been translated and published in Romanian, English, Polish, German, it has received 14 awards, including Second Prize at the Romanian National Comedy Festival for the political parody *The Textile Revolution* (Bucharest: Palimpsest, 2007), and has been reviewed in *The History of Romanian Literature: Drama* (2008) and *The History of Romanian Contemporary Literature 1941–2000* (2005), among others.

Yael Prizant is an Assistant Professor in the Department of Film, Television, and Theatre at the University of Notre Dame, USA, where she teaches dramatic literature and dramaturgy courses. Her main areas of interest include modern Cuban and Cuban-American theatre, Latino/a drama, and theories of globalization and identification. She earned her doctorate in theatre at the University of California, Los Angeles, and her master of fine arts in dramaturgy at the University of Massachusetts, Amherst. While serving as Literary Manager for The Grace Players in Hollywood and Company of Angels in Los Angeles, she assisted playwrights in developing new works and adapted texts for the stage. Her work includes production dramatugy on university and professional shows over the past 15 years. She has written for *Theatre Journal, Gestos,* and other publications.

Freddie Rokem is the Emanuel Herzikowitz Professor for nineteenth- and twentieth-century Art and teaches in the Department of Theatre

Studies at Tel Aviv University, where he served as the Dean of the Yolanda and David Katz Faculty of the Arts (2002–06). He is a permanent visiting Professor at Helsinki University, Finland, and during 2007–08 he was a visiting Professor at Stanford University, the Free University in Berlin, and the University of California, Berkeley. He is editor of *Theatre Research International* (2006–09). Rokem's book *Performing History: Theatrical Representations of the Past in Contemporary Theatre*, published by University of Iowa Press (2000), received the ATHE (Association for Theatre in Higher Education) Prize for best theatre studies book in 2001. *Strindberg's Secret Codes* was published by Norvik Press (2004) and *Philosophers and Thespians: Thinking Performance* is forthcoming (2009) from Stanford University Press. He is also a translator and a dramaturg and has published numerous articles on Israeli and European theatre as well as on theoretical issues in theatre and performance studies.

Jerry Wasserman is Professor of English and Theatre and Head of the Department of Theatre and Film at the University of British Columbia in Vancouver. He has published widely on dramatic literature and theatre history, including the books *Spectacle of Empire: Marc Lescarbot's Theatre of Neptune in New France* (2006), *Theatre and AutoBiography: Writing and Performing Lives in Theory and Practice*, co-edited with Sherrill Grace (2006), and *Modern Canadian Plays* (4th edition, 2001). Wasserman is an actor with more than 200 credits for stage, film, and television.

Introduction: Framing 'America' – Between *Exilic Imaginary* and *Exilic Collective*

Silvija Jestrovic and Yana Meerzon

An unemployed émigré writer sits in his cockroach-infested apartment in New York and reminisces, not without irony, about an anti-American exhibition he saw in his native Poland:

> The exhibit was meant to evoke horror, disgust, and hatred. It had, however, the opposite effect. Thousands of Varsovians, dressed in their holiday best, waiting everyday in lines as long as those to see Lenin's Tomb and in solemn silence looked at the display, listened respectfully to the boogie-woogie, wanting in this way, at least, to manifest their blind and hopeless love for the United States.
>
> (Glowacki: 103)

The situation of the Polish émigré in Janusz Glowacki's play *Hunting Cockroaches* embodies the complexities of exile and the ambivalence of "America" as a space one longs to reach. The world of Glowacki's protagonist encompasses a wide spectrum of the exilic phenomenon covered by the works in this collection. On the one hand, there is internal exile and an almost pleasurable dream of the remote and happier place – the 'America' of the *exilic imaginary*. On the other hand is the reality of physical exile in America that involves its politics, its economics, and its survival strategies. In both instances, albeit from different ends, 'America' is constructed through interplays, contrasts, and clashes between an immigrant's desire and actual experience, each of which helps to shape a communal body of the marginalized and of the displaced, that we will here name th*e exilic collective*.

The idea for this volume emerged from the *Exile and America* seminar that took place in Chicago in 2006 as a part of the American Association for Theatre Research Conference and more than ten years after Glowacki wrote his coming-to-America play. Some of the dreams and realities of the exilic experience depicted in this play still seem very vivid and relevant today, even with a changed political landscape in the background. Chapters in this collection deal with the 'America' of the *exilic imaginary* and of the *exilic collective,* moving from metaphor to first-hand experience and back. The chapters range in focus from studies of artists with direct experience of exile and immigration (as in Manole, Prizant, Meerzon, Jestrovic) to issues of internal or self-imposed exile (Ackerman). Some authors are interested in the representation of the *Other* (Ambros, Jaffe-Berg, Basiouny, Carlson, Wasserman); others are concerned with space and identity (Fitzpatrick, Rokem). Historical frameworks also vary – from visions of exilic America in early twentieth-century Germany to the post-9/11 United States. However, all of these chapters, each in its own unique way, deal with the dynamics of exilic 'America', the spatial-temporal continuum that appears at the crossroads of immigrants' collective and individual imaginary as well as their everyday experience as *Other* in a new land. This volume highlights the *exile/America* chronotope as the primary framework within which to situate and explore its two key aspects and their correlations – *the exilic imaginary* and the *exilic collective.*

Exile/America: the chronotope

The common point to all of the chapters in this collection is that exile and "America" emerge as a *chronotope* – a poetic, political, and performative space/time concept that Mikhail Bakhtin described in the following way:

> In the literary artistic chronotope, spatial and temporal indicators are fused into one carefully thought-out, concrete whole. Time, as it were, thickens, takes on flesh, becomes artistically visible; likewise, space becomes charged and responsive to the movements of time, plot and history.
>
> (84)

Exile/America is the chronotope of transition and transformation, concretized through countless varieties of cultural, ethnic, and political practices, but also through fantasies. This particular chronotope appears as vast and broad as its geographical and cultural dimensions, metaphors, realities, and preconceptions that stand behind its two keywords. Within this chronotope, thus, broad and somewhat open-ended questions emerge that nonetheless need to be reiterated. First, what is exile? How broadly can we frame this notion before it becomes too open-ended and loses its epistemological potential? Second, why 'America' and what turns it into such a compelling exilic metaphor? Last but not least, how do theatrical and performative dimensions concretize the *exile/America* chronotope?

Exile

The most quoted source on the subject of exile is certainly Edward Said, who in his essay "Reflections on Exile" writes that "just beyond the frontier between 'us' and the 'outsider' is the perilous territory of not-belonging: this is to where in the primitive time peoples were banished, and where in the modern era immense aggregates of humanity loiter as refugees and displaced persons" (177). Said then tries to make the meaning of the term even more specific through sub-definitions, distinguishing among refugees, expatriates, and émigrés – among those who were forced into exile and those who had a choice.[1]

While Said reminds us that exile is context-specific, political, and historical, Ellie Wiesel places the notion within the framework of an essentially existentialist trope, when he writes: "At the end, all mortals find a last exile or a last home – what do they call it, a resting place? – in the grave. Is history, then, nothing else but a journey from exile to exile? Social exile, criminal exile, political exile, religious exile" (20). Yet, to illustrate his position, Wiesel continually refers to the Jewish history of exodus, proving that even metaphysical exile cannot escape the iron wings of Walter Benjamin's angel of history.

Similarly, Svetlana Boym warns against romanticizing exile and the tendency to confuse it with various forms of social and spiritual alienation. She insists that "exile cannot be treated as a mere metaphor – otherwise one could fall into somewhat facile argument that every intellectual is always already a 'spiritual exile.' Rather, it is the other way around: actual experience of exile offers an ultimate test to the writer's metaphors and theories of estrangement" (243).

Said has argued that what distinguishes twentieth-century exile from exile in other periods is its unprecedented scale. Moreover, we might argue, at the beginning of the twenty-first century it is no longer only the scale of the exilic situation, but also its scope that has been starting to play an important role in Western cultural and political consciousness. On one side of the spectrum is the *new other* – a stronger breed of the outsider who poses a threat to locals whether by snatching high-paid jobs or by being a potential terrorist. On the other side, the figure of an uprooted, stateless person has been emerging as the major player in contemporary discourse on transnationalism, cosmopolitanism, and democracy from Hannah Arendt to reiterations of her ideas in the works of Giorgio Agamben and others.

In literature and theatre, exile is embodied through metaphor and document, metonymy and stylization. The problem is not the broad nature of the term, but the ways in which exile through discourse and performance turns too easily into a shared experience and becomes de-historicized. Even if the notion of "exile" is viewed within one geographical context – America in this case – it clearly cannot be depicted through a singular cultural/political paradigm nor can its theatrical and dramatic renderings be expressed through a universal model. "Exile" and "the exilic" only work as umbrella terms if they are used so as to make us acutely aware that there are different levels of exilic loss and pain, and no equal opportunities for experiencing *pleasures of exile* (Said, Lamming). In other words, the discourse on exile does not only concern issues of place and displacement, but also the framing of these categories along temporal and historical axes.

'America'

'America' is a contested term for a contested site, and in this book too, it appears as a euphemism for the United States. Why does the *exile/America* chronotope become so tightly framed within the geopolitical borders of the United States in this discourse? On the one hand, as the authors of the book *Why Do People Hate America*, Ziauddin Sardar and Merry Wyn Davies, point out, the explanation is in the hegemonic politics of the United States:

> [...] we are conscious that we use the word 'America', as everyone else does, repeatedly and indiscriminately. Like the 19th-century 'Monroe Doctrine', this unconscious usage ascribes all of the Americas as the natural sphere of interest of just one of its nation states, the USA. That everyone understands the word 'America' to refer to the USA is a testimony to power founded on wealth of resources, economic strength and its application to an idea of nationhood that is unique.
>
> (8)

On the other hand, possible answers to this phenomenon might stretch between the modernist past and the post-9/11 present, and between the imaginary and practiced spaces the term encompasses. Over centuries of exile and immigration and from "distant shores", the geographical space within the US borders – 'America', "where I never will be", as a Russian popular song has it – has been imagined as a promise of democracy, freedom, and opportunity. Throughout the twentieth century the United States was home to exiles and immigrants escaping Nazi Germany, running away from Stalinist purges, fleeing the conflict on the Balkans. On the other hand, the post-Cold War United States has spread way beyond its borders, making it impossible for the rest of the world to escape its TV sitcoms and its celebrities, its Big Macs and Starbucks Tall Lattes, its oil wars and its military interventions. Moreover, the United States' recent foreign politics has often been a direct cause for displacement of so many around the world.

While the number of applicants for the USA Lottery Green Card hasn't really declined in the past few years, American cultural and political context – marked by the post-9/11 traumas and anxieties, war-mongering politics of George W. Bush, and the growing anti-Americanism – has made the contradictions of 'America' as an exilic space even more complicated, giving rise to new exilic voices and different views on both 'America' and exile. This collection tries to capture the ambivalence of 'America' as an exilic space where cultural imagination and critique go hand-in-hand and where the figure of the exilic *Other* has been perpetually constructed and dismantled. It attempts to investigate the tensions in the *exile/America* chronotope embodied through the images of immigrants processing through New York's iconic Ellis Island into a new life at the turn of the twentieth century and in the images of Guantanamo Bay's detainees from the beginning of the twenty-first century.

Yet the *exile/America* chronotope is multilayered and allusive. It is impossible to capture within the covers of one volume its countless imaginaries and all of its communities that share the experiences of exile and immigration, nor is it possible to fully encompass the chronotope's ever-expending performative vocabulary and repertoire. Covering a wide chronological spectrum – from modernism to 9/11 and the war in Iraq, this volume attempts to capture the complexities of the place and its rendering through the experience of exile and through its performativity, but also to offer workable conceptual models for further explorations. Final chapter drafts for this collection were completed in the fall of 2008 on the eve of the US presidential elections. This volume, thus, emerges between 'America' as a geopathology (Chaudhuri) – a problem place – and 'America' as a place of renewed hope, whose new "utopian performatives" (Dolan) are yet to be investigated.

Theatricality and performativity of the chronotope

The chapters in this collection to some extent reflect the semantic struggle behind the terms "exile" and "America". The contributors often use and adapt a variety of theoretical concepts, not all of which were originally created to theorize exile and emerge from performance and critical theory. The articles address among others Jill Dolan's *utopian performative,* Baz Kershaw's *pathologies of hope,* and Deleuze and Guattari's *deterritorialization.* Jerry Wasserman coins the term *utopian cartographies* to relate Dolan's concept to spatial politics, but also to communal bonding and its capacity for social critique. Sigmund Freud's notion of the *unheimlich* (uncanny strangeness) and its reworking in Julia Kristeva's theory of the abject – the familiar strangeness of the immigrant – re-emerge as conceptual tools to address issues of social death and social marginalization in exilic circumstances (Fitzpatrick, Manole, Jestrovic). Exile and 'America' have also been examined in the context of cultural identity and transnationalism through contributions that draw from Homi Bhabha and Yan Haiping (Wasserman), but also by bringing into the discourse on exile and performance the recent theories on democracy of Seyla Binhabib and Ella Shohat (Jaffe-Berg). Una Chaudhuri's notion of *geopathology* proves to be the theoretical model for analyzing exilic performance in relation to home, homelessness, and homecoming (Prizant). The spatial theories of Michel Foucault, Henri Lefebvre, and Edward Soja re-occur in several contributions (Prizant, Meerzon, Jestrovic). Yet Yana Meerzon's reworking of Lefebvre's categories of Conceptual, Experienced, and Lived Space adds a fourth dimension to his theory, when she introduces the concept of *mental space*, which is theatrical and encompasses the exilic imaginary as well as the exilic experience. However, it is the encounter or collision with the adopted social space that truly prompts performative manifestations of the mental one, merging not only the conceptual with the experienced space, but also the subjective space with the collective one.

Diana Manole also offers new possibilities of theorizing exile and creativity, as well as potential new ways to approach intercultural theatre, where the immigrant writer serves as a model, in her notion of *transnational theatre.* Manole distinguishes her category from both Patrice Pavis's one-directional "hourglass model" and Jacqueline Lo and Helen Gilbert's proposition where "both partners are considered cultural sources while the target culture is positioned along the continuum between them" (44–5). Manole proposes an analogues model, based primarily on the unique double vision of the immigrant writer, where both the source culture and the target culture are ambiguous. Meerzon's *theatricality of mental space* and Manole's *transnational theatre* offer new theoretical tools and categories that could be applied further beyond the scope of this volume. In addition, several chapters in this collection already embody or at least prefigure Freddie Rokem's innovative term *American performativity*. Rokem defines *American performativity* both as "a metaphor for the anxieties awakened in the shadow of modernity and its hopes for creating new opportunities on the basis of technological inventions and economic growth as well as a theatricalized strategy for coping with exile and alienation in such situations" (Rokem, Chapter 5 in this collection).

To encompass some of the complexities of exile, performance, and 'America', the editors of this collection propose the notion of *exilic chronotope* as a framework within which to investigate various dramatizations of tension between imagined and lived *exilic America*. Within the context of the *exilic chronotope*, the concepts of theatricality and performativity emerge as, perhaps, the most telling frame to better understand the construction of *Otherness* and the self-fashioning of immigrant identity. Various theatricalizations of space and identity, as well as the materiality of the exilic experience in its own performativity, serve to undercut the vagueness and artifice inherent in both keywords – "exile" and "America". Theatre and performance once again become means of historicization, rescuing the *exile/America* chronotope from the pitfalls of turning into a mere poetic metaphor. In its focus on imagination and experience, and on theatricality and performativity of the *exile/America* chronotope, this collection aims to investigate the following questions: How has 'America' been constructed as an exilic imaginary space through theatre, drama, critical thought, and everyday life? How has this 'America' of the exilic imaginary been altered and transformed through recent cultural, political, and personal experiences as expressed through specific dramatizations and theatricalizations of the *exile/America* chronotope? Could new ways of re-imagining exilic "America" or new modes of living it be forged through performative interventions?

'America' between the exilic imaginary and the exilic collective

The aspect of the imaginary plays one of the key roles in the *exile/America* chronotope not only as a means of understanding various visions and fictionalizations of "America", but also as an active force that shapes the practices of exilic communities. In his book *Frame Analysis*, Erving Goffman points out:

> Life may not be an imitation of art, but ordinary conduct, in a sense, is an imitation of the properties, a gesture at the exemplary forms, and the primal realization of these ideals belongs more to make-believe than to reality.
>
> Moreover, what people understand to be the organization of their experience, they buttress, and perforce, self-fulfillingly. They develop a corpus of cautionary tales, games, riddles, experiments, newsy stories, and other scenarios which elegantly confirm a frame-relevant view of the working of the world.
>
> (562–3)

Goffman's notion of framing negotiates between what we imagine our existence will be and what we experience in our everyday lives. Exile foregrounds this negotiation: it reinforces the inevitable gap between what immigrants imagine of their new land and home and what they truly face after they have landed in those places. The notion of the *exilic imaginary* frames "America" within the experience of marginalization and displacement that involves some of Goffman's central categories including keying and out-of-frame activity. Both of these categories are based on transformation, which is in the very core of the *exilic imaginary*. The visions, preconceptions, and misunderstandings through which the "America" of the *exilic imaginary* becomes constructed are transformational activities and they partake in the process of transcription that Goffman calls *keying* – "a set of conventions by which a given activity meaningful in terms of some primary framework, is transformed into something patterned on this activity but seen by the participants to be something quite else" (44). Goffman's *out-of-frame activity* – described as mode or line of activity that is "segregated from what officially dominates and will be treated, if treated at all, as something apart" (201) – fully applies to the notion of marginalization and internal or self-imposed exile – a position that often precludes the construction of the *exilic imaginary*.

The concept of the *exilic collective* originates at the crossroads of the Jungian collective self, Erving Goffman's social collective self, and – particular to the exilic experience – the exilic collective self of every immigrant who simultaneously sees herself belonging to her home culture left behind, and the new culture of her diaspora found in a new land.[2] Finally the *exilic collective* emerges here as a concession between the immigrant's life as a representative of her ethnic group and as an assimilated subject of the American melting pot.

In his seminal book *Imagined Communities: Reflections on the Origin and Spread of Nationalism*, Benedict Anderson describes "nation" as "an imagined political community [...] inherently limited and sovereign" (6). He points out that national imagination is not grounded in history, but in collective myths and biography. Anderson further suggests a connection between the history of a nation and the individual biographies of its people since both are based on narratives of identity, home and memory. While Anderson's imagined communities are based on continuity of narratives and linguistic, ethnic and cultural homogeneity, the *collective exilic* suggests a counter-arrangement – a community based on rapture, heterogeneity, and a shared experience of displacement. Nevertheless, individual biography, imagination, and a process of mythologization of the experience still play the central roles in both arrangements.

Arjun Appadurai further redefines the notion of imagined communities in his analysis of the post-national nature of the contemporary nation-state as the nation characterized not by a unified ideology and economic practice, but by a variety of collective imaginaries – migratory, exilic, diasporic, and transnational. In his definition of a post-national state, Appadurai comes up with the concept of a *community of sentiment,* which describes a group of de-territorialized persons who "imagine and feel things together" (8). The appearance of personalized exilic communities, Appadurai's personalized diasporic public spheres (10), contributes to the notion of the *exilic collective* that creates the possibility of "convergences [linguistic, cultural, social, performative, among others] in translocal social action that would otherwise be hard to imagine" (8). Defining the phenomenon of *the exilic collective identity* against the backdrop of both Anderson and Appadurai's theories, this collection explores ways in which the *exilic collective* negotiates the notion of "America" both as an imaginary exilic space and as a nation-state.

Exilic imaginary and exilic collective are categories of space, time, and identity. While exilic imaginary is either turned to the chronotopes of the past (i.e., places left behind) or of the future (i.e., places one longs to reach), exilic collective incorporates also the present moment, which unfolds in the encounter between the immigrant's theatricalized *mental space* (Meerzon) and the *lived social space* (Lefebvre). This volume examines exile, "America", and performance as they oscillate between these two central categories – the utopias and dystopias of various exilic imaginaries and the experiences of the *exilic collective.*

The opening part – *"America" Between the Exilic Imaginary and Exilic Collective* – addresses, through specific case studies, some of the key conceptual features of this duality: from the trope of home and imaginary "America" as a place of transformative possibilities to the uncanny strangeness of the immigrant, the self-fashioning of identity and the "paradoxical homogeneity of the marginalized" (Manole, Chapter 3 in this volume). Part 1 opens with two chapters that deal with iconic places of the *exile/America* chronotope – Ireland, in Lisa Fitzpatrick's "Land of Air-Conditioning and Opportunity: America on the Irish Stage", who uses Kristeva's theory of the abject to examine the contrast between visions of the imaginary exilic "America" fueled by returning immigrants and reality; and Cuba, in Yael Prizant's "Ninety Miles Away: Identity and Exile in Recent Cuban-American Theatre", where home and homecoming emerge, somewhat paradoxically, as the key tropes of both the exilic imaginary and the exilic collective. Diana Manole and Yana Meerzon further investigate the relationship between the exilic imaginary and the exilic collective – which, in Manole's case, is manifested as a parody of the American Dream and in Meerzon's chapter turns into exilic performativity. In all four chapters of Part 1, "America" of the exilic imaginary is embodied in the iconography of consumerist desires, while the exilic collective always involves theatricality as the self-fashioning of identity.

In "Land of Air-Conditioning and Opportunity: America on the Irish Stage", **Lisa Fitzpatrick** describes the image of America as a promised land, "a place of escape to freedom and prosperity, and a space of transformation" (Fitzpatrick Chapter 1 in this volume), as it appears in twentieth-century Irish drama and in different stages of twentieth-century Irish history – from Margaret O'Leary and Frank Carney, to Brian Friel's classic *Philadelphia, Here I Come!*, to recent works such as Declan Hughes's play *Shiver*. She suggests that the imaginary and fictional "America" has been evolving in Irish twentieth-century writings featuring the American "promised land" as both "the transformative, the banal and the material". Her chapter focuses on "this conjunction of the spiritual and the material that representations of America offer". By examining the trauma of homecoming, the pains and the risks of return, Fitzpatrick postulates that an exilic journey consists of one accepting America not as a chronotope of *the exilic imaginary*, but as her only true home, when an emigrant recognizes her existential destiny and undertakes her social task: to build her new "America" as the state of an exilic collective.

Yael Prizant's chapter, "Ninety Miles Away: Identity and Exile in Recent Cuban-American Theatre", investigates the problems of adaptation and identity loss by children of exiles returning to the native country of their parents and the difficulties of rediscovering one's roots. In line with Fitzpatrick's contribution, Prizant questions the pleasures of homecoming and the challenges of recognizing one's place of birth as her true home. Focusing on the plays of contemporary Cuban-American playwrights Rogelio Martinez and Nilo Cruz, Prizant examines how any romantic notion of exile disintegrates when an émigré becomes a hybrid, forced to reconcile the contrapuntal nature of their identities within their spatial realities. Specifically, Prizant analyses how the complicated relationships between the United States and Cuba affect the presentation of Cuban-American and Cuban identities on stage. As she states, the geopolitical site of the United States has become the condition of exile for more than a million former Cuban citizens who now live in America, but also to those that have remained on the island. Prizant also points out that the notion of exilic imaginary is not a one-way street, showing how Cuba and Florida become architecturally shaped through exilic imaginaries from both sides. This contribution recognizes "the experience of this postmodern dislocation" and examines the techniques of making this experience visible in the Cuban-American theatre that intensely concentrates on "the interstitial space of the blended subject" (Prizant, Chapter 2 in this volume).

Diana Manole investigates the tragicomedy of immigration in the twenty-first-century United States, as depicted in Saviana Stanescu's plays *Lenin's Shoe* and *Waxing West*. The main focus of this contribution is the immigrants' collective self-definition as "Others", on the one hand, and the reinforcement of the collectively imagined "America" on the other. The demythologization of American legend and the irony of living through any ideological phantasm are at the core of Manole's chapter. As the author suggests, Stanescu, a Romanian playwright living in the United States, "chooses to ridicule the burden of [her characters'] communist/post-communist past and of their American present as she ironically re-evaluates some of the most common stereotypes and clichés of exile and immigration. Her cartoon-like characters lack genuine psychological determinations and act as if accepting the 'multiplying masks and "false selves"' (Kristeva: 8) that are imposed upon them by a US audience" (Manole, Chapter 3 in this volume). Moreover, Manole's contribution suggests the notion of immigrant playwright as a product of the exilic collective. As mentioned earlier, Manole raises the questions of national literature and genre in application to the plays written by recent exiles in America. She suggests that twenty-first-century American drama, and specifically the works of new immigrants, must be recognized as examples of transnational theatre: that is, a body of works written by "immigrant authors in their second languages, addressing social and political problems in their birth countries and/or the exilic condition of an ethnic individual or group, whose target audiences are spectators in both the playwrights' native and adoptive countries. The transnational character of their work is enhanced by worldwide access to their texts, facilitated by recent technological developments" (Manole, current volume).

Theatricalization of America has a long-standing tradition in Russian literature and art. In their novels, poetry, and plays, Russian writers (both exilic and not) concretize the theatricality of New York as "the city of Yellow Devil" and as the poeticity of its futuristic bridges and skyscrapers. **Yana Meerzon** investigates the practice and the outcomes of the theatricalization of the American landscape in the writings of Vasily Aksyonov, who saw himself as a "fellow-traveler" in the United States and went back to Russia as soon as the Soviet regime collapsed. He dramatized the American cityscape as a part of his reflection on the marginality and outsidedness of the exilic destiny. He portrayed Russian emigrants exhibiting self-theatricality through the use of their language and through their perception of the surrounding landscape. As Aksyonov found out, these diverse forms of theatrical experience (those of self, space, time, and linguistic expression) are inevitably linked to the change of the social and existential roles any émigré is forced to live through once he has landed in a new country. As Meerzon suggests, the idiosyncrasy of the exilic experience provided Aksyonov with the possibility of anticipated and welcomed self-alienation and self-theatricalization in the performatively perceived and presented city-scene (Chapter 4 in this volume). This exilic self- and city-theatricalization becomes, therefore, in the words of Alexander Etkind, the émigré author's desire for the "other", an intellectual yearning that always "devaluates their own culture, which is perceived as fictional and unsubstantial, like a simulacrum" (9).

Part 2 borrows its title, *American Performativity*, from Freddie Rokem's chapter in this volume and it investigates this notion as a specific case of exilic imaginary – the one whose final destination is theatre whether it be on stage or in everyday life. *American Performativity* is also an organic follow-up to Meerzon's identification of the exilic experience as theatrical. However, in this part the outsider's and the insider's perspectives are somewhat confronted as *American Performativity* unfolds in two directions – "America" as a means of theatricalization of the European exilic imaginary (Rokem, Ambros) and "exile" as a means of self-fashioning of American intellectual identity in the 1950s (Ackerman).

Freddie Rokem's contribution examines the works of Brecht and Kafka as examples of imagined theatre and performance in America. This article takes the discussion onto existential and metaphysical levels, emphasizing the idea that Kafka and Brecht envision their imagined theatre as expressions of the "universal life drama and in particular the confrontation of the individual with death" (Rokem, Chapter 5 in this volume). Moreover, Kafka and Brecht's imagined theatres constitute a form of "existential, exilic performance" (Rokem, current volume), where, as Walter Benjamin stated, "everyone is hired" because this place "is the last refuge, which does not preclude it from being their salvation" (Benjamin: 804). For Rokem, works of Kafka and Brecht, although very different from each other, "both have a strong cinematographic quality of montage, which in combination with their deep sense of alienation have created the basis for a provocative and even subversive understanding of American performativity through which the final stages of the life-drama of the exiled individual are acted out as theatre" (Rokem, current volume).

Veronika Ambros's contribution embodies a different kind of *American performativity* that oscillates between Americanization of Europe and theatricalization of America. The chapter looks at three images of 'America' as they are manifested in early 1920s avant-garde theatre and film from Fritz Lang's *Metropolis* to the Broadway staging of Karel Čapek's *R.U.R.* Ambros explores imaginary dimensions of exile and 'America' focusing in particular on dislocation of the notion of "America" in Čapek's *R.U.R.* and on the cultural transfer through the play's subsequent productions in Prague, Berlin, Vienna, and new York. Using William James's theory of pragmatism that inspired Čapek, Ambros discusses how the idea of the biologically produced androids named "robots" informed "the German expressionist nightmares of the new man, but also the American dream of great experiments, which remodel the existing world" (Ambros, Chapter 6 in this volume). Although the exilic situation in Čapek's play is metaphoric, Ambros relates exile to issues of technology and democracy. The article suggests that in his text, "Čapek created a bridge between utopia and dystopia, between the fantasies of the Old world and the science-fiction of the New world" (Ambros, current volume), thus projecting the modernist excitement and fear of either fictional or real exilic experience. In other words, "America" is dislocated in European modernist imagination to become a dramaturgical device and a cultural reference, but also to foreground the notion of exilic "America" as a paradoxical trope that oscillates between the Utopia of the promised land and the dystopia of capitalist oppression.

Alan Ackerman's study, entitled "At Home in Exile", shifts the focus of the *exile/America* chronotope to the analysis of the so-called inner exilic experience in application to the American cultural practice, and further enriches the scope of *American performativity* by suggesting theatrical models as vital to understand "America" . Looking at the classic Hollywood film *Casablanca* and Tennessee Williams's response to the movie in his play *Camino Real*, Ackerman indicates that "the idea of America that emerged in the works of intellectuals and artists, many of them former communists themselves, was thus inextricably linked to a war-torn Europe characterized by flight and fragmentation, by exile and return, and to a humanistic culture and 'struggle for men's minds' that centered paradoxically on the mobility or freedom of the individual" (Ackerman, Chapter 7 in this volume). For Ackerman, Williams's play functions as a commentary on the themes of American cultural identity, isolationism, and exile, as well as internationalism and geopolitical determinism. While Rokem and Ambros look at visions of "America" shaped through European exilic imaginary, Ackerman points to a "quasi-exilic" America imagined internally, but inspired by the ethos of exile and displacement in war-torn Europe. Ackerman foregrounds the paradox of this exilic imaginary, suggesting that the "quasi-exilic imagination" is another version of US nationalism of the era. Moreover, the problematic of internal exile, as Ackerman argues, is almost fully ignored in Tennessee Williams scholarship. This chapter fleshes out a specific kind of internal exile by looking at the intellectual's theatricalization of self, while his self-imposed exilic experience unfolds against the background of the familiar American landscape. Ackerman argues that in the work of Williams, the exilic condition emerges as an expensive artistic paradigm through which the native speaker is viewed as a "linguistically amputated exile" (Ackerman, current volume).

The last section of this volume, Part 3: *America and the Other: From Representation to Intervention*, examines specific aspects of the exilic collective that do not only unfold on the axes of the imaginary and experiential, but also through problems of representation and presence as means of political critique and performative intervention. Like Ackerman, yet in a very different context, Erith Jaffe-Berg's chapter, opening Part 3, focuses on American playwrights and their representation of the Other, in this case Middle Eastern women post-9/11. In return, Dalia Basiouny and Marvin Carlson examine the presence and self-representation of Arabic-immigrant playwrights, especially women, on the American stage. In Jerry Wasserman's chapter, the deliberately caricature-like Other is a critical vehicle for a radical political satire of

George W. Bush's America, while Silvija Jestrovic further explores satire in performing otherness through the urban interventions of the Polish immigrant artist Krszystof Wodiczko. All four contributions touch on the subject of stereotyping and address overt political dimensions related to the issues of exile, 'America' and performance: Jaffe-Berg examines multilingualism as a means of going beyond stereotypical representation of the Other; Basiouny and Carlson point out how the relative prominence of Arab voices on the American stage post-9/11 helps to offset the one-dimensional representations of the Arab and Muslim world fuelled by the media; Wasserman looks at deliberately created stereotypes as a means of exploring racial politics, particularly in the light of the invasion of Iraq; and Jestrovic explores estrangement as a means of confronting the colonial gaze that shapes the Other into a cultural, social, and/or racial stereotype.

In her contribution "De-Territorializing Voices: Staging the Middle East in American Theatre", **Erith Jaffe-Berg** reflects on the post-9/11 context by looking at theatricalizations of exilic identities as vehicles and forms of political and cultural critique, but also as transformational possibilities, invoking again Jill Dolan's notion of *utopian performative* (455). The chapter argues that although "the promise of globalization appeared to make the language of territories obsolete, detaching 'deterritorialization' from its partner-term 'reterritorialization,' recent quagmires faced by the United States in its activities in the Middle East suggest otherwise. How American playwrights stage the Middle East, and particularly how they represent Muslim characters has become increasingly important as the question of Americans' relation to others has been unsatisfactorily answered in other forums" (Jaffe-Berg, Chapter 8 in this volume). Examining works by Naomi Wallace, Karen Hartman and Tony Kushner and their productions before and after 9/11, Jaffe-Berg investigates ways in which these playwrights confront the construction of Otherness in US politics and media. The chapter also focuses on the idea of a female character not only as an exilic Other, but also as a "cultural go-between", and looks at "linguistic hybridity" (Jaffe-Berg current volume) and its transformative potential.

In their chapter "Current Trends in Contemporary Arab-American Theatre", **Marvin Carlson and Dalia Basiouny** investigate the issues of cultural appropriation and how ethnic stereotypes are featured on the American stage as they have been propagated by US foreign policies. This time, it is the "global war of terror" that functions as the hastening of this diminutive racial practice, "within which members of the Arab world have been not only generically cast as 'the Other', but as the global enemy by many in the West and particularly in America" (Carlson and Basiouny, Chapter 9 in this volume). This study offers an overview of the recent theatrical practice of the Arab community in the United States, focusing on the works of its prominent theatre and performance makers. As the authors state, various forms of cultural caricaturing and racial profiling have made it more important than ever before for Arab American theatre writers and performers to create works that explore their identity and their place in American society both for themselves and their generally non-Arab-American audiences. These performances attempt to shed light on the complexities of these hybrid identities, define and present the self, and correct the stereotypical misrepresentations portrayed in the media.

Invoking Canada's (and Canadian theatre's) historically ambivalent position on the margins of US imperial power, **Jerry Wasserman** discusses Marcus Youssef, Guillermo Verdecchia, and Camyar Chai's agitprop cabaret, *The Adventures of Ali & Ali and the aXes of Evil*, a metatheatrical satire on the War on Terror that has toured across Canada for the past several years. In his chapter, Wasserman approaches the controversy of current American foreign policy through discussion of the relationship between Canada and the United States; and Canadian domestic issues with its multicultural and emigration practices. The production in question, as Wasserman suggests, targets in equal measure the horror and stupidity of the American response to 9/11 and Canada's own hypocritical embeddedness in the misadventures of the new American imperium: "the play enacts a series of mock-physical confrontations, political lessons, and emotional engagements with the plight of real-life refugees and victims of statist violence" (Wasserman, Chapter 10 in this volume). Re-embodying the Canadian nation and its national cross-border gaze in non-white, diasporic, Canadian performing bodies, the play ultimately imagines a "trans-nation", in Yan Haiping's useful term: "a material space of alternative temporality, where new alliances and forms of citizenry as flexible social solidarity become tangible" (241). Moreover, in its controversy, the play aims for those transformational moments in which performers and audience join in the experience of the *utopian performative*.

In her closing chapter, "Exiles and the City: Krzysztof Wodiczko's New York Interventions of Making the Familiar Strange", **Silvija Jestrovic** revisits some of the main themes of this volume including self-presentation of exilic identity, space, and homelessness in the context of site-specific political performance and through the lens of Brechtian estrangement strategies. Looking at performance projects by Polish-born immigrant artist Krzysztof Wodiczko – *Alien Staff, Homeless Vehicles*, and *Homeless Projection: Proposal for the City of New York* – the chapter tackles different aspects of the exilic experience including immigration as a form of physical exile and homelessness as marginalization within, and as an instance of, internal exile. In both cases, as Jestrovic argues, Wodiczko explores the exilic situation as a way of rethinking the encounters between strangers and a means of proposing new communicational practices through performative interventions. The essay foregrounds Brechtian estrangement as a key strategy in these interventions that rely on adopting an immigrant perspective, of seeing the world from the margin, from the border, from a place of political, cultural, and linguistic in-between-ness. In analyzing Wodiczko's work, Jestrovic explores the links between exile and social marginalization and the American metropolis as an exilic site, where the experience of immigration, displacement, and homelessness turns into a form of performance that asserts the presence of the marginalized and decolonizes the Other. The city also appears as an intrinsically political and theatrical space where exilic identities could be performed and reconstituted, but also a site where existing social relationships and preconceived perceptions could be constantly challenged. In other words, through the interplay between immigrant and the city, theatricality and performativity, imagination and experience, a "third space" emerges as space of intervention that might hold a promise for a community of the displaced.

*   *   *

In conclusion, this book proposes to render an exilic paradigm as a mode of collective social consciousness based on the immigrants' everyday experience at home, their dreaming of leaving their homeland, their new experience and their new dreaming about this experience in their newly acquired homeland. The chapters in this collection point to the construction of *the exilic collective* in the context of America *imagined* as a transnational state of deterritorialized peoples – the state in which the battles over English language and rights for immigrants are no longer just examples of "the politics of pluralism, they are about the capability of American politics to contain the diasporic politics of Mexicans in Southern California, Haitians in Miami, Colombians in New York, and Koreans in Los Angeles" (Appadurai: 11). Yet 'America' also emerges here *vis-à-vis* Edward Said's notion of exile as a "contrapuntal" state, comprised on the one hand of a "crippling sorrow of estrangement" and on the other of the "liberating pleasure" of a point-of-view from the liminal condition

(Said: 173–87). America/"America" therefore appears in this collection in its ambiguous form: both a nation-state – a construct embodied in Anderson's notion of imagined communities – and a transnational or a post-national place inhabited by misplaced and deterritorialized people – a community formed through the exilic imaginary.

Notes

1. These categories could of course be made even more precise in the light of the legal weight that terms such as "asylum seekers", "refugees", "immigrants", "expatriates", and others carry.
2. The Merriam-Webster dictionary provides several definitions for the term diaspora: 1. as a description of a historical phenomenon: "the settling of scattered colonies of Jews outside Palestine after the Babylonian exile", 2. as a geographical location: "the area outside Palestine settled by Jews, and the Jews living outside Palestine or modern Israel", and 3. as a social dynamic for the contemporary world of global migration, i.e., diaspora as "the movement, migration, or scattering of a people away from an established or ancestral homeland" (http://aolsvc.merriam-webster.aol.com; accessed 25 November 2008).

Works cited

Agamben, Giorgio. *Homo Sacer: Sovereign Power and Bare Life*. Trans. Danile Heller-Roazen. Stanford, CA: Stanford University Press, 1998.

Anderson, Benedict. *Imagined Communities: Reflections on the Origin and Spread of Nationalism*. Rev. edn. London and New York: Verso, 1991.

Appadurai, Arjun, *Modernity at Large: Cultural Dimensions of Globalization*. Minneapolis: University of Minnesota Press, 1996.

Bakhtin, M. M. *The Dialogic Imagination: Four Essays by M. M. Bakhtin*. Ed. M. Holquist. Trans. C. Emerson and M. Holquist. Austin: University of Texas Press, 1981.

Benjamin, Walter. *Selected Writings*, vol. 2, Cambridge, MA, and London: Harvard University Press, 1999.

Boym, Svetlana. "Estrangement as a Life Style: Shklovsky and Brodsky", *Poetics Today: International Journal of Theory and Analysis of Literature and Communication* 17.4 (Winter 1996): 511–24.

Deleuze, Gilles and Felix Guattari. *The Thousand Plateaus: Capitalism and Schizophrenia*. Trans. Brian Massumi. London and New York: Continuum, 1987.

Dolan, Jill. "Performance, Utopia, and the 'Utopian Performative'", *Theatre Journal* 53.3 (2001): 455–79.

Etkind, Alexander. *Tolkovanie puteshestvii: Rossiya i Amerika v travelogakh i intertekstakh*. Moscow: Novoe Literaturnoe Obozrenie, 2001.

Glowacki, Janusz. *Hunting Cockroaches and Other Plays*. Evanstone, NJ: Northwestern University Press, 1990.

Goffman, Erving. *Frame Analysis: An Essay on the Organization of Experience*. Boston, MA: Northwestern University Press, 1986 [1974].

Haiping, Yan. "Other Transnationals: An Introductory Essay", *Modern Drama* 48 (Summer 2005): 225–48.

Kershaw, Baz. *The Radical in Performance: Between Brecht and Baudrillard*. London: Routledge, 1999.

Kristeva, Julia. *Strangers to Ourselves*. New York: Columbia University Press, 1994.

Lamming, George. *The Pleasures of Exile*. London: Michael Joseph, 1960.

Lefebvre, Henri. *The Production of Space*. Trans. Donald Nicholson-Smith. Oxford: Blackwell, 1992.

Lo, Jacqueline and Helen Gilbert. "Toward a Topography of Cross-Cultural Theatre Praxis", *The Drama Review* 46.3 (T175), Fall 2002. New York University and the Massachusetts Institute of Technology, 2002.

Said, Edward. *Reflections on Exile and Other Essays*. Cambridge, MA: Harvard University Press, 2000

Sardar, Ziauddin and Merry Wyn Davies. *Why Do People Hate America?*. Cambridge: Icon Books, 2002.

Wiesel, Elie. "Longing for Home". Ed. L. S. Rouner. *The Longing for Home*. Notre Dame, IN: University of Notre Dame Press, 1996: 17–29.

Part 1
'America' Between the Exilic Imaginary and the Exilic Collective

1
The Land of Air-Conditioning and Opportunity: America on the Irish Stage

Lisa Fitzpatrick
University of Ulster

Introduction: constructing emigration as exile

In her essay, *Daughters of Colony*, Irish poet Eavan Boland recounts a story her mother heard as a small child, from an old woman. This woman had survived the Irish Famine of 1846–52, when an estimated one million people died of starvation and a further million emigrated to Canada, the United States, and England:[1]

> She had dragged though the hunger, the emigration, the aftershock. Her children had died. Her husband was dead. [… H]er only son, who had emigrated earlier, managed to send her the passage money to join him in New York […] She had reached New York only to find him dead. Then began years and years of work […] Finally she had enough [money] to return to Ireland. A woman alone. No doubt her village gone. No doubt the last vestiges of what she knew and recognized gone. Everything gone but the words in which to tell the terrible story. Everything gone but that air, and space into which the words carried their freight.
>
> (11)

I have quoted Boland at length because one of the features of emigration from Ireland to America has historically been its construction as exile. The woman's story illustrates a loss that intimately defines the experience of the emigrant: for him or her, home is unchanging, crystallized in memory as one moment in time. Even when return is effected, he or she has been transformed by experience into an alien element that cannot be readily reabsorbed by the home place. But the home they left has also been transformed. This figure of the 'returned Yank' recurs in Irish drama, and functions as a plot device in three of the four plays discussed here. But he or she is not a figure of success. In these and other plays, emigration is represented in terms of distress, failure, and alienation.

This chapter examines the representation of emigration in four plays written between 1959 and 1992: *The Country Boy* by John Murphy (1959), Brian Friel's *Philadelphia Here I Come!* (1964), Tom Murphy's *Conversations on a Homecoming* (1985), and Sebastian Barry's *White Woman Street* (1992). All of them are part of the repertoire on the Irish stage and the contemporary canon of Irish drama, and all but one is set entirely in Ireland. Therefore they address the issue of emigration predominantly from an internal perspective, largely maintaining a silence around the subjective experiences of the emigrant. The plays represent America mainly through the diegesis, and its materialization on stage is effected through the representation of items brought back by the emigrants, signifying their material wealth, and occasionally through their Americanized speech and physicality. But the wealth is revealed as illusory, just as America, in its construction as Utopia, is revealed as a no-where. This no-place is imagined by the emigrant characters as a false Utopia of endless opportunity. It offers a possibility of personal transformation, but the result is a dystopia of alienation and placelessness. The return 'home' brings with it a realization that their experience has marked them with a difference that precludes reintegration into the originary culture.

Claeys and Sargent note that "the primary characteristic of the utopia is its non-existence combined with a *topos* – a location in time and space" (1). Louis Marin situates Utopia "in the place of a gap" (404); "*Outopos, Outopia* is a paradoxical, even giddy toponym since as a term it negates with its name the very place it is naming [...] the term as the name of a place designates a no-place; it designates *another* referent, the 'other' of any place" (411). By situating Utopia in a "gap", and describing it as "nam[ing] the limit" between worlds, as "nam[ing] the way of the *limes* traveling between two edges that will never join together" (411), Marin's analysis is suggestive of a space that in Irish theatre is often associated with the supernatural and the fantastic. This is a space that harbors ghosts and other spirits, and it may invade or overlap with the natural world. In eliding Utopia with the space more often associated with death, and given that the absence of exile is often imagined in Irish culture as analogous to the absence associated with death, the returned emigrant is to an extent an abjected, *unheimlich* revenant who disrupts normal life.

The old woman in Boland's story is a revenant, a ghost who haunts later generations with her tale of distant but dreadful national trauma.

Her words are carried forward by Boland's mother, and Boland in turn tells the story to her readers. Similarly, the emigrant figures remind both the other characters and the audience of the traumatic loss of generations of Irish people. They are reminders of famine and poverty, and the failure of the state to provide employment and opportunity. Historian Joseph Lee writes that "the psychic impact of emigration on those who stayed, the price paid by the society for the subterfuges to which it had to resort to preserve its self-respect while scattering its children, has only begun to be explored" (375). The dramatic figure of the emigrant functions to reawaken and exacerbate this trauma, and the grief and loss expressed in these plays are those both of the population left bereft at home, and of those who leave. Plays commonly include the emigrant leaving again, having realized that they do not belong in the home place. Their absence is a necessary precondition for a return to normality, offering as it does a comforting conclusion that it is they – rather than the society – which is at fault. This can also be read as a reflection of hegemonic discourses that represent emigration as a means of expelling disruptive elements, and of maintaining existing social and economic systems.

Emigration was a defining Irish experience for over a century.[2] Ferriter records that "by 1911 one-third of all people born in Ireland were living elsewhere" (44), and this hemorrhage continued throughout the 1900s, with over 40,000 emigrants and one-quarter of all university graduates leaving Ireland each year into the late 1980s. Prior to political independence, emigration is identified in popular memory and song with the political and religious persecution associated with colonization, and with poverty and famine; and post-independence it continued to be motivated by poverty and unemployment, oppressive social and moral attitudes, and the censorship of artists on 'moral' grounds – though by the late 1980s the lack of employment was undoubtedly the main motivating factor. Nonetheless, hegemonic discourses of the early and mid-twentieth century constructed emigration as an irrational and selfish act by those who "must obviously be deluded, if not depraved, to desert God's own island", as Lee caustically writes; emigration was "an otherwise baffling indictment of an axiomatically innocent society, basking contentedly in its own smug sense of moral superiority" (376).

America in the popular imagination

Although Irish people emigrated in large numbers to Australia and Britain, amongst other countries, America appears to have functioned continuously as the main imaginative site of exile. This is unsurprising, given that in the 1800s and early 1900s trading links with America facilitated the movement of population, as boats bringing goods to Ireland sold space to emigrants for the return journey. Stories of the Gold Rush and of the adventures and opportunities that awaited pioneers in the western states filtered back in the form of newspaper reports and letters since the 1800s, while since the early twentieth century most of the population had access to American popular culture in the form of pulp fiction and Hollywood cinema, with no language barrier to hinder the flow of information. As Mary Trotter notes, even the Proclamation of Independence, signed by the leaders of the 1916 Uprising, refers to support for Ireland's struggle for independence from "her exiled children in America" (35), attesting to the perceived connection with America as a place of refuge. In the theatre, James Carney's *The Righteous Are Bold* (1946) contrasts America as non-corrupting space with the depravity of England: the children who emigrate across the Atlantic remain true to their Catholic faith, unlike the daughter who returns from England possessed by demons. And indeed, America is often imagined as a neighboring country – albeit rather a distant one on the other side of the ocean. The playwright J. M. Synge, traveling in the Aran Islands in the West of Ireland at the turn of the twentieth century, records this sense of America as simultaneously distant and familiar in his record of an island woman whose son had emigrated:

> [...] a letter came from the son who is in America, to say [...] that he was leaving New York and going a few hundred miles up the country. All the evening afterwards the old woman sat on her stool at the corner of the fire with her shawl over her head, keening piteously to herself. America appeared far away, yet she seems to have felt that, after all, it was only the other edge of the Atlantic, and now when she hears them talking of railroads and inland cities where there is no sea, things she cannot understand, it comes home to her that her son is gone forever.
>
> (107–8)

Folksongs celebrate the wealth awaiting the emigrant in that promised land, in contrast to the hardship of life at home. One popular song includes the refrain:

> [...] as sure as my name is Carney, I'll be off to Californ-ey,
> Where instead of digging praties I'll be digging lumps of gold.[3]

Figure 1.1 Map: "Ireland: Famine, Misery, Poverty"; "America: Hope, Wealth, Opportunity". Courtesy of Derry City Council, Heritage and Museum Service.

It is in this confluence of the banal (potatoes) and the fabulous (lumps of gold) that the Irish dream of America emerges. Other cultural artifacts often offer a specific substitution of one set of values or material situations for another: nineteenth-century advertisements for passage to America juxtapose the text "Ireland: Famine, Misery, Poverty" and "America: Hope, Wealth, Opportunity" over a crude map representing the two landmasses, the ocean, with the ship's journey represented by arrows directing the imagination towards the promised land.[4]

This promised wealth appears in the dramas as the promise of personal transformation of the individual into a successful professional and a great lover, imbuing him with eloquence and sophistication. The circumstances that will allow this transformation, however, are expressed in terms of the banal and the material: air conditioners, ice-boxes, elevators, and private bathrooms.

Emigration, death, and abjection

Historically, most emigrants never returned from America, and in acknowledgement of that fact it was customary in rural areas to hold an "American Wake", modeled on the traditional bacchanal normally held on the nights between the person's death and burial.[5] Thus, as emigration becomes conflated with exile, it is also conflated with death through the shared ritual of the 'Wake', recognizing and marking the permanence of absence. One play that makes that connection explicitly is Margaret O'Leary's 1929 drama *The Woman*.[6] O'Leary's protagonist, Ellen, dreams of a place where "it is never cold", "the lovely country where all the sun is" (n.p.), a place that her lover Maurice assumes is America, but that she appears to understand as death, since she speaks with the same longing of the lake, Poulgorm, where her grandmother drowned herself. Finally Maurice agrees to go away with her:

> ELLEN: And we will meet each other at the bend of the road by the hawthorn bush.
> MAURICE *sadly*: By the hawthorn bush.
> ELLEN: In the evening time after the cows are milked.
> MAURICE: Yes, in the evening time we will go away together.
> ELLEN: That will be grand. *Dreamily*: and it will be quiet, and your arms around me will be as soft as the dark waters of Poulgorm.
>
> (n.p.)

The reference to the "dark waters of Poulgorm" suggests that in Maurice's embrace, Ellen will find death: not only the *petite morte* of orgasm, but something more sinister. In the same section of dialogue she also invokes the hawthorn, a plant believed to belong to the spirit world, and twilight, 'after the cows are milked', a liminal time when the worlds of the living and the dead overlap.

Although the linking of exile/death/America is not explicit in the plays discussed here, the uneasy response of the Irish characters to the returned emigrants demonstrates an awareness of their Otherness, an Otherness which can be understood in terms of the Freud's *unheimlich* or uncanny, and of the concept of abjection. Freud describes the uncanny as "that class of the frightening which leads back to what is known of old and long familiar" (121), and is particularly related to death and dead bodies (142). Thus the return to the family home of a person whose departure from everyday life has already been mourned seems to mimic the fear of the dead returning, and suggests an awareness that their reappearance is somehow disruptive, however seemingly joyful the family reunions may be. Freud's remark that "the *unheimlich* is what was once *heimisch*, familiar; the prefix *un* is the token of repression" (146) seems significant in relation to Lee's belief that the history of mass emigration has inflicted a national psychic damage which has yet to be acknowledged or investigated. The return of the emigrant figure, therefore, provokes a discomfiting awareness of what is otherwise repressed: the relationship between the survival of the state, the status of those who stay, and the sacrifice of those who leave.

Kristeva writes that the "abject has only one quality of the object – that of being opposed to *I*" (1). In the dramatic representation of emigrants on the stage, their defining feature is their difference from the 'I' who did not leave; and this difference is embodied in performance through an alien *parole*, and through an emotional expressiveness – in word or gesture – which is in opposition to the silence and repressive physicality of the Irish characters. But the difference is not absolute or fixed; the emigrant is familiar as well as Other; it is this familiar strangeness which is at the root of the danger. The corpse, Kristeva argues, is the "utmost of abjection" if seen outside of God or science; it is "death infecting life [...] Imaginary uncanniness and real threat, it beckons to us and ends up engulfing us" (4). The returned emigrant as revenant, moreover, is a source of both fascination and disgust; familiar and unfamiliar; safely dead – having been waked – and yet, somehow, still present amongst the living. Writing of the uncanny, Kristeva defines it as "the strange within the familiar", continuing, "that which *is* strangely uncanny would be that which *was* (the past tense is important) familiar and, under certain conditions (which ones?), emerges" (283).

The transformed self: *Philadelphia, Here I Come!* (1964)

Philadelphia, Here I Come!, now an iconic Irish play, explores the transformative experience of emigration in an ironic portrayal of the protagonist Gar's anticipated metamorphosis from gauche Irishman to sophisticated American. His imaginary persona is juxtaposed with the figure of returned emigrant Aunt Lizzy, an unhappy woman caught between the two cultures of Ireland and America, and fully comfortable in neither. The play was first performed in Dublin in 1964 at the Gaiety Theatre, directed by Hilton Edwards for the Dublin Theatre Festival, and it went on to productions in London and New York (Grene 197). It was a huge popular success and the year of its premier is often signposted as "a new beginning in Irish theatre" (Grene: 195). Set, like almost all Friel's plays, in the small town of Ballybeg, *Philadelphia* tells the story of the last night at home of Gar O'Donnell. The play's central conceit is that the character of Gar is split, and played by two actors, one of whom performs the taciturn, socially awkward Gar Public, and the other the bitterly witty and expressive Gar Private, who speaks the character's innermost thoughts, rallying him when he succumbs to his anxiety and nerves. Gar lives with his father S.B. (whom he nicknames Screwballs), a grocer who employs his son for a pittance, and Madge the housekeeper. His mother Máire died when he was a small child. Flashback sequences show key moments that motivate Gar to leave. These include the ending of his relationship with Senator Doogan's daughter Kate, because his lack of money means he cannot hope to support a family; and the visit of his mother's sister Lizzy with her husband Con and their friend Ben Burton, during which Lizzy invites him to join them in Philadelphia.

By the time of the play's premiere, although emigration figures remained high, the economic situation in much of the country was improving, evidenced in Gar's having gone to university in Dublin – though he failed his first year examinations and returned to Ballybeg. His motivation to leave, therefore, is to be found primarily in the breakdown of communication within the family: Madge, S.B., and Gar himself are all unable to express the love that binds them. Gar longs for a word from his father that will stop him leaving: a shared memory or a word of affection. At the end of Episode 2 Gar begs, "(*in a whispered shout*) Screwballs, say something! Say something, father!" (80). He makes his last desperate attempt to connect emotionally late at night, when he and his father, neither of them able to sleep, sit together in the kitchen. But S.B.'s grief at the loss of his child is expressed only to Madge, in his memory of his son as a small child "the two of us, hand in hand, as happy as larks" (97); he cannot form a connection to his son.

America as a site of transformation is materialized on stage through the physical presences of Gar's aunt Lizzy, and through Gar's imagined American persona. Lizzy is described as "a small energetic woman, heavily made up" who "has a habit of putting her arm around, or catching the elbow of, the person she is addressing. This constant physical touching is new and disquieting to [Gar]" (60). The alien physicality and the makeup mark Lizzy's transformation to 'Elise', the name she uses in America. She drinks alcohol during her scene, and is garrulous and emotional, behavior which marks her hybrid, Americanized self and draws Madge's disapproval. The stage directions read, Lizzy "puts her arm around [her friend Ben] and kisses the crown of his head" four times in a short scene, and when Gar agrees to go to America she "opens her arms and approaches him [...] throws her arms around him and cries happily" (66). None of the family members ever touch each other. Lizzy's behavior therefore materializes on stage an alien culture where the expression of emotion in words and gesture is acceptable. Apart from this, America is located diegetically in her lists of possessions – a ground-floor apartment, an air-conditioned car, a color TV, investments, a deep freezer, snow in winter, a big cherry tree, and a "big collection of all the Irish records you ever heard" (65). Later she writes to tell him that he has a job in a local hotel and that he will have "the spare room which has TV and air-conditioning and window meshes and your own bathroom with a shower" (59).

Though her only scene on stage is short, Lizzy's character functions as a catalyst for the dramatic action. Her presence offers Gar a connection to his dead mother, and much of Lizzy's dialogue is memories of her sister and of their life in Ballybeg. In this way, Lizzy functions to offer Gar access both to the dead, and to the Other, absent space of America, and in both instances she disrupts the normality of the O'Donnell household. She is aware that she is an unwelcome presence. S.B. does not meet her, and Madge "refuses to look at the visitors. Her face is tight with disapproval." This response has little naturalistic justification, since Lizzy is Gar's aunt, and family ties and the demands of hospitality would normally take precedence over Madge's reservations. Reading Lizzy in terms of the abject, however, through her connection with the world of the dead, offers a way of making sense of the scene. This connection is emphasized by her identification of *herself* as dead. Weeping for her sisters, she cries: "Poor Aggie – dead. Máire – dead. Rose, Una, Lizzy – dead – all gone – all dead and gone [...]" (64). Her husband reminds her, "Honey, you're Lizzy" (64). Though comic in performance – and Lizzy is a comic character – there is a clear sense in which her statement is true. Lizzy, the country girl from Donegal, is indeed dead and gone, and her place has been taken by a sort of changeling[7] in the form of garrulous, heavily made-up Elise from Philadelphia. She is a figure who is simultaneously familiar and strange; part of Gar's family, yet unlike them in dress, behavior, and language. The familiarity within the difference fascinates Gar, who hopes to catch in her a glimpse of his dead mother; as one both dead and alive, Lizzy is an *unheimlich* figure.

Having decided to emigrate, the dialogue between Gar Private and Public rehearses various transformative possibilities that result from this decision. Although his timidity has resulted in failure and unhappiness at home, the America of his imagination offers an opportunity for reinvention. These rehearsals, however, mirror the tensions in the dramatic present between diffident and taciturn Gar Public and witty and eloquent Gar Private, and the flashback sequences and scene where Gar meets his friends confirm the gap between his image of himself, and the reality. The "boys", Ned, Tom, and Joe, are all in their mid-twenties, living at home, and lacking both the financial independence to marry and the sexual confidence and maturity to form relationships with women. They are trapped in infantile relationships with their mothers, who exert considerable control over their sons' actions. Thus Joe tells Gar, "I wish I was you". When Gar points out that there is nothing stopping him leaving, he replies, "Only the mammy planted sycamore trees last year, and she says I can't go till they're tall enough to shelter the house" (76). Gar Private's comments reveal to the audience the sad truth behind the "boys"' tales of conquest, saying "the girls' names were Gladys and Susan. And they sat on the rocks dangling their feet in the water. And we sat in the cave, peeping out at them [...]" (73). Yet Gar's awareness of his sexual failure in Ballybeg does not prevent him indulging in fantasy scenarios:

> PUBLIC: (*In absurd Hollywood style*) Hi, gorgeous! You live in my block?
> PRIVATE: (*Matching the accent*) Yeah, big handsome boy. Sure do.
> PUBLIC: Mind if I walk you past the incinerator, to the elevator?
> PRIVATE: You're welcome, slick operator.
>
> (46)

The audience are therefore ironically aware that the transformation Gar anticipates is unlikely to materialize. Instead, as Private warns him, he is already engaging in a process of mythopoeisis that will involve a very different transformation from adventurous migrant into the tragic hero of exile. Private warns him that he is "collecting memories and images and impressions that are going to make you bloody miserable" (58), and comments on the emigrant's nostalgic memories of home: "Just the memory of it – that's all you have now – just the memory; and even now, even so soon, it is being distilled of its coarseness; and what's left is going to be precious, precious gold [...]" (77).

Faking the American Dream: *The Country Boy* (1959) and *Conversations on a Homecoming* (1985)

Gar's imagined transformation into the embodiment of the American Dream is in ironic juxtaposition with many plays that represent the figure of the returned American in terms of failure and alienation, rather than success. Both *The Country Boy* by John Murphy and *Conversations on a Homecoming* by Tom Murphy, discussed below, show a dark side to emigration that *Philadelphia* only hints at: loneliness, heart-break, alcoholism, and the death of the American Dream. The first of these plays explores the social pressures that contribute to a culture of emigration, while the second represents the death of the American Dream and of the dream of America, in its portrayal of Ireland at a particular historical moment of cynicism and hopelessness. It is, perhaps, also reflective of the increasingly publicized plight of the undocumented Irish living illegally in the United States: people for whom the American Dream is tantalizingly close, yet unattainable.

In *Philadelphia* Gar's reluctance to pursue his beloved Kate because he earns less than £4 a week is a predicament that is reiterated in a number of plays as late as the 1980s. Religious and cultural prohibitions around romantic love and sexuality, and economic obstacles to marriage are recurring themes, mirroring lived realities. Ferriter reports that in the mid-1950s only 30 percent of the population were married (479), and Lee argues that "marriage rate and emigration rate are inversely related, not directly related, in Irish experience [...] Emigrants essentially left for the chance of a job that would in turn give them a better chance of marriage than at home" (382). Particularly in rural areas, late marriage and life-long celibacy were commonplace. Lee writes of this demographic, "Some might eventually inherit property, but at too advanced an age to found a family of their own. In general they lingered through life [...] mute victims to the failure of the society to create sufficient work to provide for even a dwindling population to give its members a decent chance at personal fulfilment" (649). He writes that "four out of every five children born in Ireland between 1931 and 1941 emigrated in the 1950s" seeking "the 'luxury' of a family of their own, the 'luxury' of a job where they need not constantly touch the forelock, the 'luxury' of decent medical treatment" (379–80). His scathing analysis critiques the role of the Irish Catholic Church in enforcing repressive social mores that denied many the opportunity of a normal life. Seeking to express the quality of life for the rural poor, Lee quotes Patrick Kavanagh's poem *The Great Hunger*, whose protagonist Maguire "will hardly remember that life happened to him". This work was later dramatized by Tom McIntyre:

> Like the after-birth of a cow stretched on a branch in the wind
> Life dried in the veins of these women and men:
> The grey and grief and unlove
> The bones in the backs of their hands
> And the chapel pressing its low ceiling over them.
>
> (Kavanagh 2005)

In the theatre, Murphy's *The Country Boy* represents the prohibitions around early marriage as leading to heartbreak and emigration for one young couple, while threatening the future happiness of another. This poignant comedy was first performed at the Group Theatre in Belfast, before opening at the National Theatre of Ireland, the Abbey, in 1959, and has remained in the repertoire ever since. It was written late in a period of mass emigration, which was to continue, though in diminished numbers, into the 1960s. The play centers around a family, Tom and Mary and their sons Eddie, who has lived in America for the past 15 years, and Curly, who lives at home and works the farm for his father. The play begins on the eve of Eddie's visit home. Like many Irish emigrants, he has been sending money back[8] which has allowed his parents to replace their old-fashioned thatch cottage with a modern slate-roofed house (4). He brings with him his American wife Julia, and initially intends to bring Curly back to America when they return. Curly is in love with a local girl, Eileen, but his father is resolutely opposed to the marriage which will involve the girl coming to live in the family home, and his signing over of the farm to his son; and Curly has no independent means of support. For Tom, it will be time enough for Curly to marry when he and his wife Mary are no longer able to care for themselves:

> TOM: You'd swear the way you talk we were crippled or something and had to have someone else in …
> MARY: Is that the only reason you can think of for marriage? …
> TOM: Is there a better reason for a fella his age to be getting' married? None!
>
> (4)

But Curly's story mirrors that of his older brother's: Eddie was in love with a local girl, Katie O'Hara, and went to America to earn money so that he could marry her. But time passed, and Katie married another man from the village. As the play begins she is dangerously ill, exhausted from repeated childbirths, and she dies. Eddie tries to talk Curly out of leaving, hinting that life in America is more difficult than Curly realizes, and pointing out what he will lose by going, but Curly cannot see any opportunity at home. His speech summarizes the situation of many young men at the time:

> I've had to ask him for every shillin' I needed [...] I've worked twelve and sixteen hours of a stretch above in the fields or in the bogs[...] and at the end of it, if I wanted to go out for an hour for the crack I had to sneak through the door [...] And when I'm about thirty-five

years of age or forty [...] he'll tell me it's time I started castin' round
for a wife. Not getting' married mind you. Just "castin'" around [...]
And he'll be the one to tell me who I should bring in and how much
she'll bring with her [...]

(32–3)

In contrast, America appears to offer the opportunity to work for
himself (30).

Eddie's American prosperity is represented on stage through the objects
he brings home with him: "a very large cabin trunk [...] American type
shower proofs" (13), cigarettes, and a cine camera. The camera cost
$250 (£65), and his father comments that "Any man that pays sixty-five
pounds for a camera to take pictures with must be getting his money soft.
'Tis easy known it's not in Ireland you are [...]" (14). The Irish characters'
expectations of America, and their worry about providing properly for
their guests, are comically expressed in the opening scenes where Mary
and Eileen prepare for Eddie's arrival. Eileen enters with the announce-
ment that another emigrant, Delia, has returned home. Delia looks "like
a film star" and has flown back by airplane. "It's great surely to be Yanks",
Mary replies (8). She worries that Eddie's wife won't drink porter and will
never have seen cabbage and potatoes, a staple food of the family. Eileen
reports on American food: "In summer it's cold salads and iced tea and
trifles [...] so Delia Riley says. And cheese and biscuits and coffee afterwards. And for breakfast [...] pancakes and maple syrup [...]" (9). The
characters' casual remarks to and about Eddie and his wife Julia similarly
express their stereotypical assumptions about the luxuriousness of American life, which might be assumed to be largely shared by the theatre
audience of the time. Finally, Eddie, drunk, reveals the truth: he has not
been successful in America. This scene unfolds with the Irish characters'
assumptions juxtaposed with the reality, as Eileen and Julia chat together
and Eddie, unheard by the women, speaks to himself and partly to the
audience.

The scene begins with Eileen asking "Tell me all about America, Julia,
and all the posh style" (46). As Julia expounds on the largeness of everything in America, Eddie remembers falling in love with Katie; but he
then interrupts the women with a shout that begins the second half of
the scene, in which he reveals their poverty. Calling himself "a no-good-
stinkin' bum", he describes living in a tower block with no elevator:
"you got to push your way up the stairs [...] making sure where you
put your foot [...]'cause the kids make a lavatory of the steps." This is

juxtaposed with Julia's comment to Eileen that all the high-rise buildings have elevators (48). Eileen remarks that she would love to have a refrigerator; and as Julia assures her that Americans could not consider living without a "cooler", Eddie reveals that they have a freezer, but "it don't freeze"; they keep all the food in it so that "the rats don't get at it". The camera has been rented for $20 a week, a confession prompted by Julia's description of American romance as "Parties [...] dances [...] and in to the country on a summer's evening in a smart car [...] movies [...]" (49). Prompted by the disjunction between the life his family imagines he leads and his reality, Eddie reflects that the fine cabin trunks are empty because they cannot afford to buy clothes to fill them; they are part of an elaborate pretence to save his pride:

> You can't come back with a shirt and two pairs of socks locked in a wooden box your father made for you when you went [...] No sir, you got have three or four bags with 'Cabin' and 'Stateroom' labels stuck all over them [...] and you got to buy the biggest goddamn stateroom trunk you can afford [...] only things is ... there's no goddamn clothes in it.
>
> (49)

The play also addresses the false expectations of America and the pressure on emigrants to present idealized images of their lives there, lest they be rejected for their failure by their friends and families at home. Eddie drinks away most of his income. The truth, he tells his brother, is that "you'll hit liquor because it's the only out for you when it's too late to do the things you first set out to do" (51). The play offers him a resolution, however: he decides to be a loving husband to his wife, and celebrates this by taking her to the lane where he and Katie went courting. Curly recounts how he found him there, lying with Julia in the long grass. Eddie returns to America having, it seems, reconciled himself to the reality of his life and having decided that he will be happy with what he has. But he arrives at this realization by experiencing his alienation from his home-place, and the death of Katie removes his last fantasy of a happy return. Persuading his brother not to emigrate, he warns him of the paradoxical experience of the exile:

> EDDIE: Do you think that if you do [go] you'll come back to the same place you left?
> CURLEY: It'll be here ...

EDDIE: Sure … it'll be here. But that's about all that will be here. The
same house … but in a different field, in a different country, in a
different world. And you'll go searching for the other things … like
me … And let me tell you sumthin' … when you go back again and
see that New York skyline … you'll be so sorry you'll laugh … 'cos
you're really back home then …

(31–2)

Returning "home" to New York, Eddie's departure allows for the restoration of an improved normality, in which Curly marries the girl he loves
and the life of the family and community is re-established.

Premiering almost 30 years after *The Country Boy*, but set in the early
1970s, Tom Murphy's *Conversations on a Homecoming* also represents a
returned emigrant who tries to conceal his failure. The critic Fintan
O'Toole describes the play as "perfectly poised between despair and
hope", "set in the backwash of an illusion, Ireland's infatuation with
American modernity as embodied by Jack Kennedy", the first American
president of Irish descent, and the first to visit Ireland in 1963 (1997: xi).
The action takes place in a pub called The White House, which was
founded by the absent character J. J. Kilkelly, as a "vague version of
Camelot where art and culture and intelligence […] would flourish amid
the bigotry and crassness of small-town Ireland" (O'Toole 2003: 37), but
which attracts only a few customers. The stage directions describe "a
forgotten looking place" (Murphy: 3) and a landlady in a dirty house-
coat. The men who gather that night – Tom, Liam, and Junior – are JJ's
former acolytes, now older and cynical, their despair expressed in their
disillusionment with America and their lack of belief in possibility at
home or overseas. Of the three, only Junior is married; Liam is courting
JJ's schoolgirl daughter and Tom has been engaged for ten years but is
reluctant to marry, his immaturity and alienation expressed physically
in his opening posture "hunched in his overcoat […] almost foetal" (3).
They have assembled to welcome Michael home from New York, where
he is supposedly a successful actor. *Conversations* represents the despair
of a society in turmoil both economically and politically, with the civil
unrest in Northern Ireland referenced in the text, and the desperation
both of those who stay and those who go. O'Toole describes it as "a poor
man's Purgatory, where God in the broken-down shape of JJ will not
show his face, where Michael avoids the fires of hell with which he has
tried to burn himself, and Tom lives out an eternal suspended adoles-
cence" (1997: xi). Though many of the problems that drive emigration
are mentioned – lack of opportunity and impediments to marriage being

two of them – the characters also voice their disenchantment with the American Dream and are aware of the disparity between what Michael tells them, and the reality of his situation.

Michael tries to explain why he has come home, but like Eddie in *The Country Boy* he finds the gap between his experience and that of his friends is too wide, and his attempts at communication fail. He says, "you'd be surprised at how dicked-up one can get – I mean, how meaningless things can become for one – occasionally of course – away from one's – you know." Tom replies, "I suppose 'one' can. (*Awkward moment's pause*)" (Murphy: 12–3). He fails to understand his friends' passionate response to the events in Northern Ireland, thinking at first that they are joking about joining the IRA and only slowly realizing that they seriously considered it (13). He can only reach them by evoking their shared past, but while he believes in JJ's vision for the White House, his friends have become cynical. Isolated from the group, he resorts to tales of life in New York, but fails to impress them: the first story he tells is one they heard from him ten years previously (25); the second is a joke about Christ that his friends find blasphemous (26), and the third is of a drunken man in a bar, that the characters realize is Michael (28–30). Their awareness of his financial failure is confirmed by the landlady's cutting remark, when he pulls out money to pay for a round of drinks, that "your mother is delighted; I was talking to her for a minute this morning in the post office and she drawing out a wad of money. (*All get the implications of her remark*)" (60). However, as Tom tells him, none of them have any more than he does (74); his experiences in America are no more than a dismal reiteration of theirs at home. The pervasive sense of hopelessness is apparent in Tom's reluctance to marry, though he and his fiancée are both 40; it is apparent in the deserted bar, and it is coupled with a terrifying loneliness in Michael's story about the man in the bar who "took off his clothes. Well, bollocks naked, jumping on tables and chairs, and then he started to shout 'No! No! This isn't it at all … Then he tried to set himself on fire […] Then he started crying, put on his clothes I suppose, and left. I thought it was a good one" (29–30).

Like *The Country Boy*, the play addresses the pressure on emigrants to succeed, with Michael caught in a dilemma of wanting to impress his friends while needing to confide in them. They are alternately supportive and dismissive of his putative success: Tom says of America that it is a "Ridiculous country. The luck is on me I never left here" (42). Later in the play, however, his ambivalence is captured in two contrasting exchanges between him and Michael: the first in which Michael insists, "I've been having a great time", and Tom replies, "No! – No! –", saying, "You came home to stay, to *die*, Michael" (51–2). But the dynamic is reversed when Michael confesses to Tom that he was the man in the bar:

TOM: …But you're doing well.
MICHAEL: No.
TOM: No! You are!
MICHAEL: Setting myself on fire.
TOM: You're doing well, you're doing well, someone has to be doing
   well, and we're all delighted, we are, we are, we really are…

(77)

These exchanges identify Michael as a source of fascination and repulsion for the local characters. His knowledge of strange and wonderful places, and his potential status as a famous and successful friend, attracts them to him yet reminds them of their own failures; his success angers them, yet his comforting failure angers them too since he has squandered a chance that they did not have. As with Eddie in *The Country Boy*, his departure will allow a return to normality; his unwelcome evocation of their shared past will be put aside and he will return to the nowhere land, the lost Utopia of America.

America as death: *White Woman Street* (1992)

Sebastian Barry's *White Woman Street* also presents a dystopic vision of America, but the play is unusual in setting the dramatic action entirely in America. The time is Easter 1916, the same time as the Rising in Dublin that ultimately led to the founding of the Irish Free State. This event is obliquely referred to in the text, but the Easter setting is made explicit and its significance as a time of sacrifice and redemption, with its promise of spring and of new hope, also holds a very particular meaning for the central character, Trooper. Originally from Sligo in the West of Ireland, he has spent his entire adult life in America, firstly as a soldier fighting in the Indian wars, and later, following a traumatic event which is not fully revealed until late in the play, as a wanderer and an outlaw. Together with his band of four companions – Blakely, Mo, Nathaniel, and James – he is camped in the wilderness in Ohio, near the town of White Woman Street, waiting for the gold train which is due in two days. The group plan to rob the train, and Trooper dreams of using his share of the wealth to return home to Ireland. This is the only one of these plays set in an exterior space, furnished with "five rough bed-sites ranged about a wood fire, burned down to a redness", with a coffee can, cups, blankets, leathers, guns, hats, and horses listed as the stage properties. The scene is immediately familiar as America from filmic representations of the Wild West.[9]

Yet despite the familiarity of the scene, America in Barry's play is placeless. Lesley Hill comments that America has been "developing the art of placelessness right from the beginning" (4), seeing the division of America into six-mile squares for the settlers regardless of topography as an indication that only private property had value, so that "the public realm was considered worthless if it was considered at all, giving it a placeless sort of status" (4). Hill's commentary seems apposite in the light of Trooper's contribution to the pioneer project. But the landscape in which the play is set is also a distinctively Irish theatrical one, recalling Beckett's roadside and the empty bogland spaces of Marina Carr's plays,[10] amongst others. Daniel Gerould quotes Jean Duvignaud's comment that "countries like Belgium and Ireland [...] produce legendary topologies, obsessional psychic landscapes that lend themselves to poetic visualisation" (Duvignaud: 59–64, qtd in Gerould: 306), and as the play continues it is clear its aesthetic draws upon expressionism to create a dramatic world which is both an internal, lyrical space and a supranatural space between the world of the living and that of the dead.

The play begins with a soliloquy in which Trooper reflects upon his life. It is a drama of atonement, in which he retraces his steps to White Woman Street, seeking forgiveness from the ghost of a young Native girl for whose death he holds himself responsible:

> [O]ne day and the darkest of my life I rode into a young town of those days called White Woman Street, where the canal workers and the troopers went to visit the famous whore, the only white woman for five hundred miles. And I was keen to see her and my heart was sore and I was needing a hint of home. And in I went to her.
>
> (126)

His experience there has altered the course of his life: "So thirty years ago not far from here I saw the worst sight of all my days and I hit the roads of America as a simple outlaw and followed that trade" (126). He longs to return home to Sligo, but cannot do so "till peace be made, till I stand again in White Woman Street and beg a certain ghost for her good word" (126).

The men's visit to the brothel in White Woman Street leads to the gradual revelation of Trooper's secret. The barman in the brothel is a Native man named Clarke, who tells the group about the murder of a "girl – sixteen, little Ohio river girl [...] Little Indian girl" killed 30 years before in one of the rooms. "Fella drew his knife across her throat, just like she was a pig to bleed" (155). Nobody was caught for the crime. In the final scenes of the play, in the shadowy streets of the pioneer town, Trooper tells his friend Mo what happened. Thinking the girl was the legendary white woman, he paid to sleep with her, but in the dusk of the room he saw that she was a light-skinned, green-eyed "Indian girl" (*sic*). He had sex with her anyway, then:

> I looks down [...] and that woman is bleeding the way a first-time woman does, and she not crying in her face but I see the thing worse than tears [...] Then fast as a wolf she dips down to take my cold English blade from my breeches belt, and dragged it flashing like a kingfisher across her throat [...] She just choked and died in front of me.
>
> (163)

He had hoped that, by returning, "Trooper O'Hara can wipe the slate clean and go back to being what he was" (162); that he could "say something to her, I could do something kinder". But the girl, as Mo reminds him, is "dead thirty years" (163). The play ends with the raid on the train, and the shooting of Trooper. Dying, Trooper sees "that shining hawthorne", a landscape from his childhood; crouching beside him, Mo talks to him until he dies, saying "You sleep, Trooper ... Look, Trooper – Ireland" (167).

Barry's play represents Trooper's sense of exile, his experience of being outcast from both his home and his host societies, and his longing for the landscape of his childhood echoes through the interweaving of his soliloquy with the dialogue. His homesickness takes the form of vivid memories expressed in the language of the senses, of color and smell, taste, sound, and touch. He left Sligo in search of adventure when he began to "fume with youth" (126), but now cannot offer any other rationale for his decision. The American Dream has eluded him, and in its place is a darker, largely disremembered history of the role of Irish emigrants in the colonial project, and the poverty of the laborers who worked on the railroads and canals. Recognizing a similarity between his experience as Irish and the plight of the Native Americans,

Trooper tells his companions, "Never could shoot an Indian … the tent towns … put in me in mind of certain Sligo hills, and certain men in Sligo hills. The English done for us, I was thinking, and now we're doing for the Indians" (143–4). The Native barman, Clarke, voices the same sense of comradeship when he tells Trooper the news of the Easter Rising: "Fighting the English. My grandpa fighting the English too. English won" (161).

The play recognizes the role of Irish emigrants in the American Army, fighting against the First Nations. But its characters also reflect on the position of the Irish in that society. Blakely, one of Trooper's companions, muses, "I seen Irish … holed up in the crevices of America just as cockroaches do, or the very lice on my body, and I never saw an Indian as bad as an Irish" (145). This description of the Irish in America accords with Noel Ignatiev's analysis of American racial attitudes towards Africans and the Irish in the nineteenth century, though it is very much at odds with the dominant discourses in Ireland, which represented America as a land of unlimited opportunity. But Trooper speaks of the laborers "pushing spades and hauling up axes in America, digging and cutting like pigs and dogs", for whom the prostitutes on White Woman Street were the only comfort (148–9).

In contrast to the richness of his remembered Ireland, Trooper's America is a land of weariness, darkness, bare earth and dust: a limbo, a purgatorial space, where he is left to lament and to make reparations for his treatment of the young Native girl. He describes "a filthied land of thinning trees" (126), "empty lands", and "fields without a harvest sown" (127). And he states, "I aim to head for home again [...] But I can't go till peace be made" (126). This need to seek forgiveness before he can go, read against the play's final moments in which his going "home" is experienced in his death, suggests the conflation of America with the world of the dead. Trooper's America is an expressionistic representation of his internal landscape; a purgatory in which he expiates his guilt through suffering. He is already dead, his promised land almost visible just beyond his reach, vividly expressed in his memories of Ireland. He is twice abjected: he is an outcast in America, living a life of crime, and his sin – for though innocent of the crime he accuses himself of wrong-doing – prevents him from "rest[ing] a local man in Sligo" (126). He cannot go home until he has been forgiven, his psychological torment mirroring Catholic teaching that the soul cannot progress to heaven until it has expiated its sins in purgatory.

Conclusion

Irish plays of the late twentieth century repeatedly engage with the folk-image of America as Utopia, only to dismantle it, uncovering a dystopia of frustrated ambition, homesickness and alienation. All the returned emigrants reveal the limitations of their lives overseas: Lizzy is childless; Eddie and Michael have turned to alcohol for comfort from their loneliness and failure; Trooper is an outlaw and an outcast; and Gar is aware that his dreams of greatness will founder into a job at a hotel and a room in his aunt's apartment. Emigration becomes exile – as Eddie warns his brother – and coming home will bring no relief: neither Lizzy, nor Michael, nor Eddie can recapture their youthful experiences of home, while Trooper dies far from the gorse fires and hawthorns of his memory.

This experience of alienation, however, is not purely naturalistic in its representation. America as Utopia, as it exists in Irish folk culture, is revealed here as an unreachable nowhere, a space that is neither here nor there, that exists "in the place of a gap", in Marin's words. This "gap", the space associated with the world of the supernatural in Irish culture, is represented in Barry's tragedy as a space in-between the worlds, where his character repents until he is allowed to transcend his human guilt and suffering; or, in O'Leary's *The Woman*, as death. The emigrant characters, returning from that nowhere space to the kitchens and pubs and interior spaces of their homeland, create disruption and discomfort. They have been transformed by their experience, and the difference within the familiar both fascinates and repels the other characters, as in Declan Hughes's *Shiver* or, comically, in Martin McDonagh's *Cripple of Inishmaan*. Having returned from an Other place – America/Utopia/Death – they bring with them unwelcome reminders of the failures of their homeland, as Lee argues; they provoke the spectators and the other characters to reflect on the failures of the Irish state. But they also haunt the living with tales of the past, as Michael in *Conversations* reminds his friends of their idealistic, youthful selves; they attempt to bring others back with them, as Aunt Lizzy does in *Philadelphia*, or as Eddie first intends to do in *The Country Boy*; and they constitute an uncanny, inassimilable element with their American mannerisms, physicalities, clothes and cosmetics embodying a strangeness within the familiar. Their departure brings relief, both to themselves and to their families; as *The Country Boy* demonstrates, it is in their acceptance of their exilic state that the dramatic resolution can be reached.

Notes

1. There are no precise figures on record. See Roy Foster, *Modern Ireland 1600–1972*; Joseph Lee, *The Modernisation of Irish Society*; Liam Kennedy, *Mapping the Great Irish Famine.*
2. There are an estimated 80 million people of Irish or partially-Irish descent worldwide.
3. Popular folk song, "Goodbye Muirsheen Durkin". Lyrics and music available at http://www.lyricsdownload.com.
4. Image provided courtesy of Derry City Council, Heritage and Museum Service.
5. For more information on Irish Wakes, see Sean Ó Súilleabháin, *Irish Wake Amusements*, Cork: Mercier Press, 1969.
6. Margaret O'Leary, *The Woman*. Unpublished. National Library of Ireland, MSS 21,437 acc.3250
7. A changeling is a fairy or other malevolent spirit, left in place of the human. Usually this happens when the fairies steal a human child and leave one of their own in its place; but it may also occur with adults. See Angela Bourke, *The Burning of Bridget Cleary*, and Tom McIntyre's play *What Happened Bridgie Cleary*, for a murder case in the late 1800s which references the idea of the adult changeling.
8. Ferriter cites Catherine Dunne's *Unconsidered People: The Irish in London* to estimate that "in 1961 alone emigrants sent £13.5 million home in remittances to relatives, almost equalling the £14 million spent on primary and secondary education in Ireland" that year (Dunne qtd in Ferriter: 10).
9. John Wayne films *Big Jake*, and *Cowboys* both include scenes of the men sitting around a campfire. The iconicity of this image is apparent from its parodic representation in Mel Brooks's Wild West comedy, *Blazing Saddles.*
10. See, for example, Marina Carr *By the Bog of Cats*. The opening stage directions read, "Dawn. On the Bog of Cats. A bleak white landscape of ice and snow. Music, a lone violin. Hester Swane trails the corpse of a black swan after her, leaving a trail of blood in the snow", or Samuel Beckett's "A country road. A tree. Evening" in *Waiting for Godot.*

Works cited

Proclamation of Independence. Available online at: http://www.taoiseach.gov.ie/eng/index.asp?docID=2521. In response to recent immigration into Ireland – a previously unknown phenomenon – the Proclamation is also available on this government site in Polish and Chinese.

Anon. "Goodbye Muirsheen Durkin". Traditional. Words and music available online at: http://www.lyricsdownload.com (accessed 4/3/2008).

Barry, Sebastian. "White Woman Street". In *Sebastian Barry: Plays 1*. London: Methuen, 1997.

Beckett, Samuel. *Waiting for Godot* London: Faber & Faber, 1965.

Boland, Eavan. "Daughters of Colony: A Personal Interpretation of the Place of Gender Issues in the Postcolonial Interpretation of Irish Literature", *Éire-Ireland* Samhradh/Fomhar (1997): 7–20.

Bourke, Angela. *The Burning of Bridget Cleary: A True Story*. London: Pimlico, 1999.

Carney, Frank. *The Righteous Are Bold*. New York, London, and Toronto: Samuel French, 1951, 1956.

Carr, Marina "By the Bog of Cats …". In *Plays 1*. London: Faber & Faber, 1999

Claeys, G. and L. T. Sargent. "Introduction". *The Utopia Reader*. New York and London: New York University Press, 1999.

Ferriter, Diarmaid. *The Transformation of Ireland, 1900–2000*. London: Profile Books, 2004.

Foster, Roy. *Modern Ireland, 1600–1972*. London: Penguin, 1988.

Freud, Sigmund. "The Uncanny". Trans. Alix Strachey. In *Psychological Writings and Letters*. Ed. Sander L. Gilman. New York: Continuum, 1995, pp. 120–53.

Friel, Brian. "Philadelphia, Here I Come!". *Selected Plays*. Buckinghamshire: Colin Smythe; Washington: Catholic University of America Press, 1986.

Gerould, Daniel. "Landscapes of the Unseen". In *Land/Scape/Theater*. Ed. Elinor Fuchs and Una Chaudhuri. Ann Arbor: University of Michigan Press, 2002, pp. 303–21.

Grene, Nicholas. *The Politics of Irish Drama*. Cambridge: Cambridge University Press, 1999.

Hill, Lesley and Helen Paris. "Introduction". In *Performance and Place*. Basingstoke: Palgrave Macmillan, 2006.

Hughes, Declan. *Shiver*. London: Methuen, 2003.

Ignatiev, Noel. *How the Irish Became White*. London and New York: Routledge, 1995.

Kavanagh, Patrick. *Collected Poems*. London: Penguin, 2005.

Kennedy, Liam. *Mapping the Great Irish Famine*. Dublin: Four Courts Press, 1999.

Kristeva, Julia. *Strangers to Ourselves*. New York: Columbia University Press, 1994.

Lee, J. J. *Ireland, 1912–1985*. Cambridge: Cambridge University Press, 1989.

Marin, Louis. "Frontiers of Utopia: Past and Present", *Critical Enquiry* 19.3 (Spring 1993): 397–420.

McDonagh, Martin. *The Cripple of Inishmaan*. London: Methuen Drama, 1997.

More, Thomas. *Utopia*. Trans. Peter K. Marshall. New York: Washington Square Press, 1965.

Murphy, John. *The Country Boy*. Dublin: Progress House, n.d.

Murphy, Tom. "A Crucial Week in the Life of a Grocer's Assistant". In *Plays 4*. London: Methuen, 1997.

Murphy, Tom. "Conversations on a Homecoming". In *Plays 2*. London: Methuen, 1993.

Murray, Christopher. ""Such a Sense of Home": The Poetic Drama of Sebastian Barry", *Colby Quarterly* 27 (December 1991): 242–8.

O'Leary, Margaret. *The Woman*. First performed Abbey Theatre, 1929. Unpublished. National Library of Ireland.

Ó Súilleabháin, Sean. *Irish Wake Amusements*. Cork: Mercier Press, 1969.

O'Toole, Fintan. "Sebastian Barry". In *Critical Moments: Fintan O'Toole on Modern Irish Theatre*. Ed. Julia Furay and Redmond O'Hanlon. Dublin: Carysfort, 2003, pp. 313–5. (First published *The Irish Times*, 13 June 1992.)

———. "Conversations on a Homecoming by Tom Murphy". In *Critical Moments: Fintan O'Toole on Modern Irish Theatre*. Ed. Julia Furay and Redmond O'Hanlon. Dublin: Carysfort, 2003, pp. 37–9. (First published *The Irish Times*, 21 April 1985.)

————. "Introduction". In *Tom Murphy: Plays: 2*. London: Methuen Drama, 1997, pp. ix–xiv.

Roche, Anthony. "Introduction". In *Cambridge Companion to Brian Friel*. Ed. A. Roche. Cambridge: Cambridge University Press, 2006.

Synge, J. M. *Collected Works. Vol 2: Prose*. Ed. Alan Price. London: Oxford University Press, 1966.

O Lochlainn, Colm. *Goodbye Muirsheen Durkin*. Traditional. Music and lyrics available at: www.mysongbook.de.

Trotter, Mary. "Re-Imagining the Emigrant / Exile in Contemporary Irish Drama", *Modern Drama* 46.1 (2003): 35–54.

2

Ninety Miles Away: Exile and Identity in Recent Cuban-American Theatre

Yael Prizant
University of Notre Dame

> *We are in the epoch of simultaneity: we are in the epoch of juxta-position, the epoch of the near and far, of the side-by-side, of the dispersed.*
>
> Michel Foucault, in his essay "Of Other Spaces", 1986

On 13 August 2006, Cuban President Fidel Castro, although recovering from major surgery and ominously absent from view, celebrated his eightieth birthday. Miami Cubans who identified as political refugees danced in the streets at the news of Castro's failing health but were also forced, yet again, to acknowledge his spectacular longevity as Cuba's charismatic leader. By the time Fidel Castro's ailing health led him to relinquish power to his brother Raúl in February 2008, the response from Florida was far more subdued. These reactions added to the extensive, problematic relationship between Cuba and the United States that deeply informs the entire Cuban diaspora, far beyond the Miami–Havana nexus that Juan Flores insists is, "incomplete without Washington, and New York, and by extension San Juan, Los Angeles, Mexico City, Madrid, Tokyo" (in De la Campa: vi) and recently (I might add) Caracas or Beijing. Years of exchange and influence have linked the island and America, its northern neighbor. Yet since the Cuban Revolution of 1959, decades of unresolved political clashes, ideological disagreements, economic sanctions, and immigration crises have marred the two countries' once enormously affable political, financial, and social affiliations. The Cuban Revolution has certainly, according to scholar Román de la Campa, "found its primary source of inspiration in confronting American brawn" (13) and ten American presidents encountered a resolute, fiercely independent Fidel Castro. While more than one million former Cuban citizens live in exile *in* the United States, other Cubans have undeniably been exiled *by* the United States. This project considers how the experience of this postmodern dislocation is making itself heard in the theatrical language of two contemporary Cuban-American playwrights, Rogelio Martinez and Nilo Cruz, both of whom concentrate on the interstitial space of the blended subject.

While exile may provide a ground of possibility, it can also engender severe estrangement – its participants are not fully at ease in any country. Rogelio Martinez and Nilo Cruz vividly express the inherent tension of living at a murky, hyphenated crossroads. Both artists come from families that were ruptured by exile from Cuba to the United States. Rogelio Martinez and his mother came to America from Cuba when he was nine years old, during the Mariel boatlift of 1980, but his father was unable to join them until ten years later. Nilo Cruz also left Cuba before his tenth birthday. He emigrated from Matanzas to Miami with his parents, but left two older sisters behind on the island. Martinez and Cruz reaffirm what theorist Edward Soja contends, that "'life-stories' have a geography too; they have milieux, immediate locales, provocative emplacements which affect thought and action" (14). The hope for a reconstitution of the self and of the homeland is accentuated as multiple competing exile conditions (internal, external, by a country and within a country) are considered in their plays. Both artists write about self-imposed exile and exile *by* the United States, both inside of Cuba and out. Their works incorporate a keen personal awareness as exiles that, as scholar Alberto Moreiras puts it, "Self-reproduction without mutation is no longer politically viable" (3) for any of their characters. Since the Cuban Missile Crisis of the early 1960s, Cuba has been notably positioned as peripheral to America and the personal consequences of the island's distinct positionality are manifest in these playwrights' works. Both Cruz and Martinez engage the ways in which various views of America as a "home" to the exile are translated, transferred, and transformed by Cubans in the United States and in Cuba.

In his play *Illuminating Veronica* (2000), Martinez explores Cuba just after the Revolution, when the title character remains on the island although her family has relocated to Miami. Martinez portrays Veronica's exile, her efforts to embrace the revolutionary socialist system in Cuba, to re-envision her home and family, and to reconcile the personal sacrifices she will have to make to participate in Cuba's newly constructed community. In *Hortensia and the Museum of Dreams* (2004) by Nilo Cruz, a pair of siblings, who were exiled to the United States during Operación Pedro

Pan (Operation Peter Pan), return to Cuba seeking recollection, recuperation, closure, and conservation. Sent to America as children (without their families), their homecomings are observably burdened by questions of identification and belonging.

Both of these plays examine how Cubans in America view themselves, how they view Cuba (in memory and in actuality), and their relationships with it. Wrestling with what theatre scholar Una Chaudhuri recognizes as, "the unsentimental recognition of home *as* a discourse, replete with ideological antecedents and consequences" (xiii), Martinez and Cruz illustrate how the enduring, intricate relationship between place and personhood, between the United States and Cuba, has irrevocably shaped the exilic identities of their characters. The plays portray the hybridity that Renato Rosaldo claims "can be understood as the ongoing condition of all human cultures, which contain no zones of purity because they undergo continuous processes of transculturation (two-way borrowing and lending between cultures)" (qtd in García Canclini: xv). "Broken" English, and the relationship with America it represents, serves as an apt metaphor for the continual fusion of Cuban identity and American exile that frame these plays.

Illuminating Veronica by Rogelio Martinez begins in Havana in December 1960, nearly two years after Fidel Castro became the leader of revolutionary Cuba. This socialist revolution has transformed the small capitalist island and Veronica's entire family has emigrated to Miami, the most popular destination among Cuban émigrés of the era. According to Cuba historian Louis Pérez: "Miami began as an imitation of Havana in the 1920s and 1930s, then was imitated by Havana during the 1940s and 1950s; in the 1960s it was a copy of a copy that was copied" (1999: 502). Cuban culture dictated much of Florida's imaginary, just as American culture shaped a great deal of Cuba's aesthetic. For example, most of Key West reflects early twentieth-century Cuban architecture and much of Havana imitates the American art deco style of the 1920s. De la Campa, however, questions the particular choice of Miami as a popular exile destination to begin with. He writes, "I am not sure why Cubans went there instead of New York, Europe, or Latin America [...]. Perhaps it was the unconscious return of the possessive gaze: Cubans looking to Miami as the United States historically looked at Cuba" (23). It is precisely how the Cuban characters who remain in Cuba respond to this gaze that Martinez's play investigates. Well educated and pregnant, Veronica remains on the island because for her "revolution", as Chaudhuri writes, "is not just an event; it is a painful turn in a long, ongoing narrative that has a logic of its own" (153). This 'turn' must *find* its meaning within a particular cultural narrative – in Martinez's play, that narrative includes the unambiguous division between Cuba and the United States after the Revolution. Soja artfully explains this kind of ideological and political schism in terms of space:

> Those seeking the demise of capitalism ... tended to see in spatial consciousness and identity – in localisms and regionalisms or nationalisms – a dangerous fetter on the rise of a united world proletariat, a false consciousness inherently antagonistic to the revolutionary subjectivity and objective historical project of the working class. Only one form of territorial consciousness was acceptable – loyalty to the socialist state [...].
>
> (35)

Martinez's work traces the processes of re-identification that the revolution demands of Veronica, of her marriage, of her home. Veronica compares Lenin's portrait with that of American movie star Yul Brynner, although the former familiarity that had allowed the United States and Cuba to influence each other, "to imitate each other, to borrow from each other, to become somewhat like each other", notes Pérez (1999: 6), had recently been altered. Here a theatrical and spatial framework is created; both the Soviet Union and America are ever-present in this Cuban world, despite their distance and antagonism toward each other. Cubans in the play live with what May Joseph asserts is the "impossibility of full citizenship by constituting its absences, its longings, its elsewheres" (7). America is ubiquitous, yet Veronica does not seem particularly anxious in the play that the "Yankees will attack at any moment" (96). However, she also reveals that she and her husband are the only members of her immediate family and friends who did not leave Cuba for Miami. An ideological rift, followed by physical separation, has fractured her family and exiled her from them.

The vestiges of a different life, of a pre-revolutionary (capitalist) society are still visible in Veronica's home. Abandoned objects that belonged to her family and correspondences by mail are the only links Veronica has with her family now. The definition of home becomes malleable throughout the play. Despite her revolutionary resolve, Veronica grows pensive while poring over her father's copy of Proust, confessing, "All of a sudden I miss home" (103). When her husband Manuel, who works as a government censor rewriting books in a "socialist context" (101), reminds her that she *is* "home", she gently concedes, "Yes. I know.

Isn't that silly"(103). Veronica suffers from what Chaudhuri calls *"static exilic consciousness"* or the condition of being homesick while at home. As Chaudhuri notes, "Here the sentimental image of home – as an actual place correlated with a strong and desirable emotional experience (the sense of 'belonging') – unravels [...]" (11). The play raises important questions about what a home entails and whether or not it can be (re)constructed (physically and/or emotionally) in exile to suit one's needs or situation.

Although Soja suggests that in the recent past, "national patriotism and citizenship were usually couched more in a cultural than a geographical identity and ideology" (35), Martinez's Veronica views Miami as a space that is distinctly disconnected from Havana. America is only a consumerist text to Veronica, a fractured dystopia that has been determined, corrupted and transformed by commodity capitalism and personal hubris. No matter how many Cubans create enclaves there, Veronica realizes that Florida can never replicate Cuba. Manuel contends that Veronica does not "belong" in Cuba, but belongs "with [her] father", that is, in Miami (100). However, Veronica deems it impossible to cultivate what De la Campa calls "an alternative Cuba through Miami" (9). Her thinking corresponds with Foucault's insistence that "we live inside a set of relations that delineates sites which are irreducible to one another and absolutely not superimposable on one another" (qtd in Soja: 17). A rift emerges between Veronica and Manuel in the play as he embraces the connections between the countries, openly discussing "how the Yankees just lost the World Series to the Pirates" (Martinez 101) with his boss, the Minister of Culture, Pepin. Is this discord unavoidable if, as Chaudhuri might suggest, Veronica has been exiled *to* where she belongs, not *from* it (12)? The comparisons between Cuba and the United States continue, as Veronica demands, "I want color television, Manuel ... My father has one in Miami" (106). No matter her ideology, American consumerism still fuels her desires. Manuel's immediate response reiterates his earlier opinion – "Then maybe that's where you belong" (106). Is Manuel's comment sarcastic? Or is he choosing to ignore that "the immediate purpose [of departing for Miami] was to get away from an uncertain – and in some cases threatening – future, but it was also a way to communicate opposition to Castro's regime", by doing what De la Campa calls "voting with one's feet" (26)?

America remains in the conversation, as a palpable adversary, when Veronica meets Pepin. Pepin accuses her of being afraid to destroy a decidedly bourgeois painting her aunt has left behind. He firmly warns

Veronica, "You can't live in two worlds" (113), flatly rejecting Chaudhuri's notion of "inhabiting two or more homes simultaneously" (212). Veronica implores Pepin:

> Do you ever get – do you ever remember things from your past. Things you had forgotten. Like a painting has the – to remember what you were like. It happens sometimes when I'm alone. I go into my older sister's room – she has this little music box that I open and Schumann plays. And just as it gets – I think she's going to walk through the door. I wait and wait, but she never comes back.
>
> (113)

Veronica's memories are a critical link to her identity and to her relationships within her family. She still calls a space in her house "my older sister's room" although that sister is no longer present. Her home, as Chaudhuri asserts, exists in relation to a familiar group of people. Yet it is the deepening uncertainty of home as an unstable container that leads Veronica to wonder if a house is still a home without her family in it. This exile grows deeper, as Pepin insists Veronica "can't have revolution under the values taught to [her] by [her] father" (114). He goes on to demand that Veronica "prove" that she can "let go of everything" in her past in order to secure a promotion for her husband. Veronica must negotiate her own identity by proving she can overcome her past and change. As her formidable response, Veronica violently slashes her aunt's painting with a knife. Despite this strong display of her will to transform, to join this new society, Veronica's self-definition remains geographically centered, tethered to what Chaudhuri calls the "power of place" (156) and her desire to reterritorialize her own home.[1] Her ex-servant Rosario, like others, gruffly points out that Veronica is "too sentimentally attached [...] to the way things used to be" (116). However, within a month, Veronica significantly modifies her view. She brazenly informs Pepin:

> This isn't even my house. Everything in it belongs to my father. Is it too much to ask to be taken seriously? Papi thought it was. Then I read Marx and quickly learned everything Papi had taught me was wrong. Submission. Grace. Weakness. They were nothing but antiquated beliefs. Now there are new ideas. Fulfillment. Equality. Strength. Ideas that have taken hold of me. That have filled me. And I don't ever see me letting them go.
>
> (124)

"The transformation of the family", notes Chaudhuri, "from a living receptacle of the individual's memory to the site of its being forgotten [...]"(107) denotes a crucial shift here. Veronica views herself as having been enlightened, having been schooled anew. The price of her ideological re-education, of her new national identity, is her familial one. She has shed one to incorporate the other, has exiled her family and been exiled herself.

Manuel, on the other hand, has begun to appreciate the markers of the past. Where he once criticized Veronica for her sentimentality, he now clings to what was before. When Manuel finally asserts, "I can't live here – I want to go" and explains that pouring cement for 70 hours a week since losing his government position was not "what he bought into", Veronica insists that he doesn't understand the immense sacrifices that are called for and reminds him that she "gave up her family" (138) to further the revolutionary project. Surprisingly, Manuel tells her that he has arranged for their clandestine departure and relocation to Miami. Veronica painfully admits that she thought her husband was "another man" (139). The binary of staying on the island as opposed to leaving for Florida has created profound fissures in their relationship, leaving no room for complicated nuances. Veronica and Manuel take sides, unfortunately against one another.

Veronica's reaction when explosions are suddenly heard is particularly revealing. She assumes that Cubans in America have decided to attack the island, that her father has not abandoned her but will reclaim his homeland and reinstate the "dynamic adaptation and accommodation" that existed between the United States and Cuba, argues Pérez, for centuries before the Revolution (1999: 6). The explosions are not an attack after all, but rather are the celebratory fireworks of Cuban carnival. However, the scene exposes Veronica's innermost feelings. The audience sees the glimmer of the naïve hope she has preserved. Furthermore, this deliberate conflation of celebration with destruction exposes a major paradox of the Cuban Revolution and of exile: Does the past have to be obliterated for a re-envisioning of the future? Must a definitive line be drawn between participants and exiles? What is left of identity when the general uncertainty of the time actively erodes it? The ideological differences between characters in the play become especially tumultuous as the play continues. Veronica reports her husband's plan to leave the country to government authorities, resulting in his arrest and imprisonment for five years. It is unclear whether she does this out of spite, fear of his departure, fear for her own safety if the government views her as his accomplice, or her belief in the burgeoning new society. (A complex blend of these motivations seems most probable.) Rosario rationalizes the losses required for Veronica to move forward, as she tells her, "I want you to kiss your husband goodbye so you can get on with your life" (147). De la Campa's assertion that "nationalism begets a sense of isolation, if not arrogance, that may well keep all Cubans from any sense of belonging" (14) reflects Veronica's particular exilic experience. Her internal exile, complete with emotional isolation, seems required for change. Yet her perplexed response to blended influences also illustrates Pérez's notion of national identity, "not as a fixed and immutable construct but as cultural artifact, as contested" (1999: 8). The supposedly safe haven of exile creates a torturous longing for the homeland, while those who have remained "at home" attempt to reconfigure it. The yearning for connections, for belonging, drives Sofia to offer to become Veronica's family, to attempt to "revive small enclaves of familiarity, intimacy, security, intelligibility, organic-sensory interaction in which to mirror him/herself", according to scholar Zdravko Mlinar (4). Martinez's Sofia tells Veronica, "I don't want to give up the chance to have something genuine" (151). Is she implying that they have not had sincere relationships with their actual relatives? Or that family can be chosen or fabricated? An earlier reference to Goldilocks re-emerges, as the characters admit that they don't know how the lost girl's search for identity and belonging was actually resolved. This metaphor bolsters the provisional, unfixed nature of the postmodern exile identity.

The fracture of the home is completed by the last letter Veronica's father writes to her. He explains that "memory either narrows a place to the point of disappearing or causes it to grow in your imagination" (157). He admits that he can find no way to retain actual experiences. He reveals, "I've decided to let go because for me Havana is a house on a quiet street – a house that no longer belongs fully to me" (157). Yet his most chilling admission is that his own daughter grows faint in his memory, that he feels he must relinquish her along with Cuba itself, to live fully in the present:

> Last night I forgot what you look like and though the thought of forgetting you rattled me a little I soon decided that you were like the house that no longer belonged to me. With love, your father. PS. This is my last letter to you. I have grown sentimental and I am embarrassed by everything I do or say in respect to Cuba.
>
> (157)

Her father has incorporated the "combination of nostalgia and refusal" (9) that De la Campa argues defines the Cuban exile community in

Miami. He also chooses, according to De la Campa, "the creation of an alternative community, another homeland, perhaps a Cuba we never had or could have, in the United States" (64). The letter makes Veronica fully aware of her father's decision to embrace another community entirely. Hence, in a brief exchange between Veronica and Ernesto, Veronica adopts a new family, a new father, a new identity. "The possibility of being exposed", Milnar claims, "to the near infinity of places, persons, things, ideas, ma[de] it all the more necessary to have a center in which to cultivate one's self" (4), to reterritorialize the local. Veronica replaces her lost relatives with those who already share the house with her, who accept her choices, as if families were interchangeable. The scene appropriately ends with the sound of Veronica's twin babies crying, of the family that will surround her in the future. She remarks:

> The man who wrote that letter and his friends. When they come back we will turn off all the lights and close all our doors and then we will hope they don't recognize their old homes. That they have forgotten them. We will hope they go away.

> (158)

The alteration of Veronica's identity and belonging have come full circle. Veronica's home is transformed into what Chaudhuri calls "a place of discovery, a place to be discovered" (135) rather than the site of her physical and metaphoric exile from her family and her self. New alliances are forged that disregard the old, that utterly reject those who were once so vital. The rupture is severe enough that it has destroyed all of Veronica's ties, yet it has also engendered significant new bonds to replace them. Is this severity necessary to form new identifications surrounding exile? Is this what is required to find belonging in a new society? Martinez's work demonstrates that, as Ann Pelligrini contends, "Processes of identification are the subject's constitutive condition. Through identification, individuals effectively solder their egos to others, both real and imagined" (10). The tension remains unresolved, "Less a matter of arriving at a fixed and final destination as it is of stopping off at points along the way to a somewhere or someone else", as Pelligrini suggests (10).

Nilo Cruz's play *Hortensia and the Museum of Dreams* occurs in 1998, during the Pope's historic first visit to Cuba. "The fact that Pope John Paul II", according to De la Campa, "has regularly critiqued the excesses of capitalism as well as those of socialism provides a telling index of how these forces have crisscrossed" (31) and serves as an important backdrop for two Cuban-Americans exiles who visit their homeland. The play deals

with the loss intrinsic in exile and especially within the experience of
the children who were part of Operación Pedro Pan, the 1960–62 exodus
of over 14,000 Cuban children to the United States. In the play, Luca
and his estranged sister, Luciana, return to their native Cuba after living
in the United States for nearly 35 years. Cruz uses theatrical elements to
express the paradoxes and complexities of exile and reterritorialization as
envisioned by cultural theorist Néstor García Canclini, despite the loss of
immediate relations to geography. Cuba was, is, and always will be a part
of who they are. The crucial relationship between place and personhood
emerges in the first few moments of the play, making it clear that exile
has hybridity at its core. Cruz explains that Luciana and Luca "should
look younger than their actual age, as if their lost childhood has stopped
them from aging"(4). He physically presents their bodies, as Pelligrini
might describe them, "as contested discursive site[s] through which ideological concepts are naturalized as biology" (6). The Cuban-American
siblings also embark on separate, very personal journeys, as they seek to
make sense of their abstracted childhoods, experiences that Kaja Silverman notes are "dominated by identification and duality" (157). Where
the United States was once the Utopia they dreamed of, now they both
imagine Cuba as their Utopia. As Chaudhuri astutely articulates, their
Cuban "identities have to be negotiated out of a welter of myths and
stereotypes and desires and dreams and daydreams" (147). While there
are moments of theatrical realism throughout the play, ambient sounds
and commingled spaces often create an impressionistic stage environment. For instance, the play begins with Luca and Luciana both on stage,
but completely unaware of each other and clearly in separate environ-
ments while having simultaneous, parallel traveling experiences. They
go from the United States to Cuba, but their physical environment does
not change. They also write in travel journals and impart their thoughts
directly to the audience.

Cruz's characters come to the island with different purposes and separate visions of their Cubanness and of Cubanidad in general. Luca
explains to the Cuban airport agents that he has come to the island
to visit relatives, with whom he will stay. Luciana discloses that she
is a journalist and will stay at the Hotel Capri. One sibling has come
home as a Cuban returning from America, the other has come to Cuba
as an American tourist. Their varied perspectives are instantly evident:
the Hotel Capri, once run by Miami mobsters, is open only to non-Cuban
tourists. What does Luciana's choice signify if, as Chaudhuri contends,
"tourism is a method of experiencing other places in terms one already
understands, a method of canceling out unfamiliarity" (150)? Doesn't

an exile inherently approach with a remembered, or possibly imagined, familiarity? In the play Luciana insists, "I didn't come here to retrace the past, I came to see the new generation ... The new island ..." (9). Her statement begs the question of whether or not there is something contemporary in Cuba for her to see and just how her past may be reflected or obscured there. Her remoteness reiterates Chaudhuri's view that the meaning of exile is usefully ambivalent, that "exile is branded by the negatives of loss and separation; on the other [hand] it is distinguished by distance, detachment, perspective" (12). Considering the contentious relationship between the United States and Cuba, what kind of "perspective" might Luciana have?

Basic privileges in America surely alter Luca's perception of Cuba as well. In a section entitled "A Place Called Home", Luca's uncle Tio Lalo explains to Luca that, "It's better to bathe in the morning because the electricity is cut off after six" (9). Here the reality of daily life in Cuba in the 1990s is conveyed. Blackouts, shortages and desperate innovations shape Havana. These hardships are strange to the siblings because, since their departure in the 1960s, these Cuban-Americans have had little contact with the island. In a scene entitled Maps and the City, the siblings grapple with memory:

> LUCA: I'm remembering the streets ...
> LUCIANA: The streets are remembering me ...
> LUCA: Blue skies, faded awnings, orange tiles...
> LUCIANA: The world is not forgetful ... A sidewalk never forgets to be a sidewalk ... A tree never forgets to be a tree.
>
> (10)

Are one's memories affected by whether or not one is remembered? Whether conditions remain the same? Is there an exchange, or conversation, of memory? As Chaudhuri observes, "Although the act of returning home is an archetypally regressive act – 'going home is always going *back* home,' [...] it is used [...] not to recuperate identity but rather to stage the difficulties, even impossibility, of such a recuperation" (92). Hence, while Luca reveals that he and Luciana should "settle the past" (Cruz 10), Luciana is only concerned with what she can presently cull from the island. She remarks, "In a secret way I'm collecting faces, streets and romantic corners ..." (11). Luciana's exile is complete in her definition of herself; she tells Samuel, a stranger she encounters, "I'm not from here. I'm from the United States" and insists she is on the island "for the Pope's visit" (13). Cruz does not allow her to admit that her trip has any personal significance or that she was born in Cuba. When Samuel's brother, Basilio, insists that her birthplace, "makes [her] one of [them] ...," Luciana tellingly does not respond. She resists the "new hybrid identity" that Joseph suggests may "continuously produce discursive critiques of the state, of patriarchy, and of capitalism" (5).

Basilio, a man in his twenties, welcomes Luciana to his mother's house and to the Museum of Dreams in the same breath. The two, home and museum, are conflated. How is their home like a museum and/or their museum like a home? "It is not the same thing, of course, to preserve the memory in individual form or to pose the problem of assuming the collective representation of the past", writes García Canclini (140). How might one family represent the dreams of all of Cuba? Chaudhuri asserts that, "Only those things are put in a museum that have no 'organic' place within a society, because they either belong to a different time or a different place" (120). Do dreams belong in "a different time and place" than present-day Cuba? Meanwhile, Luca tries to explain to Delita, a Cuban girl, why he often doesn't know how old he is – in the play he tells her that his "body has stopped recognizing" (15) his age. This idea, that he has been physically unable to grow due to his unexplored identity, resonates throughout the play. Luca's fervent attempt to "adjust" (16) to life in Cuba echoes his past, in which he was forced to adjust to life outside of Cuba. He is dejected when confronted with what Soja identifies as "urgent awareness of geographically uneven development and the revived sense of [his] personal political responsibility for it [...]." This awareness, writes Soja, "spatializes the contemporary moment and reveals the insights to be derived from a deeper understanding of contemporary crisis and restructuring [...]" (23). Luca's intense memories of the island as it was 30 years before must be reconsidered. Because Luca looks younger than his age, the audience is confronted with a physical paradox as well: although Luca still appears youthful, years have significantly altered the world around him and his perception of it. The ethereal nature of these conversations materializes as the scene is punctuated with the sound of a wave that "takes Luca and Delita away" (16).

Luciana is also exploring Cuba, her homeland, but as a tourist and adventurer rather than as a native. She is unable to "'return' completely", according to Guillermo Gomez-Peña (21), and therefore gets lost in Havana. Luciana is utterly lost while at "home" in Cuba and describes how "the thrill and the fear of the unknown take over" (16) in Cruz's play.

This specific language, that her homeland is 'unknown' to her, pointedly reflects her experience. When Luciana meets Hortensia, Hortensia calls her "a woman from a foreign country" (17). It is only Luca who consistently positions Luciana as a native of Cuba. He tells an absent Luciana, "I went back to our old house. I found you in every room. Even if you have chosen to remove yourself, you were there in the patio, in the living room, standing by the window ..." (20). The place is marked for Luca and, in his estimation, his sister still belongs in it. His memory is crafted around her presence, in sharp contrast to the fact that she has chosen to distance herself from him and from Cuba.

Even Basilio and his brother Samuel, born after the Revolution and therefore too young to remember any other system, understand and use American references throughout the play. If they do so for Luciana's sake only, it becomes evident that her American background actively changes the communication between them. This moment is juxtaposed with Tio Lalo explaining to Luca just why he and his sister were sent to America. Lalo describes the perception on the island: "Everybody thought there was going to be a war, you see. And there were rumors that the government planned to send children to work on Soviet farms, so [your mother] wanted to protect you" (24). The binary between America and the Soviet Union emerges here – America is viewed as a safe haven for the children while the Soviet Union is feared. Cuba is isolated between these super powers. Although they leave the island, Luciana and Luca suffer similar isolation in exile.[2] Basilio soon shares a file of "a few of the miracles that came last month" with Luciana. One in particular is staged. In this man's story, departure from Cuba to a foreign land is central. Luciana is pensive as she hears the rest. Elsewhere, Luca opens a suitcase as he asks Delita, "Tell me what do you want to eat?" (29). This suitcase is overstuffed with food and toiletries. Luca ironically adds, "I told you I came prepared" (29). Delita eats a biscuit and quizzically comments, "They taste like paradise" (29). Cuba is often discussed as a paradise, with its warm tropical weather and sandy beaches. Instead, Delita views American goods this way. To soothe Delita's extremely emotional reaction to the wealth of food, Luca gently says, "We have everything we need, and what we don't have we'll do without" (29). Although Luca has a suitcase full of products and Luciana has the freedom to travel, the access and excess of American capitalism do not soothe the emotional ruptures of exile and isolation.

The angst that the trip to Cuba has created for Luciana is evident when Samuel and Basilio share parts of Luciana's travel diary aloud. They note that she is "in a quandary"(30) that causes her to wander through the streets. The psychic toll of rediscovery, of attempting to reconcile the past, has disoriented her. Her identity is clearly in flux, as Luca enters the stage and remarks:

> I went to the house we used to visit every summer ... The place looked withered and old, as if the sea had entered the house ... The old swing was still there swaying in the breeze ... And the hum of mother's song in the air, telling you to come back.

(32)

Because Luca and Luciana have been estranged, Luca chooses to imagine his sister through his early childhood memories of places and things, clearly equating her with Cuban locations and climes. Luciana remarks, "Because I can only love you best when you're far away, I've chosen to love you in the distance" (33). This is true of her feelings for both Luca and Cuba. The fracture of involuntary relocation, combined with an ominous secret from their childhood, creates the internal exile that Cruz portrays. Luciana tells Hortensia, "Little by little I realize why I am playing this role, why I can't face myself ... Why I am living a lie ..." (35). She has been exiled from her own feelings as well as her country.

Luciana's quest for self-discovery and recovery is troubled by General Viamonte of the Interior Ministry. He ruthlessly interrogates Luciana and Hortensia. Although Hortensia insists that Luciana is "not a foreigner" because she was born in Cuba, the General replies, "She's a foreigner to me!" (37) marking Luciana's distinct difference from those who stayed on the island. Viamonte also points out that the processes of childhood exile manufactured identifications, as he comments "So, the Pedro Pan project, they called it, like the children's book about the boy who runs away to never-never land and never grows up ..." (38). Because their childhoods were irrevocably altered, many of the Pedro Pan children who were separated from their families and raised by strangers feel as if they never fully experienced childhood.[3] Even if sarcastically, America is positioned as a far-away land where all is supposedly well, a Utopia where no one ages and new identifications can be created. The General later refers to Luciana as a "tourist" and blatantly rejects the dreams Hortensia has collected, all while praising the material accomplishments of the Revolution. Yet his unsentimental, illuminating assessment of the struggles of modern Cuba troubles Luciana's utopian vision of her homeland.

Upon their return to the museum, Luciana criticizes Hortensia's passive response to the interrogation:

> LUCIANA: (*With contained anger*) It seems like this whole island is always waiting! Waiting! Waiting for something to happen. And nothing ever happens. Who's going to be the first one to stop waiting! Who's going to be the first!
> HORTENSIA: You have your ways ... You come from a different world.
> LUCIANA: No, I come from the same world.
>
> (41)

Their disagreement over the form of action reflects their unique perspectives. Do Cubans have a very different world view than Americans? The play begs the critical question May Joseph asks – "How are hybrid identities shaped in excess of, and in relation to, the boundaries of nation" (4)? It is indicative that in this exchange Luciana reveals that her two experiences, as a Cuban exile and as a hyphenated American, are not separate. She finally acknowledges her connection with a Cuban world just as Hortensia denies it. This characterization affirms Homi Bhabha's observation that identification is "always the production of an image of identity and the transformation of the subject in assuming that image" (45). Luciana is accepting her Cuban identity. When Hortensia asks Luciana why she chose to stay in Oriente rather than Havana, Luciana replies: "Because for a moment I needed a sense of place, to belong" (42). Hortensia informs Luciana of the play's central concern, that "everything in life is trying to find its place but also its absence. And already from the beginning the absence had begun ..." (42).

The following and most impressionistic scene in the play, "Entering the Night Without Electricity", takes place in near darkness. Cruz writes two conversations that overlap considerably, often making it unclear exactly who is being spoken to, or spoken of:

> DELITA: You must not remember much about this place.
> BASILIO: You're almost American ...
> LUCA: Are you saying that I'm American?
> BASILIO: You were so young when you left.
> LUCIANA: But I don't feel American.
>
> (44)

What does it mean to "feel" Cuban or American? How do these cultures coexist in one's body/perspective/memory? Can one decide to be neither? Is one's self-definition a choice or circumstantial? Both Luca and Luciana experience what Mae G. Henderson calls "the outsidedness of insidedness" (17). They are trapped between rootedness and estrangement, from their homeland, from their adopted nation, and from themselves. Is their dichotomy of consciousness because, as Chaudhuri argues, "the most fundamental rift between the figure of America and the old discourse of exile comes [...] from the grim reality of home – and homelessness – that greets the already unhomed immigrant" (200)? Delita exposes Luca's exile when she admits: "I never thought that life would be difficult up there" (in America). Luca replies: "It was. I remember it as if it was yesterday. A cold town in Ohio. And old building falling apart ... Children and more children. The stench of urine." Here Luca incisively dismantles the utopic fantasy of America. Luciana poignantly adds, "In Ohio my heart was circumcised" (45). The "sense of trauma" that De la Campa considers irrevocable for exiles has definitely molded these adults.

Luciana and Luca's young-looking bodies act as the sites of inscription of their exilic experiences. When Basilio asks Luciana if she loves Luca, she tells him, "He was my mother, my father, my brother, my sister, and also nothing. Nothing. So he could be everything. Everything. On his mouth the seaside. On his eyebrows my old school" (46). She explains that Luca became the vessel for her memories, physically as well as emotionally. As De la Campa explains: "Behind their anxieties lies a need to come to grips with a complicated national history that affected them so deeply at an age at which they could not act for themselves" (55). As music plays and Luciana says farewell to the museum, she reads: "I write this as though I am claiming and taking back with me a box of embraces ... A box of dreams ... A jar of memories ..." (48). The notion of claiming, or reclaiming, one's heritage or identity is crucial. Taking something back infers it was once lost, once separated from the individual. Yet Cruz's play seems to suggest that it was never disconnected, never missing entirely. As she leaves to find Luca, Luciana declares: "Now it was time to find my way back to what I had left behind", keenly aware of the journey to repossess something absent. When the siblings finally meet again face to face, they share the following exchange:

LUCA: Do you regret our past?
LUCIANA: I regret nothing. But you and I ... We have to find a way ...
LUCA: For a long time I had thought about this moment, when we
would finally talk ...

LUCIANA: Me, too. I thought I had to find a way to tell it to myself, like a children's story that explains the world.
LUCA: And how would the story go?
LUCIANA: Two children dressed up in airport dreams. Two children who thought the world was going to end. Two children who only had each other.

(52)

For Luca and Luciana, the airport marks the continually shifting border that they have spent their lives negotiating. Their experience mirrors Gloria Anzaldúa's idea that "Borders are set up to define the places that are safe and unsafe [...]. A borderland is a vague and undetermined place created by the emotional residue of an unnatural boundary. It is in a constant state of transition [...]." (3). Luca and Luciana's exile shielded them from the changes in Cuba yet its residue also engendered the incest that eventually led to the upsetting fracture between them. Despite fear, loss, displacement, and disjuncture, Luca and Luciana (like many Cubans on the island) remain imaginative and hopeful, optimistically childlike. They finally embrace what Chaudhuri describes as the "possibility of entertaining two or more cultural contexts simultaneously" (212) and find comfort in it. The play ends with the miracle they send to Hortensia. In it, they choose to describe themselves by their professions (salesman and journalist, respectively) and by their present addresses (one in New York, the other in Rhode Island) rather than by their nationalities or their pasts. Luca and Luciana finally create self-definitions that do not include the rigid spatial binary that caused them such turmoil. Cruz uses the intersection of space and time as a border where subjects with ties to two identifications constitute crucial acts of self-representation.

If, as De la Campa suggests, "the most realistic way to inhabit one's nation [...] is to recognize the conflictive pluralities it contains" (19), then the characters in these plays prosper. Their geographical and emotional displacements are eventually subsumed into their daily realities. In these plays, "An already-made geography sets the stage," notes Soja, "while the willful making of history dictates the action and defines the story line" (14). Veronica, Luca, and Luciana actively seek to make their own histories. They seek identities in between the binaries of impoverished Cuban and anti-Castro American. De la Campa's most difficult question is eloquently posed by these dramas: "Can [exiles] ever recapture a lost past, or register suspicions about historical events that engulfed everyone, most of all themselves" (55)? *Illuminating Veronica* and *Hortensia and the Museum of Dreams* defy closure by refusing to resolve key paradoxes. The binaries become untenable when identities are not clarified, but further complicated. Constant conditions of loss and recovery frame multiple and incomplete exilic identities, creating intricate levels of hybridity within these subjects. The result of the theatrical layering of discrete spatial domains in these plays is the exposure of enigmatic qualities extant within all recognizable relationships. Going back to Cuba or remaining there amid profound change helps these characters deconstruct their experiences in order to reveal and celebrate new possible paths. Ultimately, Martinez and Cruz use unfixed, yet confined stage spaces to challenge, incorporate, and overcome the radical insecurity of displacement. Their works position the theatrical voice of the hybrid immigrant as intact in its own right while always characterized by what has been left behind. *Illuminating Veronica* and *Hortensia and the Museum of Dreams* are significant works because they focus on the simultaneities that, as Soja duly notes: "intervene, extending our point of view outward in an infinite number of lines connecting the subject to a whole world of comparable instances [...]" (23).

Although there are only 90 miles between Cuban and American shores, the extreme division of the two countries for five decades, politically, socially, and economically, has created acute dislocation for Cubans both on the island and living in the United States. Merely being in the United States isolates Cubans – American laws separate them from their families, their culture, and their heritage, as complete assimilation is expected, encouraged, and rewarded. However, remaining in Cuba isolates Cubans as well, as access to the world has been extremely limited by their government's laws. These plays make it clear that exiles in both situations manufacture new, more palatable identities by fusing together the past and the present in the hopes of creating a viable future. Exiles constantly float in between, dispersed yet present, fervently trying to incorporate two cultures into individual, reconstituted hybrid identities shaped by profound emotional ruptures and losses. They experience a dichotomy of consciousness, brought on by the residue and proximity of previous associations, which is surely central to any exilic theory.

Notes

1. I refer to the work done by Deleuze and Guattari in this area, specifically the concept of using one's own local culture to engage, integrate, and denote an amended absorption of key ideas after deterritorialization. This ability to take active part in the production of one's own environment, after a massive paradigm shift like the Cuban Revolution, is what drives Martinez's character Veronica.

2. Román De la Campa and many others have written about the severe loneliness and isolation that children exiled from Cuba without their families suffered. For detailed information, see Yvonne M. Conde, *Operation Pedro Pan: The Untold Exodus of 14,048 Cuban Children*, New York and London; Routledge, 1999.
3. See Conde.

Works cited

Anzaldúa, Gloria. *Borderlands/La Frontera: The New Mestiza*. San Francisco: Spinsters/Aunt Lute, 1987.

Bhabha, Homi K. *The Location of Culture*. London and New York: Routledge, 1994.

Chaudhuri, Una. *Staging Place: The Geography of Modern Drama*. Ann Arbor: University of Michigan Press, 1995.

Corbett, Ben. *This is Cuba: An Outlaw Culture Survives*. Cambridge, MA: Westview Press, 2004.

Cruz, Nilo. *Hortensia and the Museum of Dreams*. New York: Dramatists Play Service, 2004.

De La Campa, Roman. *Cuba on My Mind: Journeys to a Severed Nation*. London and New York: Verso, 2000.

García Canclini, Néstor. *Hybrid Cultures: Strategies for Entering and Leaving Modernity*. Minneapolis: University of Minnesota Press, 1995.

Gomez-Peña, Guillermo. *Warrior of Gringostroika*. Saint Paul, MN: Graywolf Press, 1993.

Henderson, Mae G. ed. *Borders, Boundaries and Frames*. New York and London: Routledge, 1995.

Joseph, May. "Diaspora, New Hybrid Identities, and the Performance of Citizenship", *Women & Performance* 7.2–8.1, Nos.14/15 (1995): 3–13.

Martinez, Rogelio. *Illuminating Veronica*. New York: Broadway Play Publishing, 2000.

Mlinar, Zdravko, ed. *Globalization and Territorial Identities*. Vermont: Ashgate Publishing, 1992.

Moreiras, Alberto. *The Exhaustion of Difference: The Politics of Latin American Cultural Studies*. Durham, NC, and London: Duke University Press, 2001.

Pelligrini, Ann. *Performance Anxieties: Staging Psychoanalysis, Staging Race*. New York and London: Routledge, 1997.

Pérez, Louis. *On Becoming Cuban*. Chapel Hill: University of North Carolina Press, 1999.

———. *Cuba: Between Reform and Revolution*. New York: Oxford University Press, 1995.

Silverman, Kaja. "The Subject." In *The Subject of Semiotics*. New York: Oxford University Press, 1983, pp. 126–93.

Soja, Edward. *Postmodern Geographies: The Reassertion of Space in Critical Social Theory*. New York: Verso, 1989.

3

"An American Mile in Others' Shoes": The Tragicomedy of Immigrating to the Twenty-First-Century United States

Diana Manole
University of Toronto

Transnational drama in enriched English

In his essay "Reflections on Exile," Edward Said emphasizes an interesting paradox: although exile is "a condition of terminal loss", it has become "a potent, even enriching, motif of [Western] modern culture" (173). Furthermore, as some of the displaced persons establish themselves in their countries of adoption and become significant artists and authors, their intense embodiment of "the exile's antinomies" (Said 174) and the sense of loss and estrangement that undermines their achievements, not only actively challenges inherited stereotypes of the foreigner but also indirectly alters the host collective's perception of itself. As the border between "us" and "others" is continuously blurred and reinforced, the national space is accordingly redefined. The mutual mirroring and attempt to walk in each others' shoes gradually change international and national perspectives, hierarchies, and value scales. In addition, the effect of the resident culture and the necessity to make their experiences comprehensible on their new markets determine exilic authors to employ hybrid transnational styles. Given its direct interaction with the audience, exilic theatre particularly requires this double effort of translation and adaptation on behalf of both authors and audiences. At the same time, it openly explores and intensifies the perception of *different* and *not-so-different* characteristics of the aliens and their adoptive cultures. In *Waxing West* and *Lenin's Shoe*, the plays I will analyze in this chapter,[1] the Romanian-born and current New York resident Saviana Stanescu[2] attempts to change the stereotypical view of immigrating to twenty-first-century United States and, implicitly, of America and the American way of life. Furthermore, as they focus on the experiences of post-communist East European immigrants whose exile usually goes undocumented, these two plays indirectly respond to Katarzyna Marciniak's plea "to recover the forgotten space of the second world", whose existence was denied, or at least ignored, by most Western scholars after the fall of the Berlin Wall in 1989 (xv). In her rescue efforts, Stanescu depicts their experiences from a parodic perspective and uses laughter to "lend dignity to a condition legislated to deny dignity – to deny an identity to people" (Said: 175).

Waxing West is a postmodern parody of the post-communist East European dream to immigrate to America. Pressured by her mother and most of her acquaintances, the Bucharest-born cosmetologist Daniela comes to New York to marry Charlie, an American computer engineer. While their relationship is unsuccessful and Charlie does not feel compelled to marry her, Daniela's American tourist visa expires and she plans to return home. At the last moment, however, she decides to give her American life another chance. This plan proves impossible as Charlie most likely dies in the 9/11 terrorist attack. The play is structured as a series of flash-backs, re-enacting the events that led Daniela to her

Figure 3.1   Waxing West by Saviana Stanescu, directed by Benjamin Mosse, La MaMa Theatre, New York, April 2007. Grant Neale (Ceausescu), Marnye Young, (Daniela), Alexis McGuinness (Elena Ceausescu). Photo by Scott Eastman.

present status as a lonely illegal immigrant. The vampires of the former Romanian leaders, Nicolae and Elena Ceausescu, observe and sarcastically comment on everything she goes through, without interfering until the last scene.

Lenin's Shoe tragicomically tells the story of six East European exiles who struggle to find the means to live in America. The main characters belong to two families, one from Russia and the other from former Yugoslavia. Jasna, a former journalist and currently an illegal immigrant, is hired as a caretaker for Vlady, a 16-year-old Russian immigrant, whose legs were crushed when the shoe of Lenin's statue in Moscow fell on him at the time of its demolition. Vlady decides to kill his father, the owner of the restaurant "Uncle Vanya" in Queens, New York and an active KGB agent. Most likely, Jasna will also die in the explosion at the end of the play. My focus in this chapter is on the immigrants' self-redefinition as Others, and on the re-enactment of imagined America from an exilic point of view. Before addressing these aspects in more detail, I will briefly elaborate on my use of the terms "exile" and "immigrant", and discuss whether or not these plays belong to a particular national[3] dramatic literature, by which I understand the totality of dramatic texts written within the culture of a nation-state. *Waxing West*'s and *Lenin's Shoe*'s characters have different resident statuses, which range from war refugees and illegal residents to newly made American citizens, but their personal attitudes require further clarification. On the one hand, Stanescu's characters voluntarily live in the United States, mostly for economic reasons, and are legally allowed to return to their post-communist birth countries. Thus, they can be considered immigrants, that is, someone "who leaves one country to settle permanently in another" (see "Immigrant"). On the other hand, they treat their situation as "a condition of terminal loss" (Said: 173) and perceive themselves as living in exile, a term which traditionally means "[e]nforced removal from one's native country" (see "Exile"). Consequently, the terms "exiles", corresponding to how Stanescu's characters feel about themselves, and "immigrants", corresponding to what they are according to their legal status in the United States,[4] alternate freely in this chapter. Some post-colonial theorists such as Revathi Krishnaswamy might object to this, as they protest against the failure "to differentiate rigorously between diverse modalities of postcolonial diaspora" (94), considering that, in this way, "[p]olitically charged words such as 'diaspora' and 'exile' are being emptied of their histories of pain and suffering" (94). Nonetheless, other scholars plead for a more general understanding of the term "exile". Christine Brooke-Rose, for example, discusses new interpretations of the word's etymology and explains that the previous belief that Latin *exilium* was linked to *solum*, soil, is now abandoned in favor of a more likely relationship to the root *sal* (to go), to be found in Sanskrit *sar* and Latin *saline/saltare*, and later in "Old French, where *exilier* or *essilier* meant 'to ravage,' 'to devastate,' a shift in meaning still traceable today in *exterminate*, literally 'to drive beyond boundaries'" (7). Based on these hypotheses, Brooke-Rose concludes "the clanging connotations are of suffering in banishment, but also of springing forth into a new life, beyond the boundaries of the familiar" (7). This perspective appears quite common today, as even some dictionaries, such as *The American Heritage® Dictionary* I already mentioned in connection with the definitions of "immigrant" and "exile", explain the word's secondary meanings in a similar way: "One who lives away from one's native country, whether because of expulsion or voluntary absence" ("Exile"). In other words, this definition identifies the displacement across borders as an essential semantic marker and disregards the antinomy *enforced/free* departure from one's birth country as irrelevant. Consistent with these points of view, I argue that the specific situation of Stanescu's characters makes the alternation of terms in this chapter adequate.[5]

In addition to terminological issues, the plays' positions in the national and international dramatic literatures raise other interesting theoretical questions. Written in English after Stanescu's relocation to the United States, and developed in collaboration with an American company, the Lark Play Development Center in New York,[6] these two plays could, according to traditional taxonomies, belong to the generic category of "Twenty-First-Century American Drama". However, their author's resident status makes their position in American drama as questionable as in the Romanian one. Stanescu was accepted into the United States for her academic and literary abilities, which placed her among the foreigners that are not only tolerable, but even necessary: "I came to the U.S. a Fulbright fellow in 2001, and now I am an 'alien with extraordinary skills in arts,' meaning I hold an O1 visa for exceptional artists"[7] (2007a). While she was introduced as a "Romanian Immigrant" at the Special Panel Event "In-Between Two Cultures", organized by the Lark on 1 February 2006 in New York ("Crossing the Line"), she was included among the American playwrights at the ARTE theatre exchange project organized in Bucharest, Romania shortly after (Haraga). According to their topic, and the English as a Second Language their immigrant characters speak, the plays could be included in "theatre in broken English", a syntagm, which some North-American scholars and theatre professionals use when referring to immigrant drama and theatre. A relevant example is Broken English Theatre, an Ottawa-based "professional, multicultural theatre company that was established in September 1995 by 10 professional new Canadian theatre artists" (*Broken English Theatre*). Also, the subgroup of the 2006 ASTR seminar "Exile and America" for which this chapter was initially developed, was called "American Theatre in Broken English".[8] Thus, the question of Stanescu's *Waxing West* and *Lenin's Shoe* belonging to such a dramatic category has appeared to me somewhat necessary. The playwright, however, firmly rejected the idea: "No, my plays are not theatre in 'broken English.' Some characters speak broken English because they are immigrants and they still inhabit that space in-between cultures and languages. If we need to find a term, I would call it theatre in 'enriched English' or 'global English'" (2007b). In her essay "Exsul", Brooke-Rose makes a similar point when she comments on the contemporary immigrant writer's decision "to create in an idiom not his own, or only secondly his own" (15), a phenomenon still rare at the time she wrote her essay in 1996, but increasingly more frequent in the last decade. Brooke-Rose qualifies the writer's work as being "as fresh, as cliché-escaping, as enriching, as that of Dante" (15), when he was struggling to create a literary language out of his own native vernacular. From linguistic and political perspectives, the exilic versions of English also recall Bill Ashcroft, Gareth Griffiths and Helen Tiffin's post-colonial concept of "the linguistic code, english, which has been transformed and subverted into several distinctive varieties throughout the world" (Ashcroft, Griffiths and Tiffin 8). The similarities between Stanescu's "enriched English" and "english" are heightened by the fact that the so-called linguistic "brokenness" has political and artistic value in exilic authors' identity projects.

Dissimilarities are also relevant. As a literary language, "english" was developed and used outside England as a way of asserting the national identities of colonized people, with colonial authors writing back to the metropolitan centre, as the title of Ashcroft, Griffiths and Tiffin's book, *The Empire Writes Back*, suggests. In contrast, the versions of English I refer to in this chapter have appeared within the borders of the United States and other English-speaking countries, from where exiled authors write back to their third- or second-world birth countries, while they still strive to affirm their likeness within the difference in relationship to their adoptive countries.

I argue, subsequently, that *Waxing West* and *Lenin's Shoe* belong to a category that gains more and more importance as the number of displaced writers increases, and which can be called "transnational drama".[9] The attempt to define this concept, however, requires clarification of the term "transnational"[10] and comparison with other theoretical concepts of cross/intercultural theatre already in use. In her article "Defining Transnationalism", Patricia Clavin notes "the recent resurgence of interest in transnationalist phenomena" (421) and reviews how the term's meaning has evolved. According to Clavin, at the beginning of the twentieth century, the concept of transnationalism "took life inside nation-states and seemed to be used primarily as an alternative term for inter-states relations" (433).[11] During the 1980s, the new term "was adopted by multinational corporations that wanted to re-brand themselves as transnational", which meant "extending or having interests beyond national bounds or frontiers" (433).

Accordingly, transnational relationships were relationships in which "at least one of the members [...] represent[ed] a non-governmental organization in an encounter that spans three or more countries" (Clavin: 434), although one of the members can be a governmental agency. Clavin argues, however, that bilateral relationships might also be considered transnational at that time because they "form[ed] part of wider phenomena" (430) and were located "in a broader political and economic network" (431). In today's world, transnationalism's meaning has further evolved. The term has become an open concept preoccupied with expressing the desire to break free "from dominant national paradigms", subsequently allowing us "to reflect on, while at the same time going beyond, the confines of the nation" (434–8). In addition to this broad definition, other theorists such as Caroline R. Nagel and Lynn A. Staeheli argue that when used in studies of exile and immigration, transnationalism refers to "a process – and perhaps a strategy – as migrants negotiate the complex politics of citizenship and identity" (3). I find that these perspectives correspond to the term's meaning in contemporary literary discourse.

Accordingly, I define "transnational drama" as a body of plays written by immigrant authors in their second languages,[12] who consciously integrate traditions and cultural values, re-enact social and political problems, and address audiences from *both* their native and adoptive countries. The transnational character of their work is enhanced by worldwide access to their texts, facilitated by recent technological developments.[13] A hybrid of cross/intercultural, immigrant, and post-colonial theatre, transnational drama responds to Patrice Pavis's plea for "a conception of culture as supporter or bastion of a cultural identity, and a conception of a culture of heterogeneity and collage" (13). It also fulfills Jacqueline Lo and Helen Gilbert's prediction that "an intercultural theatre practice informed by postcolonial theory can potentially function as a site where this intersecting of cultures is both reflected and critiqued" (49). At the same time, transnational drama distinguishes itself in major ways from various kinds of cross/intercultural theatre experiences from at least three main perspectives. First, intercultural theatre, as defined by Pavis is a type of performance that "creates hybrid forms drawing upon more or less conscious and voluntary mixing of performance traditions traceable to distinct cultural areas" (8). Given its immediate more commercial purpose, intercultural theatre "also risks reinforcing national stereotypes [because of] the great temptation to produce immediately exportable productions" (Pavis: 4–5). On the contrary, transnational drama frequently employs the artistic means of intercultural theatre, but it does it with a precise political agenda. Second, although it "claims to be concerned with the cultural identity of the forms it utilizes" (9), cross/intercultural theatre creates hybrid structures in which "the original forms can no longer be distinguished" (8), because, as Lo and Gilbert also argue, the "encounter and negotiation between different cultural sensibilities" are essential, but not "the degree to which this is discernible in any performance event" (31). Furthermore, the cultural hybridization in cross/intercultural theatre reflects the "Western fascination with non-Western performing arts" (32), but ignores any possible reactions from the non-Western counterpart. In comparison, transnational drama holds both its Western and non-Western sources as equal, and relies on the integrity and recognizable character of the constitutive parts it borrows from each culture. Last but not least, Lo and Gilbert, Pavis, and other theorists discuss cross/intercultural theatre as practice and not literature. Accordingly, the performances under scrutiny are usually "site-specific" and limited to a local audience in the case of regular productions, or to a small international one in the case of festival productions. Although relying on the appropriation of resources from various traditions, these performances are not accessible to wide cross/intercultural audiences. The texts of transnational drama, however, circulate freely in at least the two cultures of the playwright's birth and host countries, and mediate cultural and political exchanges.

The differences between cross/intercultural and transnational drama can be expressed graphically. Pavis visually represents intercultural theatre through an "intercultural hourglass," in which "the mass of source culture, metaphorically situated in the upper chamber, must pass through the narrow neck controlled by the target culture of the bottom chamber with, in this neck, a whole series of filters that keep only a few elements of the source culture selected according to very precise norms" (16). Lo and Gilbert reject this graphic representation as limited because "it assumes a one-way cultural flow based on a hierarchy of privilege" (42), and propose instead another model, in which "intercultural exchange is represented as a two-way flow. Both partners are considered cultural sources while the target culture is positioned along the continuum between them" (44–5). In this case, however, the target culture is represented as an abstract concept, floating between the cultures from which the artistic product is derived. In order to avoid this ambiguity, I propose a Venn diagram as the best model (see Figure 3.2) of transnational drama because it graphically represents the fact that the immigrant author's native and host cultures simultaneously play the role of source and target, while the transnational literary texts simultaneously belong to both.[14]

Transnational playwrights share many common traits with other categories of immigrant artists and writers. Like the accented filmmakers Hamid Naficy describes in his book *An Accented Cinema: Exilic and Diasporic Filmmaking*, they "are 'situated but universal' figures who work in the interstices of social formations, cosmopolitan centres where they exist in a state of tension and dissension with both their original and current homes" (10). The Indian-born English writer Salman Rushdie[15] explains the position of immigrant authors from a similar perspective, as he considers them "capable of writing from a kind of double

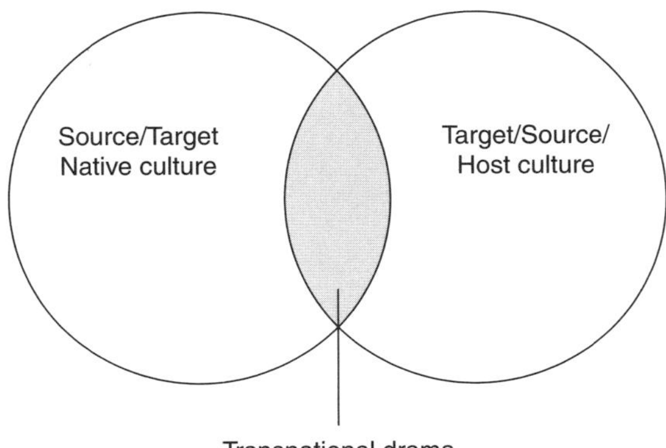

Figure 3.2 Transnational drama expressed as a Venn diagram.

perspective: because they, we, are at one and the same time insiders and outsiders in this [host] society" (19). This double viewpoint, also easily recognizable in the case of transnational playwrights, determines one of the main differences between transnational and intercultural authors. The latter's works obey "the constraints and the needs tied specifically to the [Western] target culture" in which they are produced because they are "subject to the institutional imperatives of the target culture, which tends to preserve from the foreign culture whatever suits its expectations [and] reinforces its convictions" (Pavis: 16).

In contrast, transnational authors simultaneously emphasize the differences and the similarities between the two cultures, as they consciously take on the role of mediators with a precise political agenda, while culturally, and usually administratively, they belong to both their native and adoptive countries. Following the "trajectory of their own travels of identity" (Naficy: 11), the perspectives of exilic writers are radically different from those of the majority, wherever they go. They are "capable of producing ambiguity and doubt about the taken-for-granted values of their home and host societies" (13) and are consequently acknowledged as important terms of comparison for the mainstream arts. In addition, they are even more different from each other, as they represent individual combinations of inherited and acquired cultural contexts.

The situation changes, however, when displaced artists address the theme of exile, because they tend to perceive and reflect it as a traumatic experience and, consequently, to create within a similar canon. The usual grim perspective often obliterates the specific ethnic and political differences and determines a paradoxical homogeneity of the marginalized. Stanescu makes a very interesting postmodern exception to this rule. As a journalist, when talking about her experiences living abroad, she implies that she has had her own share of exilic unhappiness. In a 2006 Romanian newspaper article, she consciously avoids the clichés: "I try not to bring to mind the immigrant life stereotypes and describe our daily melodramas" (Stanescu 2006c).[16] As a playwright, however, she intentionally mocks these clichés and also the homogenizing attitudes they represent: "I'm playing with stereotypes in order to make my plays bold dramatic/political statements and playful/entertaining theatrical experiences that deal with big topics – immigration, power dynamics, local-global, big nations – small nations etc – in an exciting way that speaks to American audiences and not only" (Stanescu 2008). In *Lenin's Shoe* and *Waxing West*, Stanescu re-enacts some of the most common political, social, and cultural clichés that have appeared in the last few decades in literature by and about exiles. The results are two postmodern tragicomedies, which parody the immigrants' "need to reassemble an identity out of refractions and discontinuities" (Said: 179), the American prejudices against foreigners, and the general East European and particular Romanian infatuation with the United States. Having been produced, read, and published in both Stanescu's native and host countries,[17] the plays' attempts to change the exilic stereotypes are accessible to both Romanian and American audiences, fulfilling the main characteristics of what I define as transnational drama.

Multiple and often contradictory redefinitions of identity and Otherness are intertwined, and result in paradoxical hierarchies, hybrid value systems, and versatile perceptions of self. The postmodern parody that structures Stanescu's perspective is similar to what Linda Hutcheon defines as a "repetition with critical distance that allows ironic signalling of difference at the very heart of similarity" (26). Furthermore, postmodern parodic texts "foreground the historical, social, ideological contexts in which they have existed and continue to exist" (24–5). This is especially relevant in the case of transnational plays, in which the re-examination of the reality they ridicule is a main objective. In Stanescu's transnational plays, the parody is naturally twofold. On the one hand, the Americans are depicted as if being recreated from a residual communist perspective, alienated by their consumerist society, insensitive, lonely, and sexually frustrated. On the other hand, the immigrants strive to meet the expectations of an imagined North-American audience – they seem to accept, in Julia Kristeva's words, the "multiplying masks and 'false selves'" (8). In spite of their tremendous efforts, Stanescu's East European characters are unable to leave behind their initial identities, from which they gradually drift away, but also fail to develop a genuine sense of belonging to the American people, who seem close, but remain unapproachable. The immigrants' progressive alienation becomes the main theme of Stanescu's dramatic discourse and is enacted from several perspectives, social, professional, familial, personal, and even fictional, but also through everyone's relationship to him/herself, to the people left behind in their home countries, to the other immigrants, and to real or imagined Americans.

American–(East) European identities

The comparison of *Waxing West*'s and *Lenin's Shoe*'s characters from the perspective of their ethnicities reveals interesting aspects of Stanescu's investigation of Otherness, and of the changes in her perception of national identities that took place over a period of only two years between their conceptions. In the 2004 version of *Waxing West,* which I discuss here, the characters are explicitly divided into "The Romanians" and "The Americans" (Stanescu 2004: 2).[18] The list of characters includes "a homeless Muslim Yugoslavian who's lost a leg in the war" (2), most likely a political refugee, among the "Americans", but it also presents two genuine American-born characters, Charlie and his sister Gloria, with an un-hyphenated nationality. Daniela, her brother Elvis, and her mother Marcela, are the Romanians. In terms of resident status in the United States, Daniela is the play's only immigrant. Moreover, Stanescu mixes together the parodies of exile and post-communism and recreates the Romanian dictators "Comrade Nicolae Ceausescu, the former Romanian president [...] and Academician Doctor Engineer Comrade Elena Ceausescu" (8) as exiled vampires, who "miss home and are nostalgic about going back to Romania and sucking some delicious Romanian blood, the blood of their human life, the blood of their 'childhood'" (8). As they are stuck somewhere in between this world and the next, I argue that they no longer belong to a precisely determined ethnic group, but to fictional stereotypes. Hence, the character ratio is balanced, with three Romanians to three Americans.

In Stanescu's 2006 version of *Lenin's Shoe,* which I discuss here, the issue of the characters' national belonging is more complicated than in *Waxing West.* In the beginning, Stanescu specifies, or at least implies, the nationality of all but one character, none of whom are American-born or have direct relationships to Americans during the play. Vanya, *Lenin's Shoe*'s main character, is introduced as a hyphenated "Russian-American" (Stanescu 2006a: 2). The ethnic identities of his son, Vlady, and of his young lover, Irina, are the same as his, as quickly becomes clear in the play. Significantly, Stanescu does not mention the nationality of *Lenin's Shoe*'s homeless exile, "KEBAB, 28" (2), as if homelessness-as-home, as Said puts it, has become a place of belonging in itself. The rest of the characters have more than two nationalities. For example, Jasna, and, consequently, her son Alex, have three nationalities by birth: "Romanian-Macedonian-Bosnian" (2), a subtle reminder of former Yugoslavia's mixed population. Like all of Stanescu's immigrant characters in these two plays, Jasna does not feel comfortable with any of her ethnicities and dreams of replacing them with an American immigrant visa. This kind of rejection is further emphasized in the case of Vlady, an allegoric victim of the communist past, the post-communist transition, and the exilic alienation. He expresses his negative feelings towards his birth country in "gansta hip-hop", such as the song "Hail, Mamma

Russia goes to jail!'": "I ain't asked, mamma/ to be born to you!/ Who shoots you?!" (8), but does not consider America any better: "Russians and Americans financed Osama Bin Laden – and they knew about each other! Compromise for the Gas Pipeline through Romania, Bulgaria and Bosnia. War for Oil. Dollars and Rubles – seed money for Terrorism" (69).

Whereas *Waxing West* focuses on a sole immigrant's struggle to adapt to the United States, *Lenin's Shoe* presents a sample of the so-called American "melting pot", which proves unable to incorporate some of its most recent ingredients. From my point of view, one possible cause of the difference in the plays' ethnic structures could be Stanescu's more realistic perspective of American society after spending two additional years there.

Furthermore, the playwright amplifies her characters' ethnic Otherness through the social and professional groups she assigns them to: the obedient East European mail-order bride (Daniela), the overqualified baby-sitter (Jasna), the limo driver who barely speaks English (Hassan), and the sexy waitress/student working at an ethnic restaurant (Irina). In addition to professional stereotypes current in the United States, Stanescu also parodies fictional clichés. Vanya recalls the Hollywood-like character of a secret double-agent. According to his son, he is a "mafioso. Number One on the CIA list of spies. Number One on the freaking KGB list with double agents" (Stanescu 2006a: 70), who buys his American citizenship with Russian military secrets. When Vlady confronts him, Vanya justifies his immigration and betrayal through his desire to protect his wife and son and offer them a better life in the United States: "That's what I've been working for. So you don't have to do something you hate" (68). Although one of the most common explanations of economic exile, Vanya's reasoning is not sound, given the fact that he continues his work as a Russian double-agent. Thus, he appears to have been sent on a mission, rather than to have immigrated for the sake of his family. Regardless of the real purpose of his presence in the United States, his actions have an unfortunate effect on his loved ones. His wife dies because of an extravagant gift: "Got Masha whatever she opened her mouth to ask for. Got her a Porsche. Last model, the one she wanted. But she was not good with gifts ... She crashed the car into a wall" (69). Vlady is not better off, as Vanya has actually "nourished his depression" (71) since they moved to New York. Indifferent to his son's suffering, he has chosen to hide the KGB microfilms in Vlady's useless "shoes' army" (10) of 80 pairs, which he smuggles out of Russia as presents: "A new pair every few months" (28). As a result, Vlady turns into a hate-filled and frustrated teenager, who regards his father as "Number One on the

Figure 3.3 The poster for "Lenin's Shoe" by Saviana Stanescu, directed by Daniella Topol, *BareBones* production at The Lark, February 2006. Poster design by Jeffrey Jackson.

black list of bad parents" (72), plots and eventually carries out a murder-suicide attack, in which they both will most likely die. Vlady's last words have an ambiguous significance and emphasize once more the allegorical character of his story. His final cry and intentional pun, "Children of communism, the party is over!" (72), recalls the failure of the Russian Communist Party and society.

If the Russian people's desire to eliminate the reminiscences of communism from the public space has accidentally determined Vlady's physical disability, Romania's political turmoil acts like the main source of Daniela's psychological frustration. After taking part in the 1989 revolution and the anti-communist demonstrations that followed shortly after, she claims she is enraged by the corruption of the so-called democratic politicians and decides to leave the country: "I've had enough of all of them" (Stanescu 2004: 38). Similar to Vanya, her reasoning also becomes questionable, when judged in context. Daniela comes to the United States for an arranged marriage to an American citizen her mother finds for her through acquaintances who already work there as housekeepers. Although Daniela tries to deny it, Marcela does not have in mind her daughter's political liberation, but financial gain and American Green Cards for the entire family. She enthusiastically explains this to Elvis, her other child: "Your sister has the chance to marry an American. An American BUSINESSMAN. Mrs Aronson's son. Charlie! Rich, decent, well-educated. American! The luck-rain has come down over Daniela. She is going to go to America and take all of us there!" (7). Unfortunately, the American fiancé-to-be is not the dream husband they hoped for, but rather the stereotypical soulless and perverse man described in anti-capitalist propaganda. Daniela and Charlie as a Romanian-American couple are defined by Charlie's "pleasure of suffering [which] is a necessary lot in such a demented whirl, and amateur *proxeni* know it unconsciously as they choose foreign partners on whom to inflict the torture of their own contempt, their condescension, or, more deceitfully, their heavy-handed charity" (Kristeva 6). Hoping for a financially secure and technologically advanced middle-class life in the United States, Daniela is in fact forced to adopt a folkloric/exotic mask, which does not correspond to her genuine identity but to the expectations of her American partner, who in turn inherits them from his mother. Mrs Aronson loves Romanians because she "had a Romanian cleaning lady for 20 years" (6) and, thus, decides to intermediate her son's marriage to a woman whose housekeeping skills are supposed to make him happy. In doing so, she actually attempts to impose onto him the more generally accepted "parameters of admissible immigrant placement within the American symbolic configuration" (Marciniak 54). In other words, Mrs Aronson's and Charlie's attitude reflects American duplicity towards second- and third-world immigrants, which Marciniak explains when talking about Mexican illegal immigrants: "The United States eagerly utilizes many Mexican migrant workers as a cheap labour force for gruelling seasonal jobs in fields and sweatshops but conveniently keeps them within the discursive and material space of alienhood" (39). Charlie's perception of Daniela and his refusal to legalize her immigrant status through marriage reflect the same treatment. He regards the Romanian woman as a maid and a cook of exotic dishes, roles she strives to accept despite her natural inclinations:

> DANIELA: I hate Romanian food, Charlie, I hate 'sarmale' and 'mamaliga' and the Romanian traditional smell, and the Romanian exotic flavours, and the Romanian claustrophobic kitchens, but for you Charlie, I stick two cotton pads in my nostrils, I play my energizing tape with applauses, and I do it for you Charlie, I cook for you.
>
> (12)

If her desperation is genuinely tragic, her attempts to fulfill Charlie's wishes are hopelessly ridiculous, especially when it comes to peculiar sexual favors, which Daniela resentfully describes as a "silly Thanksgiving-game" (12). After being rejected by Charlie, she attempts to change her sexual orientation and become Gloria's lesbian lover, but fails again (62). Her never-ending efforts to reconstruct herself trap her in a carousel of interchangeable masks[19] and eventually determine the hybridization of her identity.

From this point of view, Daniela resembles the "colonial mimic man", whom Homi Bhabha defines as "the effect of a flawed colonial mimesis, in which to be Anglicized is emphatically not to be English" (125). In the particular case of British India, the mimic man is "Indian in blood and colour, but English in tastes, in opinions, in morals and in intellect" (125). I find this concept applicable to Stanescu's Daniela, but also to Irina and Alex, who strive to adapt to US society. In this process, they inevitably retain their metaphorical and actual "blood and colour", and strenuously so, though they only superficially assume the social and cultural habits of the adoptive country. Paraphrasing Bhabha's explanation, I argue that in the case of Stanescu's characters, "to be Americanized means emphatically not to be American". Their mimetic and thus incomplete transformations are mainly determined by their conflicting desires. On the one hand, as they "feel their difference [...] as a kind of orphanhood" (Said: 182), they strive to comply with the official politics of assimilating immigrants and to acquire new American identities. On the other hand, they experience a mostly unconscious rejection of change, and, implicitly, of the host culture, which they do not understand, and which they come to know only through its most accessible stereotypes. Consequently, instead of genuinely trying to appropriate alien social and cultural codes, they attempt to impersonate Hollywood-like characters: Daniela – a perfect wife, who is great at housekeeping and open-minded at sex; Vanya – a rich husband, lover, and father, who buys expensive cars and pays nurses; Vlady and Alex – rebel teenagers and suicide bombers; Jasna – an investigative reporter who uncovers and sells a double-agent's secrets. During this mimetic process, they gradually lose their authentic national, professional, and even sexual identities, through an exilic experience "legislated to deny dignity – to deny an identity to people" (Said: 173–5).

Eventually, Stanescu's immigrants grow to be conscious of the shallowness of their lives, and start regarding themselves as fictional characters. Recalling her author's auto-irony, Daniela calls her immigration a "melodramatic incredible impractical improbable ... hairy-tale" (Stanescu 2004: 74). Furthermore, she re-enacts past events as theatre scenes, which she introduces to her audience, creating a parodic alienating effect: "Me ... At my dad's grave. Bellu Cemetery, Bucharest. Smoking like a Hamletian vamp. Hiding in the smoke" (23). Vanya also sarcastically acknowledges his life's predictable nature: "What's life, Jasna, but a pathetic fight for survival? Dog eats dog. Man kills man. Dog and man kill cat. Cat eats mouse. And we all eat cheese! (*he laughs like he made a great joke*) Life is nothing but cartoons, Jasna" (Stanescu 2006a: 5). His son's online journal plays a role similar to Daniela's commentaries. In his first entry, he speaks with contempt of the nurses his father hires to take care of him, whom he commonly regards as "Telenovella-characters called Maria" (3). The dramatic discourse is again split into multiple levels of significance as Vlady, a telenovella-like character, [20] mocks his kind without acknowledging the likeness. He despises his nurses not only for their stereotypical dreams of "desperate immigrants," but also for their ethnicities, which he sees as a source of inspiration for practical jokes: "The one before this Columbian Mariella was a Romanian called Mariana. She had huge tits and a dream to marry an American millionaire. [...] The one before the Romanian was Polish. Very religious. [...] She left after my attempt to crucify myself on the window" (2).

As the plot develops, Stanescu deepens her exploration of the immigrants' Otherness in relationship to each other. Vanya, for instance, starts his first meeting with Jasna by pointing out their differences:

> VANYA: What kind of accent is that?
> JASNA: Russian-Romanian-Macedonian-Bosnian.
>
> (Stanescu 2006a: 4)

Like Vlady, Alex also despises other immigrants. He, for instance, disrespects his boss, most likely a hero in his birth country, while the latter, in turn, responds by mocking him for his religion:

> ALEX: I take orders from a Latino guy, a moron, he can't read or write, talk or think, but he knows everything about fucking explosives, coz he started a revolution in his country, and he knows how to make dirty bombs, you can make a bomb in a fucking bottle, and he's like "you Muslim boy, you know nothing!" and I'm like "Fuck off, what's your problem if I'm Muslim ..."
>
> (16)

As Kristeva explains, the immigrants' rejection of other immigrants is determined by their insecurity and domination/exclusion fantasies: "As enclave of the other within the other, otherness becomes crystallized as pure ostracism: the foreigner excludes before being excluded, even more than he is being excluded" (24). Because they are being perceived as insignificant individuals, they project and even enforce the same perspective on their fellow exiles. Vanya firmly explains that to Jasna: "You are illegal here Jasna. You don't exist here" (Stanescu 2006a: 71). Eventually, she accepts this status as natural, and even believes this to be a requirement of survival in exile. She assumes Vanya's position and advises her stubborn husband accordingly: "We're nobody here. Get used to that. You are nobody here" (15). Daniela goes even further and completely loses her sense of self in relationship to her American partner: "I am your ashtray. Your tomb. Your Disneyland. Your past. Your present. Your future. You can do with me whatever you want. I am here to stay. I am here to endure. I am here to live" (Stanescu 2004: 59). From Stanescu's perspective, the distance between a stereotypical exilic identity and a non-identity can be covered in only one step that Jasna and Daniela become willing to take.

The imagined America of post-communist exiles

Adrift in the American "melting pot", Stanescu's caricatural exiles are overwhelmed by their different and sometimes even opposite codes of perception and systems of value. Emotionally and culturally isolated, they rely on "contradictory articulations of reality and desire – seen in racist stereotypes, statements, jokes, myths" (Bhabha: 130), which are frequent in post-colonial cultures and in their upbringing in communist countries. Consequently, one of the main factors in her characters' alienation is the fact that they continue to long for the utopic America they imagined from afar.

The idealization of Western countries appears as a frequent attitude in the case of second- and third-world peoples, especially in the zones and social groups which were under the direct influence of imperial ideologies, Soviet-style communism included. Rushdie, for example, explains the origin of his concept of an imaginary England, which preceded his actual immigration: "In common with many Bombay-raised middle-class children of my generation, I grew up with an intimate knowledge of, and even a sense of friendship with, a certain kind of England: a dream-England" (18). Somewhat predictably, when he moves there he has to accept that "the dream-England is no more than a dream" (18). His ability to recognize this discrepancy empowers him to acknowledge his own present and also past differences, that now help him adapt to his host national community, "my social class, my freak fair skin and my 'English' English accent" (18). As opposed to the Indian-born writer, Stanescu's low-class characters do not find anything in common with the American people and do not have the courage to reach out, adapt, and communicate. After decades of anti-American indoctrination, on one hand, and of waiting for the "arrival of the Americans", perceived as Messiahs, "as potential new law makers (the banishers of communism), as wise men and warriors" (Cesereanu: 195, my translation), on the other hand, the United States is perceived as a mythical place, either utopic or dystopic, in the Romanian popular imagination. Daniela's mother, Marcela, describes it like a sci-fi feminist Utopia in which women are liberated from degrading housework and poverty, and allowed to dream:

> MARCELA: She will have EVERYTHING. Robots that clean the house for you. Machines that cook by themselves. Money that is invisible numbers on a small card like this! *(she shows an imaginary card using her thumb and forefinger)* She won't have to worry about anything. She can have her mind settled in the clouds forever.
>
> (Stanescu 2004: 18)

In contrast, "Mrs. Ionescu from the 3rd floor", one of Daniela's neighbors in Bucharest, fears the Americans: "I've heard they are weird. They sleep with guns under their pillows. They have drugs for breakfast everyday. And put drugs in your coffee if you're not careful" (Stanescu 2004: 18). She, however, asks Daniela to find her a cleaning job there. She does not plan on staying there, but only on making some money to help her come back and survive in an economically wrecked Romania, where retired people have little to live on. Mrs Ionescu perceives her future American experience as a necessary, but unpleasant one, and does not consider immigration an option: "After that I'll forget about your Americans and come back home, where I belong, to die in peace" (19). Daniela has a more realistic perspective and acknowledges that she learned about the United States mostly from Hollywood movies. Yet, she cannot help but hope that reality would come close to its middle-class idealized image:

> DANIELA: Maybe in that America … it's a bit, just a bit, a tiny little bit, like in the movies. You have a nice house, two floors, four bedrooms, two cars, one for you, one for your husband … breakfast and dinner with all the family … Three main courses. Two desserts! Everybody smiling! A coffee filter, a dish-washing

> machine, a microwave … Those microwaves cook everything by
> themselves, don't they?
>
> (23)

Consequently, Daniela expects to "find 'instant happiness' in American stores" (24), and becomes frustrated when her dreams do not come true. Stanescu observes her disappointment with details:

> DANIELA: (excited) May I use the microwave?
> CHARLIE: You'll only need the stove.
> *Daniela's enthusiasm evaporates.*
>
> (55)

To different degrees and for different reasons, for all of Stanescu's alienated characters, the United States does not live up to the mythical, though clichéd, image they grew up with in their birth countries and brought with them when they immigrated. Their current "American and not quite American" standpoint sharpens their disappointment. Jasna, for example, preaches against Americans and the American way of life as she condemns what Kristeva calls "the natives' lack of perspective or eventful lives" (7) in comparison to the exile's life, "a life made up of ordeals – neither catastrophes nor adventures (although these might equally happen), but simply a life in which acts constitute events because they imply choice, surprises, breaks, adaptations, or cunning, but neither routine nor rest" (7). Yet, in the absence of an actual interaction with American society, at least during the events *Lenin's Shoe* enacts, Jasna's complaints appear as rather worn out clichés that address an abstract Western middle class she continues to imagine: "It's normal people that I can't handle anymore. I feel like shouting in their face: hey, there are people dying out there and you're eating calmly your fucking pizza in front of your stupid TV!" (Stanescu 2006a: 7). Hassan, her poet husband, has more intellectually founded objections, although they also remain unspecific and rather target the general consumerist mentality: "they not understand metaphor. No soul. No imagination. Home you cursed be poet, you cannot change, you born poet, like disease. Here you go college, you are poet! You say I am poet, you are poet!" (57). When they give up searching for the imaginary United States, they come to the conclusion that they are in fact rejected because they do not correspond to American standards. Jasna states: "America is for smiley faces, for active people with clear goals" (44). In other words, America is for Americans, as Hassan points out:

HASSAN: You are journalist, good journalist home. Here you are
servant!

JASNA: *(beat)* It's only temporary, until I get the green card, then I'm
gonna get a job as a journalist.

HASSAN: You cannot do journalist here. They have American do
journalist.

(57–8)

Hassan's avoidance of direct contact with American people and his attempt to replace the host country's reality with a hybrid product of his imagination and the ideology he was fed with become clear in his passive-aggressive behavior: "He doesn't do anything. He just sits in front of the TV, turned on mute, and declaims poems in Bosnian and Romanian" (25). The continuous reminders of the society outside the personal spaces immigrants willingly isolate themselves in enable the postmodern parody by sustaining the comparison. In *Waxing West*, the American scenes are set in fairly realistic spaces, including *"an Upper East Side New York apartment"* (Stanescu 2004: 11), *"Gloria's studio in Brooklyn"* (13), *"A bench in Central Park"* (25). *Lenin's Shoe's* main space, the restaurant "Uncle Vanya"[21] was in fact inspired by an actual Russian establishment in Queens, New York.[22] The characters' contact with the exterior world is, however, minimal in both plays. Almost all scenes take place indoors, reflecting their inner exile, in addition to the factual one, and paradoxically heightening their claustrophobia, "a way to express the painful suffocation created by social oppression and ostracism that the foreigner endures in a new culture" (Marciniak: 102). Most of Stanescu's immigrants feel incarcerated in their adoptive country, as well as in their private spaces, that is, rooms or homes, in which they take refuge. At first, Daniela springs "forth into a new life, beyond the boundaries of the familiar" (Brooke-Rose: 7) like many other immigrants at the beginning of their new lives. She is candidly fascinated by her new surroundings: "I feel like Christmas every time I enter a shop here in New York" (Stanescu 2004: 55). As she experiences what Marciniak calls a gradual but "profound defamiliarization" (42), Daniela starts feeling disoriented and eventually ashamed for her not being used to the American lifestyle. Far from being supportive, Charlie overwhelms her with his technological superiority in dealing with the microwave oven and visa cards. He abusively places himself in the position of a civilizational Other from which her East European way of life "is cast as shockingly primitive and obsolete" (Marciniak: 53). Thus, he nurtures Daniela's fears and secures his right to hold her prisoner in an "only-for-you cage" (Stanescu 2004: 13), as Gloria tries to explain to Daniela.

Lenin's Shoe presents a similar immigrant perspective of the United States. Ashamed of his disability, the "crippled" Vlady deliberately isolates himself, although he in fact hates this condition: "I don't leave this fucking room, man," (Stanescu 2006a: 11). Irina, Vanya's younger lover also dislikes her private space: "It's gross. I hate it. I totally hate it. It's like a rats' cage ..." (47). She even detests life: "Fuck 'the real life!' Real life sucks", and is able to accept people only when watching them from a safe distance, paradoxically, from Vlady's window: "Oh, you got a nice view here! I mean – the street. People. I like to watch people" (47). When they venture outside, Stanescu's characters are subjected to humiliation, rejection and failure, being symbolically or even physically quarantined in "the perilous territory of not-belonging" (Said: 177), which frames "the illegal elsewhere of exile" (Marciniak: 55), in underground spaces or wastelands, officially ignored, but painfully real within the rich and shiny space of white Anglo-American culture.

Ironically, in both plays, the two homeless characters are the only ones who do not experience a self-destructive identity crisis and refuse to restructure themselves. Their attitudes have opposite motivations. *Waxing West's* Uros is a homeless Muslim Yugoslavian who "used to teach philosophy and dead-languages before the war" (Stanescu 2004: 28). His situation symbolizes the condition of exilic intellectuals, who "are not, so to speak, 'sitting' on the border; rather, they are forced to constitute themselves as the border", as Abdul R. JanMohamed argues (103). On the one hand, Uros feels "the wanderer's insane stride toward an elsewhere that is always pushed back, unfulfilled, out of reach" (Kristeva 6) characteristic of exiles, and dreams of routes across the world, "to Iraq, Iran, Syria ... in Gilgamesh's footsteps!" (Stanescu 2004: 28). Symbolically, he inhabits an actual crossroad and makes his home in an "area with a NO-ENTRANCE sign" at "Times Square Subway station." (Stanescu 2006a: 29). On the other hand, as an unwanted immigrant from a former communist country, he is confined to a wheelchair by his past, he lost a leg in the war, and to an underground space by his present. He eventually dies in the New York subway station, without being able to overcome his exilic depreciation and make his dreams come true.

Obsessed with his failure as a "suicide bomber", another tragicomic cliché in Stanescu's plays, speechless Kebab "insists on his [...] right to refuse to belong" (Said: 182). Under Jasna's influence, however, he slowly regains his ability to perform social gestures. He tries to make himself at home on the sidewalk behind the "Uncle Vanya" restaurant, where he lives, a cynical step "up" from Uros's underground residence. During the holiday season, Kebab "decorates a little bush with trash cans and other garbage items". His "garbage Christmas tree" (Stanescu 2006a: 44) metaphorically expresses the exile's strength to empower spiritually the "human waste" zone where American society places them. Impressed by his fate, Jasna decides to teach him English as a main means towards a desired "rehabilitation and reinvention" (49). She attempts to turn Kebab into an articulate foreigner, who would "be able to start a new life, get a job, normal things that normal people do" (45). Like Charlie's death at the end of *Waxing West*, which destroys Daniela's chance to become a "legal alien" in the United States, Jasna's inevitable death at the end of *Lenin's Shoe* erases Kebab's chance to transcend his wordless exilic condition.

To different degrees and for different reasons, Stanescu's East European immigrants are denied the fulfillment of the American Dream. Although they attempt to redefine themselves and to adapt to their new country, they remain "reformed, recognizable *Other*[s]" (Bhabha: 125), "both and neither" (Naficy: 13), "alien, foreign, and not quite fully American" (Marciniak: 36), prisoners in the exilic trap they willingly or unwillingly incarcerated themselves in. Stanescu depicts their experiences from a parodic perspective that challenges stereotypical perceptions of the foreigner and warns against taking them for granted. As Said explains, however, the risk remains that the public perception focuses "on that enlightening aspect of 'their' [the exilic authors] presence among us, not on their misery or their demands [ignoring] the tragic fate of homelessness in a necessarily heartless world" (Said: 183). Like other exilic works, Stanescu's transnational tragicomedies uncover concealed aspects of twenty-first-century American society and plead for immigrants and natives' mutual acceptance of each other and of ethnic and cultural diversities.

Notes

1. The first version of this chapter was written and presented as a contribution to the 2006 ASTR seminar "Exile and America", organized by Yana Meerzon and Silvija Jestrovic. Our seminar discussions, followed by Meerzon's editorial notes, helped me clarify my theoretical frame. I am also grateful to Professor Richard Plant (University of Toronto and Queen's University) for his helpful comments on a previous draft.
2. Stanescu holds an MA in Performance Studies (2001–02 Fulbright fellow) and an MFA in Dramatic Writing (John Golden Award in Playwriting), from NYU, Tisch School of the Arts. She has published several plays and collections of plays, including *Apocalipsa Gonflabila*, Bucharest: Unitext, 2000, the Best

Romanian Play of 2000, UNITER; *Outcast,* in *After Censorship: New Romanian Plays of the '90s,* ed. Marian Popescu and Elena Popescu, trans. Alina Nelega, Bucharest: UNITEXT, 2000; *Black Milk: Patru Piese de Teatru/Black Milk: Four Plays,* English versions supervised by Richard Davies, Bucharest: Museum of Literature, 2001, Romanian–English edition; *Compte à rebours,* Paris: Espace D'Un Instant, 2002, the Antoine Vitez Center Award; *Jelly-Love and Peanut-Butter,* in *The Book of Estrogenius 2002: Short Plays by Women,* ed. Margaret Dodge Boling, Fiona Jones, and Steve Deighan Smith, New York: Play Source Press, 2002; *Aurolac Blues,* in *Plays and Playwrights,* ed. Martin Denton, New York: NYTE, 2006, and in *The Best Ten-Minute Plays – 2 Actors,* ed. D. L. Lepidus, Hanover, NH: Smith & Kraus, 2005. Her works have been produced in the United States, the United Kingdom, France, Austria, Switzerland, Hungary, Macedonia, Montenegro, and Romania.

3. In this chapter, I refer to "national" in the sense of "belonging in and to a place, a people, a heritage. It affirms the home created by a community of language, culture and customs" (Said: 176). See *The American Heritage®️ Dictionary* for the definition of terms used here.

4. The US Citizenship and Immigration Services' Glossary specifies that "the Immigration and Nationality Act (INA) broadly defines an *immigrant* as any alien in the United States, except one legally admitted under specific non-immigrant categories (INA section 101(a)(15)" ("U.S. Citizenship and Immigration Services").

5. Krishnaswamy paradoxically alternates the terms "exile" and "emigration/immigration", indirectly supporting the equivalence the article itself contests: "emigration increasingly became the supreme reward for citizens of impoverished or repressive ex-colonies. Millions of people dream of becoming exiles at any cost" (96).

6. For information regarding the Lark Play Development Center, please see the company's website at: http://www.larktheatre.org.

7. According to the US Citizenship and Immigration Services, Stanescu's status is that of an "an alien who: (i) has extraordinary ability in the sciences, arts, education, business, or athletics which has been demonstrated by sustained national or international acclaim or, with regard to motion picture and television productions a demonstrated record of extraordinary achievement, and whose achievements have been recognized in the field through extensive documentation, and seeks to enter the United States to continue work in the area of extraordinary ability" ("US Citizenship and Immigration Services").

8. For more information about participants and abstracts, please go to: http://www.astr.org/conference2006/Seminar2006_ExileAmerica.html.

9. The concept of "transnational drama" purposely echoes transnational "accented cinema," a term coined by Hamid Naficy (4), but avoids the emphasis on the "accent," which might generate unfortunate confusions in the language-based arts.

10. Dictionary definitions of "transnationalism" are quite similar. *The American Heritage®️ Dictionary of the English Language* defines "transnational" as: "1. Reaching beyond or transcending national boundaries [...]. 2. Relating to or involving several nations or nationalities" ("Transnational").

11. My thanks for this reference go to Charan Rainford of the International Centre for Ethnic Studies, in Kandy, Sri Lanka, who discusses Clavin's

definitions of transnationalism in his paper "Long Distance Nationalism: Contestations of Ethnicity, Diaspora and Transnationalism," presented at the *Transnationalism, Activism, Art* conference in March 2007 at the University of Toronto.

12. Although many literary and film works are written, produced and distributed in English, there are several immigrant authors who use French, Spanish, German, Swedish, Italian, etc. as their second languages. Writing in a language other than one's mother tongue appears to me a necessary condition of transnational authorship. I consider that exiled authors who continue writing in their mother tongues preserve their positions in the national literatures of their birth countries, without targeting a transnational audience. The authors who belong to ethnic minorities and write in the official language of their birth countries, other than their mother tongues, represent a special category of inner exiles. A discussion of their sense of national and cultural identities is beyond my purpose in this chapter.

13. Faster means of travel and communication have generally affected people's sense of belonging to a particular place and nation-state, and the significance of citizenship. In this respect, Nagel and Staeheli review some of the theoretical studies on "the role of technology in transforming the political identities and activities of immigrants" (4), in the case of Arab immigrants in the United States.

14. As defined by the *Merriam-Webster Online Dictionary*, a Venn diagram is "a graph that employs closed curves and especially circles to represent logical relations between and operations on sets and the terms of propositions by the inclusion, exclusion, or intersection of the curves" ("Venn Diagram"). I adapted the Venn diagram to represent transnational drama's relation to the authors' native and host cultures. The drawing used in this chapter is mine.

15. According to Krishnaswamy, the works of writers like Rushdie amount to the "critical archival material of alternative canons in the metropolitan academy" (93). The same phenomenon occurs in drama and theatre where the texts and performances of immigrant professionals have challenged the dominant local traditions and generated interesting theoretical investigations.

16. All translations from Romanian to English are mine.

17. The plays' American production history to date: The first draft of *Waxing West* was written in Janet Neipris's class at NYU, Dramatic Writing Department, and produced as part of the Festival of New Works, Goldberg Theatre, NYU, in 2003. The second draft of *Waxing West* and the play *Lenin's Shoe* were developed and performed at Lark Play Development Center, New York, in 2004 and 2006, respectively. The version of *Waxing West*, which I analyze in this chapter, is a later draft, produced by East Coast Artists at La MaMa Theatre, in April 2007. The play was awarded the 2007 New York Innovative Theatre Award for Outstanding Original Full-length Script. *Waxing West* was published in *Innovative Theatre Awards – Outstanding Plays of 2007* (New York: United Stages, 2007) and in *Global Foreigners*, ed. Carol Martin and Saviana Stanescu, (London, New York and Calcutta: Seagull Books, 2006). The version of *Lenin's Shoe*, which I analyze in this chapter, is the final draft of the play that was produced by Hartford University, Hartt School, in April 2006.

    The plays' Romanian production history to date: La MaMa Theatre's production of *Waxing West* was performed at Teatrul Act in Bucharest in May

2007.*Waxing West* was also produced by Teatrul Imposibil and the National Theatre Cluj in 2005, in Romanian translation under the title *Sa epilam spre Vest*; it was published in *Waxing West/Sa epilam spre Vest: trei piese de Saviana Stanescu*, editie bilingva, trans. Eugen Wohl (Cluj: Eikon, Teatrul Imposibil, 2004). *Lenin's Shoe* had a staged reading at Sibiu International Theatre Festival and was subsequently published in *Festivalul International de Teatru Sibiu (Spectacole-Lectura)/ Sibiu International Theatre Festival (Staged-Readings)*,trans. Eugen Wohl (Sibiu: Theatre Festival Readings Series, 2006).

18. All page numbers for *Waxing West* and *Lenin's Shoe* refer to the electronic copies that Stanescu emailed to me in May 2006.

19. I found a paradoxical example of the masks exiles take on striving to be accepted in their new country in the article "Paradoxes of *Hiraj* (Exile): Tales from Algerian Men in Britain" by Yvette Rocheron (Rocheron: 160–9). In order to overcome racist prejudices and become "employable", some of the Algerian men interviewed chose to adopt the masks of their ex-colonizers, i.e., to pose as French citizens who immigrated to the United Kingdom.

20. According to Anthony LaPastina, "The *telenovela* is a form of melodramatic serialized fiction produced and aired in most Latin American countries" ("Telenovela").

21. Stanescu recalls that the actual restaurant played only a minor role in the creative process: "The place has inspired me, being owned and operated by Russian immigrants. Despite this, the events in *Lenin's Shoe* are entirely fictional, based on my research on KGB agents and Russian Mafia" (Stanescu 2006b).

22. For a description of the actual restaurant, please see Daniel Maurer's online profile in *New York: Nightlife and Music* (Maurer).

Works cited

Ashcroft, Bill, Gareth Griffiths and Helen Tiffin. *The Empire Writes Back: Theory and Practice in Post-Colonial Literatures*. London and New York: Routledge, 1989.

Bhabha, Homi K. *The Location of Culture*. London and New York: Routledge, 2004.

Broken English Theatre. Updates by Caterina Ositashvili. 2006. The Broken English Theatre Company: http://www.brokenenglishtheatre.com (accessed 15 February 2007).

Brooke-Rose, Christine. "Exsul". In *Exile and Creativity: Signposts, Travelers, Outsiders, Backward Glances*. Ed. Susan Rubin Suleiman. Durham, NC, and London: Duke University Press, 1998, pp. 7–24.

Cesereanu, Ruxandra. *Imaginarul violent al românilor* [*The Romanians' Violent Imaginary*]. Bucharest: Humanitas, 2003.

Clavin, Patricia. "Defining Transnationalism", *Contemporary European History* 14.4 (November 2005): 421–39.

"Crossing the Line: Plays that Dare to Explore, Provoke and Celebrate: 2005–06 Season". 2004, Lark Play Development Center: http://www.larktheatre.org (accessed 25 February 2007).

"Exile". *The American Heritage® Dictionary of the English Language,* 4th edn. Boston: Houghton Mifflin, 2000: www.bartleby.com/61/ (accessed 14 March 2007).

"Exile and America. 2006 Conference – Seminars". *The American Society for Theatre Research (ASTR)*. Organizers Yana Meerzon and Silvija Jestrovic. 2002–06 The American Society for Theatre Research: http://www.astr.org/conference2006 (accessed 15 February 2007).

Haraga, Otilia. "American-Romanian Theater Exchange – An Insight Into Thorny Current Issues", *Daly News Romania*: http://www.dailynews.ro (accessed 15 September 2006).

Hutcheon, Linda. *Poetics of Postmodernism: History, Theory, Fiction*. New York and London: Routledge, 1988.

"Immigrant". *The American Heritage® Dictionary of the English Language*, 4th edn. Boston: Houghton Mifflin, 2000: www.bartleby.com/61/ (accessed 14 March 2007).

JanMohamed, Abdul, R. "Worldliness-without-World, Homelessness-as-Home: Toward a Definition of the Specular Border Intellectual". In *Critical Approaches to the Work of Edward W. Said*. Ed. Michael Sprinkler. Cambridge, MA: Basil Blackwell, 1992, pp. 96–120.

Krishnaswamy, Revathi. "Mythologies of Migrancy". In *Linked Histories: Postcolonial Histories in a Globalized World*. Ed. Pamela McCallum and Wendy Faith. Calgary: University of Calgary Press, 2005.

Kristeva, Julia. *Strangers to Ourselves*. New York: Columbia University Press, 1994.

LaPastina, Anthony. "Telenovela". *The Museum of Broadcast Communications*. 2005. The Museum of Broadcast Communications (MB): http://www.museum.tv/archives (accessed 18 September 2006).

Lo, Jacqueline and Helen Gilbert. "Toward a Topography of Cross-Cultural Theatre Praxis", *The Drama Review* 46.3 (T175), Fall 2002. New York University and the Massachusetts Institute of Technology, 2002, pp. 31–53.

Marciniak, Katarzyna. *Alienhood: Citizenship, Exile, and the Logic of Difference*. Minneapolis and London: University of Minnesota Press, 2006.

Maurer, Daniel. "Uncle Vanya: Profile", *New York: Nightlife and Music*. 2007. New York Magazine Holdings LLC: http://nymag.com/listings/bar/uncle-vanya (accessed 15 September 2006).

Naficy, Hamid. *An Accented Cinema: Exilic and Diasporic Filmmaking*. Princeton, NJ, and Oxford: Princeton University Press, 2001.

Nagel, Caroline R. and Lynn A. Staeheli. "Citizenship, Identity and Transnational Migration: Arab Immigrants to the United States", *Space and Polity* 8.1 (April 2004): 3–23.

Pavis, Patrice. "Introduction: Towards a Theory of Interculturalism and Theatre." In *The Intercultural Performance Reader*. Ed. Patrice Pavis. London: Routledge, pp. 1–19.

Rocheron, Yvette. "Paradoxes of *Hiraj* (Exile): Tales from Algerian Men in Britain". In *Displaced Persons: Condition of Exile in European Culture*. Studies in European Cultural Transition, vol. 14. Ed. Sharon Oudit. Burlington,VT: Ashgate, 2002, pp. 160–9.

Rushdie, Salman. *Imaginary Homelands: Essays and Criticism 1981–1991*. London: Granta Books; New York: Penguin Books, 1981.

Said, Edward. W. "Reflections on Exile". In *Reflections on Exile and Other Essays*. Cambridge, MA: Harvard University Press, 2003, pp. 173–86.

Stanescu, Saviana. "Stereotype.." Personal email to the author. 24 June 2008.

———. "American Visa". Personal email to the author. 12 January 2007a.

Stanescu, Saviana. "Broken English". Personal email to the author. 13 January 2007b.

———. *Lenin's Shoe*. Unpublished version. © the playwright 2006. Personal email to the author. 2 May 2006a.

———. "'Uncle Vanya' Restaurant". Personal email to the author. 18 September 2006b.

———. "Insemnari din West Village: Povestea de dragoste a emigrarii mele", *Gandul* 9 (September 2006c): http://www.gandul.info (accessed 20 September 2006).

———. *Waxing West*. Unpublished version. © the playwright 2004. Personal email to the author. 2 May 2006.

"The Lark's Mission". *Lark Play Development Center*. 2004. Lark Play Development Center: http://www.larktheatre.org (accessed 20 February 2007).

"Transnational". *The American Heritage® Dictionary of the English Language*, 4th edn. Boston, MA: Houghton Mifflin, 2000: www.bartleby.com/61/ (accessed 15 March 2007.

"Transnational".*Merriam-Webster's Online Dictionary*. 2007. Merriam-Webster: http://www.m-w.com/dictionary/transnational (accessed 20 February 2007).

"U.S. Citizenship and Immigration Services". November 2006. *U.S. Department of Homeland Security*: http://www.uscis.gov (accessed 13 March 2007).

"Venn Diagram". *Merriam-Webster Online Dictionary*. 2008. Merriam-Webster: http://www.merriam-webster.com/dictionary/Venn diagram (accessed 6 September 2008).

4

The American Landscape Reconsidered: On the Theatricality of Urban America in Russian Émigré Writings, with Special Focus on the Works of Vasily Aksyonov

Yana Meerzon
University of Ottawa

Exile as banishment and displacement not only changes one's social and political status but also challenges an émigré's perception of Self. The need to communicate in a second language (even if one has mastered it at home) increases an exile's insecurity not only in her own eyes, but quite often in the eyes of the residents of a newly adopted home country. Fortunately, one's "instinct of theatricality" (Evreinov 1970) serves an exile both as a protective shield and as a means of reconnecting with her sense of self, when her essential tools of communication undergo the processes of theatricalization. As a result, the quotidian practice of the exilic experience turns into a performative site of negotiation: a negotiation between the émigré's self-perception and the perception of her by the newly acquired audience.[1] The challenge of bridging the exile's habitual (original) worldview with the lingo and cultural traditions of a new country constitutes the phenomenon of exilic performance and exilic theatricality.

Theatricality of the exile's quotidian is similar to that of the cross-cultural encounter, in which the "transformative power integral to theatre (its ability to make a table into a mountain by a simple word or gesture) is extended to everyday experience in situations of cross-cultural contact" (Balme: 6). A meeting with the Other (whether this Other is a tourist, or an invited foreign guest, or an exilic newcomer) "brackets moments of action or particular places in such a way that they are imbued with extreme concentration and focus. It invariably emphasizes the visual sense and moves the beholder [a Russian exile in America, for example] to become aware of his/her act of spectating" (6). The same encounter forces an exilic artist to reflect upon her awareness of this self/other spectating. Moreover, this encounter unavoidably establishes an exilic artist (an exilic writer, specifically) as the omnipresent narrator within her stories: someone who records and reveals the theatricality of the exilic being.

In everyday practice, an exile experiences "apprehending something in theatrical terms", which at the same time "'increaseth' the sensation", the émigré's sensation of the meeting with the unknown, but "'lowereth' the ontological status", the ontological status of her experience (Balme: 6). This awareness of the increased sensation of the everyday forces an exilic author to investigate her characters' (often the emigrants' too) theatricality of self, theatricality of their language, and theatricality of their new surrounding landscapes. Thus the exilic encounter leads to the double framing of self, to the experience of self-alienation. An exile, as a performer in the *theatrum mundi* of émigré know-how, turns into a theatrical sign. This sign is framed twice: first within an émigré's own consciousness as a pariah and, secondly, within the consciousness of the inhabitants of her newly adopted country. This chapter, therefore, discusses how the emigrant's practice of putting her own Self, and the surrounding figures and objects in the double frames of her past and present experiences, marks the processes of exilic theatricalization. It examines the theatricality of exilic collective as a clash of representation and reception. Specifically, it looks at how this clash of gazes and the estranged practice of spectating are manifested in late twentieth-century Russian émigré art and literature.[2]

The works of the Russian émigré author Vasily Aksyonov, who saw himself both as a well-integrated American citizen (a cosmopolitan, rarely experiencing any nostalgia) and a *fellow traveler*[3] serve as a focal point of this paper. The problem of theatricalization of the exilic self has been an ongoing theme of investigation in Aksyonov's American writings. These works well reflect Aksyonov's early émigré years (in the 1980s United States) and his changing relationships with America, which evolved from a romantic writerly vision of a free paradise to an understanding and acceptance of his own position as both a resident of the American geopolitical realm and a marginal writer on its literary horizon.[4] This chapter examines three types of theatricalization of America found in Aksyonov's writings: theatricalization of the exile's self, theatricalization of the American landscape, and theatricalization of the novel as a literary genre. This last type of theatrical expression functions as evidence of the exilic artist's search for perfection, for a masterpiece of her performative expression. Secondly, this study describes and analyses how the Russian émigré writers, with Aksyonov as the representative example,[5] dramatized and theatricalized the American cityscape as a part of their reflection on the non-conformity and marginality of the exilic destiny, when the idiosyncrasy of the displaced experience provides an immigrant with the anticipated and welcomed self-alienation and self-theatricalization in the performatively perceived and presented cityscape. This exilic self-theatricalization, in the words of Aleksander Etkind, can be seen as the émigré authors' desire for the Other, their intellectual yearning that always "devaluates their own culture, which is perceived as fictional and unsubstantial, like a simulacrum" (9).

Exile and theatricalization of the quotidian

Adopting Josette Féral's definition of *theatricality of the quotidian*, which follows Nikolay Evreinov's vision of the human instinct to imitate and represent, this chapter explores the idea of the cultural and spatio-temporal frames and borders that manipulate our sense of belonging to the majority of public events we observe and unconsciously participate in through our everyday experience. Thus, theatricality of the quotidian is to be found "in situating the object or the other in a 'framed theatrical space' [and] in transforming a simple event into signs in such a way that it becomes a spectacle" (Féral: 98). This theatricality requires and relies on the dynamic process of "looking at or being looked at" (98), that is, the dichotomy of the gaze (that of the observer and that of the observed) characterizing any situation of displacement, and cultural and temporal alienation. This type of theatricality persists within the exilic everyday and professional experience and "appears to be more than a property": it functions as a "fantastical cognitive operation set in motion either by the observer or the observed. This theatricality is a performative act creating the virtual space of the other, the transitional space discussed by Winnicott, the threshold (*limen*) discussed by Turner, or Goffman's 'framing'" (98). It appears within the space of negotiation between the "quotidian and imaginary dimensions, the latter being founded upon the presence of the other's space" (98). In the exilic incident, theatricality of the everyday acquires a domineering position manipulating émigrés' relationships with their recently acquired landscape, both spatial and temporal.

As Edward Said suggests, any intellectual found either in the physical, outer exile or in the metaphorical, inner one is forced to experience the sense of self-alienation, the occurrence of a certain alter ego or an omnipresent narrator observing and thus telling us a story of this intellectual's outsidedness (52–3). Exile as an actual condition or a metaphorical occurrence produces intellectual-insiders, those "who belong fully to the society as it is", and intellectual-outsiders, "the individuals at odds with their society and therefore outsiders and exiles so far as privileges, power, and honors are concerned" (53). For an émigré intellectual, this distancing of the physical self from the phenomenological self manifests a certain pattern that "sets the course of the intellectual as outsider" and "is best exemplified by the condition of exile, the state of never being fully adjusted, always feeling outside the chatty, familiar world inhabited by natives, [...] tending to avoid and even dislike the trappings of accommodation and national well-being" (Said: 52–3). This alienation of self leads to theatricalization of the emigrant's actions, emotions, and expectations, making the intellectual's marginality a space for the theatrical replaying of being. This constant role-playing is the focus of investigation of Russian expatriate writers. Vasily Aksyonov's American autobiographical chronicle *V poiskah grustnogo baby / In Search of Melancholy Baby* (1987) and his 1997 novel *Novyi sladostny stil' / The New Sweet Style* are important examples of the émigré writers' literary explorations of Said's vision of an intellectual in exile, to whom forced cultural and linguistic marginalization is the condition of "restlessness, movement, constantly being unsettled, and unsetting others" (Said: 53). It is this liminal state of in-between-ness, when one "cannot go back to some earlier and perhaps more stable condition of being at home; and, alas, can never fully arrive, be at one with [her] new home or situation" (53) that Russian émigré literature embraces.

Theatricalization of America has a long-standing tradition in Russian literature and drama. Starting from the early twentieth century, the travelogues of various Russian writers *(fellow-travelers)* described American cityscapes in metaphorical language. For instance, the city of New York was described as "the city of Yellow Devil" or represented poetically by futuristic bridges and skyscrapers. In early Soviet Russia, the so-called *sotcial'ny zakaz/commissioning by the state* financed by the government and the writers' need to re-establish the identity of their readers, both "national and ideological" (Etkind: 142), motivated and explained the theatricalization of America in their travelogues. In the 1936 travelogue *Odnoetazhnaya America/Single-Storied America*, Il'ya Il'f and Evgeny Pertrov depicted both the utilitarian prosperity and commercialized carnivalesque of the American metropolis, New York specifically, and the coziness, expediency, and warm-heartened atmosphere of the single-story houses of the American countryside. The authors, however, fascinated by the signs of technological success and material wealth of the country, managed to maintain a physical and emotional distance, reminding themselves and their readers that the only purpose of this voyage was to remain outside voices, observers of the West sent there by the newly established Soviet state and its cultural politics. The theatricalization of New York is presented in this work as a point of comparison between the two countries,[6] the point of the authors' and thus their readers' estrangement from the images of "the land of Oz". The authors of the travelogue were hardly interested in creating psychological or physiological portraits of either resident or newcomer inhabitants of the American city. Instead, the American landscape is depicted mostly in its architectural, modernist characteristics, separated from the travelers or immigrants' familiarity with its theatricality.

In the late twentieth-century phase of Russian exilic art, however, the reasons for theatricalization of the American landscape had radically changed, as had their anticipated readership. During the last decades of the Soviet regime, Russian expatriate intellectuals were facing a dual dilemma: to make it in the dream-place of their youth (America) and to achieve a sense of closure in their relationships with their home country (Russia). This double aim of their exilic lives made both the immigrants' new surroundings and their own roles in this environment highly theatrical. The complex process of the expatriate's rediscovery of her identity, language, and *existential chronotope,* the "intrinsic connectedness of temporal and spatial relationships that are artistically expressed in literature", in Bakhtin's terms, and the newly acquired territory of "non-separateness of space and time [time becomes the fourth dimension of space]" (9), found dramatic expression if not in the exiles' theatre, then in their prose, poetry, critical essays, and literary memoirs.[7]

In 1960s Russia, the longing for the West, specifically for America, signified intellectuals' rejection not only of the official presentation of the United States as a monster of social and political injustice (and the USSR's primary enemy) but also of the Soviet way of life. The 1960s Soviet intellectual lived through the constant anticipation of an improbable reunion with the America of her artistic phantasms and cultural metaphors. Aksyonov was one of the best at describing the Soviet intellectuals' mythologization and metaphorization of America in his own daily theatricality and on the pages of his novels, plays, and memoirs

(2005: 248–68). According to Aksyonov, in 1960s Russia the issue of emigration, "the theme of life abroad, the dream of crossing the frontier", began to shape the living chronotope of the Soviet quotidian and to "flicker across our pages" (1991: 44). The "American Dream" – in the Russian reading of the expression – became the major focus of artists' personal quests and investigations: from the young intellectuals' idolization of American literature (especially Hemingway) and American musical culture (jazz), to their worshiping of English, the secret and sacred language of their inner resistance. As Aksyonov recalled: "The life abroad became the great dream of a generation, a generation that had been processed from childhood with a view of making it the first generation of ideal socialist citizens, grateful even for being allowed to live" (44).

However, for most of the 1970s and 1980s Russian émigré writers, the long-anticipated encounter with America proved to be disappointing, disillusioning and heart-breaking. America, as Russians had come to see it, with its cultural provincialism and open consumerism not only intimidated third-wave emigrants but also refused to grant them the socio-political status, aura of sacrifice, and dissidence they all enjoyed back at home.[8] As Joseph Brodsky wrote:

> if one were to assign the life of an exiled writer a genre, it would have to be tragicomedy. Because of his previous incarnation, he is capable of appreciating the social and material advantages of democracy far more intensely than its natives do. Yet for precisely the same reason (whose main by-product is the linguistic barrier), he finds himself totally unable to play any meaningful role in his new society. The democracy into which he has arrived provides him with physical safety but renders him insignificant. And the lack of significance is what no writer, exile or not, can take.
>
> (24)

Aksyonov's view of America, nonetheless, was different from that of many of the Russian exilic intellectuals. His view presented a sense of "faith and optimism" through the image of America as a place "not only rich and powerful, but also generous, tolerant and humane, free of xenophobia, and ready to lead the world – if not already doing so – to a new age of liberalism built on what Aksyonov has termed beneficial or even noble inequality" (McMillin: 58).[9]

In his novel *The New Sweet Style*, the quintessence of the author's American experience, Aksyonov depicts the journey of a typical Russian artist-intellectual in the United States. Like Aksyonov, 1960s Moscow avant-garde theatre director Alexander Korbach was deported from the USSR in the early 1980s. Declined his Russian citizenship, he was thus pushed to seek asylum in the United States. Alexander Korbach (the author refers to his character as AK), like many of Aksyonov's protagonists, is a cumulative character whose literary profile is semi-fictional: it is mixed with the characteristics of Russian artists of the "thaw" period,[10] as well as the author's own biography. To Aksyonov, as he stated in later interviews, "emigration [was] a difficult, horrifying experience" that he wished on no one. "Emigration is not unlike your own funeral. Only after the funeral, your vegetative system is stabilized, whereas in emigration it isn't" (2005: 431).

Back in Soviet Russia, Alexander Korbach was a worshipper of Vsevolod Meyerhold's theatre traditions, a widely acknowledged underground singer-songwriter of the Soviet intellectuals, and the seeker of moral and aesthetic freedoms. This Shakespearian fool, as Aksyonov refers to AK,[11] faces various temptations of America. The novel opens with AK's unexpected, and thus unnoticed, arrival in the United States. Due to an unforeseen turn of luck (AK is refused his Soviet citizenship while touring Paris) and an oversight of AK's agent in Paris, the American media misses his US arrival. This incident strips AK of his fame and confidence, thus turning the renowned Soviet theatre director into one in the myriad of invisible, nameless immigrants entering America daily. As a part of his exilic experience, AK has to accept the theatricality of the American quotidian he finds himself put in: Aksyonov's protagonist maintains equilibrium between the expectations he held of his mythological America and the reality of his émigré life as a Los Angeles parking valet. Secondly, deprived of any possibility of working in theatre and thus forced to accept this as an artistic refuge too, AK recognizes and welcomes as something new and original the processes of alienation of self, the loss of social niche, and gains inner peace through accepting this loss. This search for reconciliation between dream and reality that unfolds within the *mental place*[12] of the exile's consciousness becomes, for Aksyonov's character, the hunt for his only masterpiece. It takes AK years of voiceless and fruitless exile to accept his destiny: the pursuit of his only *magnum opus* that is worsened or simply made impossible by the condition of displacement. AK finds a fleeting satisfaction working in the university theatre where he directs Gogol's plays and introduces American students to the fundamentals of Russian avant-garde theatre. He conceives his own play, further developed as a Hollywood film, *Svechenie/Radiance,* not only as another interpretation of Dante's platonic love but also as a parable of the existential journey of the exiled poet. This play, however, is never consummated on stage or in film even with the mighty financial support of Korbach's American cousin, the business mogul Stanley Korbach.[13]

Again, as Féral writes, theatricality of the everyday "has little to do with the nature of the invested object – the actor, space, object or event – nor is it necessarily the result of pretense, illusion, make-believe, or fiction. Were such conditions prerequisites of theatricality, we would have been unable to identify its presence in everyday occurrences" (97). Moreover, theatricality of the quotidian as a process and as a gaze "postulates and creates a distinct space belonging to the other, from which fiction can emerge" (97). In exile, the gaze of the beholder (either an expatriate herself or those who observe her, i.e., the inhabitants of the adoptive country) creates "a spatial cleft from illusion emerged – illusion whose vehicle the spectator had selected from among events, behaviors, physical bodies, objects and space without regard for the fictional or real nature of the vehicle's origin" (97). In the alienated and thus almost fictional presence of the exile's everyday experience, the distinction between real/actual and imaginary/perceived chronotope of her new life becomes "the result of an actor's [an exile's] seizing control of the quotidian and turning it into theatrical space; it can also be the result of spectator's gaze constituting space as theatrical" (97).

By reaching a new territory, an exile finds herself continuously changing her position from that of a spectator/observer to that of an actor/doer. Since she finds herself in the constant process of performing, she also experiences the invariable need for defining this position, taking on the initiative in communication. This act identifies her theatrical perception as a life-chronotope she is forced to experience. As Féral states, "in the case where the initiative belongs to the actor [i.e., an exile], the 'other' becomes actor through an avowed act of representation; in the case where the initiative belongs to the spectator [i.e., the exile], the 'other' is unwittingly transformed into actor through a gaze that inscribes theatricality in the space surrounding him" (97). In Aksyonov's writings this act of making the other an actor of the quotidian theatre by the gaze of the beholder is presented as the basis of the characters' relationships with their new country.

Exile and theatricalizaton of city/space

Theatricality of space or urban dwelling originates in a similar fashion to the theatricality of the everyday. It requires the active presence of actors/doers and observers/onlookers. This theatricality encompasses the processes of gaze and framing, and relies on creating the *mise-en-scènes* and metaphors of cityscapes:

> [The] ways of seeing and understanding the city inevitably informs ways of acting on the space of the city, with consequences which then in turn produce a modified city which is again seen, understood and acted on. It is not just that the boundaries between reality and imagination are fuzzy and porous. In the development of cities can be discerned a traffic between the two, an economy of symbolic constructs which have material consequences that are manifested in enduring reality.
>
> (Donald: 27)

Like in a theatre production, the *theatricality of urban living* occurs within the onlooker's act of distanced observation that leads to the onlooker's creation of visual and philosophical metaphors. The spatial metaphor of urban landscape reminds the onlooker of a theatrical metaphor, the junction of iconic and indexical signs serving to represent reality, the negotiation between the symbolic account of a story and its dramatic conception. Since theatrical reality, as Fischer-Lichte states, is "intended as the representation of another reality", theatre can be seen "as a model of reality" (103). Similarly, the theatricality of urban dwelling, as it is perceived and constructed by an émigré, is "the result or product of the spectator's subjectively executed construction" (103) that demands the active role of the spectator, creating a theatrical universe through aggressive interaction with the observed site. As in a modernist performance, the role of exile-as-spectator, the creator of a mental *mise-en-scène*, is to recognize that there is "no opposition between a given reality [that of the exile's environment] and its representation (illusion) on stage [the exile's vision of this environment]; rather, there are as many realities as the different spectators can construct by relying on their own perception of the performance" (103). An exile (the protagonist and the alter ego of Aksyonov's works, for instance) perceives and interprets the city's everyday performance as "a field of experimentation where we can test our capacity for and the possibilities of constructing reality" (104), very much as a theatre spectator does. In the following passage, Aksyonov borrows ubiquitous images from the Russian literary canon in order to create his urban metaphors:

> They drove along the highway, four lanes in one direction and four in the other. [...] They slid by nondescript houses and protruding cubes

of brick without the slightest signs of an architect having worked on them, nothing but walls, windows, doors, windows [...]. To the left, skyscrapers stood pressed to each other like a phalanx about to go into battle. [...] "That's the Jewish cemetery," said Butlerov. I must be going crazy, Korbach thought. I take a nearby Jewish cemetery for faraway Manhattan. [...] "This here is Manhattan" [...]. The sight that evening was magnificent and foreboding. The stagnant hundred-degree heat lent a feeling of some vague inevitability, an approach of something fundamentally inhuman, the whole mass of stone, glass, and steel. Clarity was introduced only by the ball of the sun hanging over the rows of buildings in a murky stew of urban pollution. [...] "Perfectly," laughed Korbach. "Like in a film", he went on, still laughing. "Like in a dream".

(Aksyonov 1999: 25–6)

The hellish image of the American landscape, where Jewish graves remind the protagonist of the wealthy Manhattan skyscrapers, and the picture of the district enveloped by the "stagnant hundred-degree heat" evokes intertextual references from Dante's *Inferno* to Bulgakov's Jerusalem in *Master and Margarita*. The image also depicts the exiles' relationships with their *locales* as the signifier of their unconscious vision of the urban space as a *metaphorical location,* an *in-between, imaginary cityscape* (Donald: 6–9).

This imaginary cityscape is located in the exiles' *mental place* and is an act of negotiation between what transpires between the actual reality of a city dwelling and an émigré's interpretation of that space. In modernist aesthetics, the urban becomes *unreal* (Donald: 3); it comes to be seen and understood as the urban space of phantasmagoric or dreamlike experience of the human consciousness. The city perceived by exiles arises within the dichotomy of the projected image of the space (from their consciousness onto the reality of the place) and the space imposing itself on the people's minds (from the actual structures of the urban set up onto the onlooker's mind). This dichotomy reveals a typical set of reflections that any city dweller is bound to confer on moving into a new environment, and manifests the exile's "ability to live both here and elsewhere – a way of being encouraged in more mundane ways by new and largely urban technologies of communication" (5).

Moreover, in the exile's initial relationships with a newly acquired urban landscape, an exile acts as a tourist who is forced to constantly choose between what she perceives as her new habitat and what she imagined it to be before she arrived. Wirth-Nesher's concept of *touristic vision* defines the ahistorical perception of the city, typical for a tourist's attitude to the place of her visit. This attitude is distinguished by the tourist's "tendency to totalize, to deny history, to inhabit exclusively public space and to anticipate remembrance" (119), and is comparable to how an exile reacts to her new locale. In addition, the impression of a theatrical performance and thus an image of a theatrical set surround both tourist and émigré. The former does not seek to build any long-term relationships with the city's dwellers. The tourist views the city in the "atemporal reductiveness" (Wirth-Nesher: 117), she does not notice the demographic specificity of the place and thus does not seek to understand the quotidian dynamic of the urban living. She tends to build comparative bridges between her home-space and the place she is visiting, so she views "the objects of the foreign culture [...] in light of similar landmarks at home, [that] are measured against, compared, and understood only in terms of what is already familiar" (117). Therefore, for both a tourist and an expatriate, a momentously observed cityscape (from Vladimir Nabokov's Berlin, to Joseph Brodsky's Venice, to Vasily Aksyonov's Washington, to Sergei Dovlatov's New York) presents itself not as an administrative structure, or "an abstraction that claims to identify what, if anything, is common to all cities [...] a space produced by the interaction of historically and geographically specific institutions, social relations of production and reproduction, practices of government, forms and media of communication" (Donald: 8), but as a *performative text,* a necessary production of audio and visual signs.

Although exiles begin relationships with the new place in the same way as tourists, they gradually find a personal kinetic and psychological topography within the new metropolis and thus change their relationships with it. The processes of the émigré's gradual absorption into a new place, turning an unfamiliar dwelling into a familiar universe of life – the processes opposing the defamiliarization of space and time practices – constitute the change in the exile's tourist-like relationships with the city. Gradually, an exile begins to impress herself onto the architectural, social, and demographic setup of her new landscape. The more time she spends in the new place, the less she sees it as a piece of theatre *scenographie,* identifying the temporal frames and the events of her life with the ones that occurred in this particular space. In this instance, an exile not only adapts her Self to the Other but also performs a mental operation upon the city: she begins to recognize and appreciate the historical consistency of the place by acknowledging it not as a *mental place* of dreams and metaphors but as a *social space* (Lefebvre: 73).

In his definition of *social space,* a constituent of urban living, Lefebvre distinguishes between *communal space,* the product of peoples' collective efforts, and the *space of dreams and metaphors* constituted through the dwellers' imagination about their habitat. Social space, therefore, is never imagined, unreal, or ideal. As the "outcome of past actions", social space "subsumes things produced, and encompasses their interrelationships in their coexistence and simultaneity" (Lefebvre: 73). Moreover, it permits "fresh actions to occur, while suggesting others and prohibiting yet others" (73). Consequently, any city becomes a product of particular temporal and cultural efforts, the manifestations of the generations of its inhabitants, "a space which is fashioned, shaped and invested by social activities during a finite historical period" (73). As Lefebvre suggests, "our space has strange effects. For one thing, it unleashes desire. It presents desire with a 'transparency' which encourages it to surge forth in an attempt to lay claim to an apparently clear field. [...] Disillusion leaves space empty – an emptiness that words convey" (97). For this reason, our cities' spatial layout presupposes both the logic of visualization and the logic of metaphor. The layout suggests manifestation and representation of power: "the arrogant verticality of skyscrapers, and especially of public and state buildings, introduces a phallic or more precisely a phallocratic element into the visual realm; the purpose of this display, of this need to impress, is to convey an impression of authority to each spectator. Verticality and great height have ever been the spatial expression of potentially violent power" (98). At the same time, it implies the dwellers' constant negotiation between the presence of this power and the processes of its *metaphorization,* represented in various forms of urban and spatial theatricalization. Although verticality may seem "normal" and acceptable for city residents, it encompasses "a twofold strategy towards spectator. On the one hand, it embodies a metonymic logic consisting in a continual to-and-fro movement [...] between the part and the whole" (98), and it represents itself as a theatrical sign:

Living bodies, the bodies of "users" – are caught up not only in the toils of parcellized space, but also in the web of what philosophers call "analogons": images, signs and symbols. These bodies are transported out of themselves, transferred and emptied out, as it were, via the eyes: every kind of appeal, incitement, and seduction is mobilized to tempt them with doubles of themselves in prettified, smiling and happy poses; and this campaign to void them succeeds exactly to the degree that the images proposed correspond to "needs" that those same images have helped to fashion.

(98)

Thus, in its second incarnation, the spatial (vertical or any other) arrangement of the city structures dictates an approach that is both practical and creative. In the case of the exilic quotidian, creating a metaphor of space and thus a metaphor of life takes over any practical needs in the émigré's mind. In order not only to learn about but also to adjust and feel secure, belonging to a new place, the recently arrived expatriates reinvent, rename and reshape in their heads the names of the streets and districts where they happen to live, work and build social, personal, and communal relationships.[14]

In his semi-fictional memoir *In Search of Melancholic Baby*, Aksyonov describers how a typical émigré, similarly to a child kinetically memorizing her way home, looks for an apartment that simultaneously must remind her of her past residence and at the same time be authentically local, that is, American. "Apartment hunting brings home, so to speak, the duality of émigré existence: you want something that reminds you of your former life yet something you did not have – could not have – in that life" (Aksyonov 1987b:73). The phantasmagorical monster of a theatrical city-space invented by the exilic mind belongs at the same time to, and represents, no actual environment. In Aksyonov's example, the Washington, DC, apartment the author finally comes across and decides to rent reflects rather the 1960s Soviet intellectual's dreamscape that he lived by fantasizing about his America: "A white-walled duplex complete with spiral staircase and view to the Capitol, the Washington Monument, and the colonnade of the Lincoln Memorial, it could not have existed in Moscow and evoked vague visions of our Muscovite dreams" (73). In this sentence, the reader finds both the emigrant's subscription to the verticality of the urban landscape and his fascination with his own illusory belonging to it. "For this smashing pad on the border between Dupont Circle and the popular Adams Morgan section of town [Washington] we agreed to pay what at the time seemed a fortune: $1200 a month" (74).

Similarly, an inciting scene in Aksyonov's novel *The New Sweet Style* takes place at the meeting of the protagonist AK with his own name displayed above the entrance of a mega-department-store, the headquarters of the Korbach Corporation. "Suddenly there appeared to him [AK] a sight in the centre of which, in huge, burning letters standing out against a dark sky, was his own name: ALEXANDER KORBACH. Well that's it. My time has come" (Aksyonov 1999: 41). AK perceives the skyscraper in the American commercial paradise in its everyday theatricality. Moreover, he acknowledges and accepts the fact that he is standing in front of not merely a centre of urban culture new to him, but in front of the contemporary place of worship, the superstore equal in its functions to those of a medieval cathedral, "the symbolic centre of medieval town" (Carlson: 14).

A medieval cathedral, the place of religious reverence, stood during its times (as a superstore does today) for "a trove of symbolic referents" concentrated in that place with such might as "nowhere else in the city" (Carlson: 14). In the exilic landscape of Alexander Korbach's New York, his encounter with the department store entitled with his own name grotesquely indicates a shift of this symbolic city-centre in today's metropolis. The symbolic function of the cathedral in the medieval city manifested in its architectural layout[15] is repeated and ironically commented on in Korbach's superstore building's appointment and utilitarian significance. Korbach Co. will enter the life of AK as does Dante's Virgil, who guides the poet on his voyage of self-discovery. With the discovery of Korbach's dynasty and his own belonging to it, AK's exilic journey acquires the elements of a morality play, representing the exilic Everyman's journey to self-acceptance, to the acceptance of the artistic and life genres he is subjected to live through in his newly acquired American paradise.

Theatricalizaton of genre

One of the difficulties an exilic artist faces is to remain true to the original chosen genre of her creative expression.[16] In his later writings, Aksyonov stages the tragedy of an exilic artist's search for masterpiece. Although this pursuit of artistic closure is an existential not a social dilemma, an intellectual in exile is ready, and somewhat right, to blame her linguistic marginalization and the life outside both her native and newly acquired cultural metropolis for her inability to attain success. Aksyonov, like some expatriate writers, cherishes this marginal position of an exilic artist able to live in the cultural suburbs and thus benefit from an opportunity to sharpen his craft and ideas. He understands at the same time the exilic catastrophe of a theatre practitioner bound to create theatre only in the present time of her present audience. Hence, in *The New Sweet Style*, AK, like many theatre people in exile, never reaches a sense of closure, though he is happy when the theatricality of his profession finds its way into the everyday. Although Aksyonov proposes an alternative scenario to this situation and sends AK back home to receive a standing ovation from his company and former admirers, he still maintains the notion that once an artist experiences emigration, he cannot ultimately fulfill his artistic destiny. The novel does not present a happy picture of reconciliation between Mother-Russia and her prodigal son.

AK never crosses the threshold of his Moscow theatre. Instead, acting as the representative of the Korbach charity foundation in post-1991 Russia, AK symbolizes American economic prosperity and political influence. Finally, he chooses not to witness the commercialization or the newly found forms of corruption in his motherland and deserts it for the second time. The life journey of AK continues beyond the fictional time frame of the novel, thus making its readers wonder about his final destination.

Aksyonov himself, the author of prose and drama at home, was able to succeed in the once-chosen genre of what he calls a novel of self-investigation and self-expression, writing mostly in Russian, publishing in translation, in America. The linguistic peculiarities of his characters speaking in various tongues of the countries of their author's habitat, as well as the experiments with traditional forms of novel composition become Aksyonov's fields of artistic expression based upon "freeing oneself from the conventions of traditional prose, [...] and creating a form in which bits of rhymed and rhythmic prose and elements of drama are combined" (Briker 149). These tendencies signify Aksyonov's challenging of the essential devices of novel writing, something what he calls "an establishment of new narrative forms", or a new type of narratology based on the use of meta-narrative techniques and characterized by the novel's fundamental "incompleteness and harmony at the same time" (Aksyonov 2005: 453). In his émigré works, Aksyonov employs "instead of a plot underlying the movement of the prose, [...] a chain of associations or reminiscences, and excerpts from favorite classical works. Over all of this reigns irony, which figures in Aksyonov's scenes not only as a literary device, but even as a literary image. [...] To borrow analogies from Aksyonov himself, we can compare these scenes and devices with jazz improvisations" (Briker: 149).

Moreover, the more time Aksyonov spends away from Russia, the more his prose gains the qualities and characteristics of drama or a theatrical presentation in prose that exhibits the performativity of the narrative's spatial and temporal elements, the chronotopes of the characters' journeys. The appearance of various meta-narrative devices (from omnipresent narrator's voiceover, to plot digressions, flashbacks, and flash-forwards, to name a few) attests to the playfulness and the theatricality of Aksyonov's prose. The author's position toward the subject he dramatizes – his America – is seen through Aksyonov's irony towards his own life as a Russian expatriate writer, a university professor, a citizen of the United States. This phenomenon finds its expression in the adventurisms of Hemingway, the phantasmagoria of Gogol, Bely, and Bulgakov, and Chekhov's theatrical impressionism in Aksyonov's pages featuring Russian immigrants surviving within the American landscape.

In the chapter "Preispodnyaya"/"The Netherworld" in *The New Sweet Style*, AK makes his first extensive trip around New York observing its grotesquely distorted streets with his own figure theatrically imprinted onto them. The exilic topography of Aksyonov's protagonist consists of the author's reflections on the biographical details of Dante's life and on the structure of *The Divine Comedy* that he interprets in the context of Bakhtin's theories of carnivalesque:

> In the gathering twilight, he slowly trudged toward Times Square. [...] A stream of red fire poured out on the board heights of a wall of yellow fire, to be replaced by one blue flame. [...] The ground floors shone with their hundreds of brightly lit caves – in one, a thousand cameras; in another, a thousand radios; in a third, a thousand suitcases. [...] Up there, on the ledge of the fiftieth floor, it would be good to join that symbolist dwarf [Russian symbolist poet Alexander Blok] with the fiery tongue stuck to the sky. [...] In an acute stage of nervous breakdown, he hadn't noticed that he'd turned off the triangle glittering with commercial blandishments into one of the soberly lit side streets. Now he was moving along it, at one moment striding like the Futurist poet Mayakovsky, at another shuffling like Beckett. [...] Just have a look in a reflecting mirror – don't you see anything? There was a reflection of a man covered with sweat, in a short jacket, a bulging forehead like on a Boeing 747, long locks of hair clinging to his cheeks, and in his long mouth there might even have been a red tongue that could roll out to cover half the sky. Or the complete absence of a tongue.
>
> (Aksyonov 1999: 39–41)

As a scholar and practitioner of Bakhtin's literary theory, to whom a novel, unlike poetry or drama, presents the most flexible and thus the most undetermined literary genre, open for various experiments with its stylistic demands and canons (Bakhtin: 195–8), Aksyonov employs dramatization and theatricalization of his stories creating a unique literary event structured in accordance with the poetics of drama and performance. Specifically, Aksyonov's 2001 novel *Kesarevo svechenie/Caesarian Luminescence*, the writer's post-American or post-exilic epic presupposes the readers' active interaction with it. In line with the practice of *post-dramatic theatre* (Lehmann: 2006), Aksyonov's work rejects a mimetic representation of reality in favour of a theatrical presentation or tableau of various landscapes. Aksyonov's dramatically constructed novel presents the collision of a range of equally important and well-determined forces – the forces of stage-text, audience-text, and stage/audience context – that constitute a theatrical event. *Caesarian Luminescence*, a mixture of prose, poetry, drama, and semi-biographical memoirs, consists of three separate plays combined together by the journey of a single character. Each play, if necessary, can be cut from the text, staged separately, or switched with any other section in the narrative. The prosaic interludes, poetic excerpts, socio-political essays, and semi-fictional or autobiographical stories organize a highly dynamic text that makes the described reality more literary, more artistic, thus giving the "banality-weary human vision [...] an eye of Adam, crafting an epiphany of everyday objects".[17]

Consequently, in his exilic experiments Aksyonov more than ever anticipates the readers' counter-reaction: he employs forms of stage-audience or novel-reader relationships similar to post-dramatic theatre, seeking a reader – the co-participant of the writer's creative act. Aksyonov hopes to establish a new readership able to vigorously and imaginatively communicate with literature and thus create its own hyper-text. Therefore, if the post-dramatic theatre seeks an active spectator creating her own meaning and inner connections within the stage-text presented, Aksyonov seeks the dynamic readership able to follow intertextual connections encoded within his texts and further build her own. As his model, Aksyonov refers to the writing style of Andrey Bely, the leading figure of Russian symbolism, who "would admit to not striving for broad readership but for an 'active reader', that is, a co-author. This hypothetical artistic reader does not read with his eyes only, nor does he just skim the pages looking for some stories or moral issues. He also reads with his lips, muttering through the text, a word, a sentence at a time, experiencing the pleasure of prose".[18] In other words, Aksyonov expects his active reader to turn into the actor, turning her act of readership into one of actor-ship. Reading, therefore, takes on a variety of theatrical forms: it turns into the experience of monodrama where a reader acts as both an actor and a spectator.

However, this approach evokes a criticism related to Aksyonov's target audience. Since his novels are first written in Russian and only later translated into English, his primary readership is the Russian-speaking populace both in the mother country and in the diaspora, those who are the most familiar with the realities of both worlds: here/there in the United States and there/here at home. Those who cannot visualize, recognize, and identify with the codified American or Russian landscapes in

Aksyonov's texts find themselves back in the universe of the here/there dichotomy (that the author claims to have overcome thanks to his position of an émigré), an artist constantly working in the space of *in between*. Indeed, Aksyonov's exilic experience marks the writer's self-distancing from the reality of his novels and stimulates theatricalization of his prose. Moreover, the mythologization of America that characterized the 1960s Russian intellectual's view of the United States comes back in Aksyonov's texts as the artist's self- and genre-theatricalization, reflected in the new mythology of America reconstructed and reconstituted in today's Russia.

Aksyonov closes *The New Sweet Style* with a typical meta-dramatic device. He has AK comment on the nature of the novel and on his own place in this narrative as its leading character and as a semi-fictional replica of the exilic author. Perhaps the author unwittingly identifies himself with his protagonist, the Russian émigré, theatre director, who has never found his home in America, the country that gave him political and physical shelter:

> If everything that's gone before our eyes and with our participation is a novel, then it must be reaching its end: such were Alexander's [...] thoughts. If, of course, there is such a thing as the end of a novel. In the theatre I bring down the curtain or I turn on the lights: that's the end, dear ladies and gentlemen, please go home now. In a novel, no one goes home, everyone makes up an epilogue. What's to become of this character who throughout these pages has stubbornly opposed the author's intentions, unexpectedly turning into now a hopeless loser, now a favorite of Fortune: [...]? Am I, Alexander Korbach, of whose life fourteen years have passed before your eyes, real, O Theophilus? [...] Everything is lost, including my motherland, and I haven't managed to find a new home either. [...] Instead of becoming a law-abiding apartment renter, a valet in a parking garage, a professor in a university theater department, I insist on remaining a character in a novel with its anarchic plot.
>
> (Aksyonov 1999: 456–7)

In one of his literary-philosophical digressions, the émigré author allows himself to discuss the problem of exile as an existential category of life, stating that exile as banishment was among the fundamental ideas of God's creation. Aksyonov, who says that he never experienced the pangs of nostalgia, sees exile in its biblical context as the other side of temptation, exile and temptation "occur[ing] at one and the same time" (1999: 429). Time itself turns into the act of exile: time "created this world of ours, the sphere of mortals. Time/Banishment [or Time/Exile] created biology [...] and thus we can consider DNA to be the formula of banishment from Paradise. [...] Air, earth, and water formed the elements of every living, and consequently mortal, thing. Time, then, came immediately after that. The countdown from Banishment began" (429). This acceptance of exile as the existential state marks Aksyonov's thinking as inevitably Russian, with its spiritual searches and finds. It makes his philosophy inescapably gnostic and melancholic, similar to that of one of his favorite Americans – Ernest Hemingway.

Notes

1. Here, I use the word "audience" to interchangeably indicate the Other of everyday communication, and the public of theatrical performance.
2. Christopher B. Balme's views on the theatricality of cross-cultural encounter in tourist performance can serve here as a useful frame in discussing the Russian-Soviet writers' views of America, in understanding their need to position themselves outside the landscape, and thus their need to consciously seek and perform the act of spectating (Balme: 174–91).
3. The epithet *"fellow traveler"* refers to 1920s Russian "left-wing intellectuals who, while not members of the Communist Party, were sympathetic to its political project" (Bronner and Jacobsen 2004). This term was applied to both the state's political enemies and certain intellectuals who accepted the 1917 Revolution but were not active participants in the building of the new country, and to the outside intellectuals who were eager to discover the new Russia. The writers – *fellow travelers* – such as Vladimir Mayakovsky and Sergey Yesenin in the 1920s, and Il'ya Ilf and Evgeny Petrov in the 1930s, were chosen by the State to travel to the West, specifically to the United States, to collect and bring back home their impressions of what they witnessed outside the iron curtain. These travelogues were censored by the state: they provided a gloomy picture of the lagging behind capitalist societies, highlighting therefore the prosperous present of a newly established socialist state.
4. Aksyonov lived for about 25 years in the United States, working at George Mason University in Virginia. However, the latest phase of Aksyonov's relationship with the United States (beyond the scope of this study) constitutes his discontent with the new publishing politics in the country that focuses on commercialization of its book market and rejects in Aksyonov's words, the so-called novel of "self-expressivity". Until his death on 6 July 2009 in Moscow, Aksyonov lived between several countries. After he left America, Aksyonov bought a small house in Biarritz, France, and regularly visited Moscow, actively participating in Russian political and cultural events and publishing his novels in Russian and French.
5. Among the different voices of modern Russian literature abroad, the three writers (Vasily Aksyonov, Sergey Dovlatov, and Joseph Brodsky) had very particular relationships with America. Dovlatov, for example, who died in 1990, before acts of homecoming were popularized within the émigré community, established himself as the voice of the Russian diaspora. The Nobel

Prize laureate, the Russian-Ameican poet Brodsky lived the life of an existential philosopher, to whom the dimensions of time and language were more significant than those of space. He died in 1996 without contemplating the possibility of return to his native country.

6. This is the description of New York's transit system, as seen by Soviet intellectuals: "The major currents of pedestrians and automobiles make their way along the wide avenues. Beneath them are dug the coal mine black and damp four-track tunnels of the subway. Above them rattles "the EL" (the elevated train). Here there are all possible types of public transport – the somewhat old-fashioned double-decker buses along with the streetcars. In Kiev, the city that did away with streetcar traffic on its main thoroughfare, they would have probably been shocked had they found out that streetcars run even on Broadway, the busiest street in the world" (Il'f and Petrov: 33).

7. Through the juxtaposition of Self to Other, with the emphasis on seeing and vision, temporal and spatial architectonics in peoples' relationships, expatriates face a dialogicity of displacement that leads to estrangement and thus theatricality of the exilic chronotope. Bakhtin described the chronotope of Self (either in literature or in life) as never fulfilled without its positioning on the background of the chronotope of the Other, the formula reflecting newcomers' situating themselves toward their Selves and Others in a new country. To Bakhtin, as to anyone who has experienced life as an exile, "the recognition of this difference through the performance of such an architectonics is precisely the significance of alterity and outsideness. Yet while the Self completes the Other, the Self will never be brought into stasis and fixity. The Self will always exceed that which is necessarily derived from alterity precisely because its place in existence is unique" (Holloway and Kneale: 75).

8. With regard to the romantic myth of America that Soviet intellectuals have created collectively, the realities of life in the country were rather disappointing for them: "as with many of his generation, Aksyonov's first impressions of America were derived from films, scraps of music and information over the Western radio, and not least, indeed, perhaps more than anything else, the idealization which is typically, albeit paradoxically, produced by Soviet anti-American propaganda" (McMillin: 52).

9. In this aspect, Aksyonov's post-9/11 interviews are very symptomatic. They present a Russian-American patriot, a most loyal follower of President Bush's foreign politics. Vasiliy Aksyonov, "Amerikanskim pisatelem ya tak I ne stal", *Inostrannaya literatura* 1 (2003): http://magazines.russ.ru/inostran/2003/1/aksen.html (accessed 4 January 2007).

10. There are numerous examples of 1960s artists, the representatives of the Soviet Renaissance, on the pages of Aksyonov's works. The figure of Yuri Lubimov, founder and artistic director of Moscow's Taganka Theatre, is one of AK's prototypes. Lubimov, who tried to resurrect the traditions of Meyerhold and Brecht on the Soviet stage in the 1960s, was forced to leave Russia in the 1980s. He went back in the 1990s. The tragic figure of Vladimir Vysotsky (who died in 1980), leading actor of the same theatre company and singer-songwriter (the most famous voice of freedom in 1970s Russia), is mentioned many times in the novel. The figure of Andrey Tarkovsky, the dissident filmmaker, is recognizable among other Soviet intellectuals (theatre, film, literary, and music icons) to whom AK longs to return in his time of exile.

11. It is through his mask that we see Rabelais's characters concretized by Bakhtin's theory of carnivalesque (Aksyonov: 1999).

12. The concept of *mental place* belongs to Henri Lefebvre, who describes it as a philosophical category that negotiates the difference between the onlooker's image of reality, reality itself, and the onlooker's perception of it. Mental place, therefore, "may connote logical coherence, practical consistency, self-regulation and the relations of the parts to the whole, the engendering of like by like in a set of places, the logic of container versus contents, and so on" (Lefebvre: 3).

13. The figure of Stanley Korbach, Alexander Korbach's American cousin, is again semi-fictional: a tycoon driven by the search for genealogical roots on the one hand and by the desire of constant charity on the other, refers to the infamous Russian oligarch and Aksyonov's acquaintance, Boris Berezovsky. "I wouldn't say that Boris Abramovich [Berezovsky] is as cuckoo as Stanley Korbach, but he has in him this Byronic desire of self-expression. He does his best to play a role in the spiritual and cultural revival of his country, as well as its political development" (2005: 443).

14. Similar mechanisms of creative relationships with the city space are practiced by young children establishing their personal kinetic and cognitive coordinates through their exposure to the city landscapes. Children are more creative than adults since their actions are triggered by the act of maturation: the first time a child finds, memorizes, and sustains in her mind and imagination, the path to the school indicates the means of making the estranged landscapes familiar, and thus fully inhabiting or adopting them (Walmsley: 1988). In Brian Friel's play *Translations*, British soldiers rename Gaelic places (villages, hills, and rivers) into English (Brien Friel, *Translations*, London: Faber & Faber, 1981). This action signifies not only the unchallengeable victory of the colonizers but also the processes of reinventing the conquered Ireland. These actions of the British soldiers in the play are paradoxically similar to what all immigrants do to the places they come to inhabit. Unconsciously, they reorganize linguistically, economically, and culturally the territory they come to live to.

15. "The tripartite division of the cathedral east-centre-west into choir, nave and narthex provided a supplementary spatial orientation. Between the altar of the savior, with its evocation of the passion, the resurrection, and the last judgment, and the eastern altar of the virgin, suggesting the nativity and the church itself, the middle of the nave or the crossing of the transepts provided a less heavily charged religious space, the space not only of processions toward one end of the church or the other, but of more 'earthly' locations required by the liturgical dramas" (Carlson: 15).

16. Artists less bound by linguistic restrictions of a particular art form – painters and musicians, for instance – seem to be more fortunate in sustaining their profession. Theatre people, however, are less fortunate. Many stop their artistic work, others change their professional occupation. Some – Michael Chekhov, Joseph Brodsky, and Vasiliy Aksyonov, among others – were able to manage their integration into the new society (the field of professional pedagogy, either in private enterprises or universities, became the most welcoming for the expatriates) and still express themselves artistically.

17. Vasiliy Aksyonov, "Chudo ili chudachestvo. O sud'be romana", *Octyabr'*
    8 (2002): http://magazines.russ.ru/october/2002/8/aks.html (accessed 4 January 2007).
18. Ibid.

Works cited

Aksyonov, Vasily. *Zenitsa Oka. Vmesto memuorov*. Moscow: Vagrius, 2005.

———. "Chudo ili chudachestvo. O sud'be romana", *Octyabr'*. 8 (2002):
http://magazines.russ.ru/october/2002/8/aks.html (accessed 4 January 2007).

———. *The New Sweet Style*. Trans. Christopher Morris. New York: Random House,
1999.

———. "Moi dom tam, gde moi rabochii stol", *Voprosy Literatury* 2 (1999):
http://magazines.russ.ru/voplit/1999/2/aksen.html (accessed 4 January 2007).

———. "Residents and Refugees". Trans. Aplin Galya and Hugh. In *Under Eastern
Eyes: The West as Reflected in Recent Russian Émigré Writing*. Ed. Arnold McMillin.
London: Macmillan, 1991, pp. 42–50.

———. *In Search of Melancholy Baby*. Trans. Michael Henry Heim and Antonina
W. Bouis. New York: Random House, 1987.

———. "Tzaplya". *Aristofaniana s lagushkami. Sobranie Pies*. Ann Arbor, MI:
Hermitage, 1981, pp. 313–80.

Bakhtin, Mikhail. *Epos i Roman*. St Peterburg: Asbuka, 2000.

Balme, Christopher B. *Pacific Performances: Theatricality and Cross-Cultural
Encounter in the South Seas*. Basingstoke: Palgrave, 2007.

Briker, B. "In Search of a Genre: The Meaning of the Title and the Idea of a 'Genre'".
In *Vasiliy Pavlovich Aksyonov: A Writer in Quest of Himself*. Ed. Edward Mozejko.
Columbus, OH: Slavica Publishers, 1986, pp. 148–65.

Brodsky, Josef. *On Grief and Reason: Essays*. New York: Farrar, Straus & Giroux,
1995.

Bronner, Stephen Eric and Jacobsen, Kurt. "Dubya's Fellow Travelers: Left Intellectuals and Mr. Bush's War", *Logos* 3–4 (2004): http://www.logosjournal.com/
bronner_jacobsen_election.htm (accessed 14 July 2008).

Carlson, Marvin. *Places of Performance: The Semiotics of Theatre Architecture*. New
York: Cornell University Press, 1989.

Donald, James. *Imagining the Modern City*. London: The Athlone Press, 1999.

Etkind, Alexander. *Tolkovanie puteshestvii: Rossiya i Amerika v travelogakh i intertekstakh*. Moscow: Novoe Literaturnoe Obozrenie, 2001.

Evreinov, Nikolay. *The Theatre in Life*. Ed. and trans. Alexander I. Nazaroff. New
York: Bloom. 1970.

Féral, Josette. "Theatricality: The Specificity of Theatrical Language". Trans.
Ronald P. Bermingham. *Substance* 31.2/3 (2002): 95–108.

Fischer-Lichte, Erika. "From Theatre to Theatricality", *Theatre Research International* 20.2 (1995): 97–105.

Holloway, Julian and Kneale, James. "Mikhail Bakthin: Dialogics of Space". In
Thinking Space. Ed. Mike Crang and Nigel Thrift. London and New York:
Routledge. 2000, pp. 71–88.

Il'f, Il'ya and Petrov, Evgenii. "Odnoetazhnaya America". In *Sobranie sochinenii.
Tom 4*. Moscow: Khudozhestvennaya Literatura, 1961, pp. 7–451.

Lefebvre, Henri. *The Production of Space*. Trans. Donald Nicholson-Smith. Oxford: Blackwell, 1992.

Lehmann, Hans-Thies. *Postdramatic Theatre*. Trans. Karen Jürs-Munby. London: Routledge. 2006.

McMillin Arnold. "Western Life as Reflected in Aksyonov's Work before and after Exile". In *Under Eastern Eyes: The West as Reflected in Recent Russian Émigré Writing*. Ed. Arnold McMillin. London: Macmillan, 1991, pp. 50–62.

Said, Edward W. *Representations of the Intellectual*. New York: Vintage Books. 1994.

Walmsley, D. J. *Urban Living: The Individual in the City*. Essex: Longman Scientific & Technical, 1988.

Wirth-Nesher, Hana. *City Codes*. Cambridge and New York: Cambridge University Press, 1996.

Part 2
American Performativity

5
Theatres in America: Brecht and Kafka

Freddie Rokem
Tel Aviv University

> *I called for my horse to be brought from the stable. The servant did not understand me. I myself went into the stable, saddled my horse and mounted. In the distance I heard a trumpet blast. I asked him what it meant but he did not know and had not heard it. By the gate he stopped me and asked "where are you riding to sir?" I answered "away from here, away from here, always away from here. Only by doing so can I reach my destination." "Then you know your destination" he asked. "Yes" I said "I have already said so, 'Away-From-Here' [Weg-von-hier] that is my destination." "You have no provisions with you" he said. "I don't need any" I said. "The journey is so long that I will die of hunger if I do not get something along the way. It is, fortunately, a truly immense journey."*
>
> Franz Kafka, "My Destination"[1]

Walter Benjamin's essay on Franz Kafka was published in *Jüdische Rundschau* on the occasion of the tenth anniversary of Kafka's death, in 1934. Besides being one of the first comprehensive attempts to interpret Kafka's enigmatic writings, Benjamin's text also contains many important insights about the theatre, drawing the conclusion that "Kafka's world is a world theatre" (1999a: 804). Kafka's own interest in the theatre has been independently studied in depth (e.g., Beck: 1971). Benjamin's claim concerning Kafka's theatricality – which in reverse also indirectly implies that the theatre itself is in some sense "Kafkaesque" – is primarily based on his reading of the final, fragmentary section of Kafka's novel *Amerika*, titled "The Great Theater of Oklahama" [sic!], but also on some of Kafka's short stories. *Amerika*, which is actually called *The Man who Disappeared* (*Der Verschollene*; literally "The Missing One"[2]), depicting

Karl Rossmann's journey into the maze of the American continent – in a gesture similar to the "Away-From-Here", the enigmatic "goal" of the journey in the short story quoted as the epigraph for this essay – was written during 1912–14, but it was not published until 1927, three years after Kafka's death. In his essay Benjamin remarks that because of its visionary quality, "The Great Theater of Oklahama", where Karl Rossman, as everyone else, it seems, who wishes to join this theatre, is hired, "is the last refuge, which does not preclude it from being their salvation" (1999a: 804)

Besides considering "The Great Theatre of Oklahama", mainly through the lens of Benjamin's reading of Kafka, this chapter will also examine certain closely related features of Bertolt Brecht's opera *The Rise and Fall of the City of Mahagonny*. This play, just like Kafka's novel, is situated in an imagined America of decadence, exploitation, and a gradually growing exilic estrangement.[3] Besides the extreme theatricality of Brecht's dramatic text/libretto for which Kurt Weill wrote the music, one of its last scenes also contains a play-within-the-play: "The God in Mahagonny Play", which just like Kafka's American theatre, somewhat unexpectedly perhaps in the larger context of Brecht's *oeuvre*, contains a clear metaphysical dimension, or at least refers to such a dimension. The opera, for which Brecht had written poems and sketches beginning already in the mid-1920s, including *The Little Mahagonny*, was completed in 1929–30 and it was first performed in 1930, in Leipzig. The following year it was performed in the famous production featuring Lotte Lenya at the Theater am Schiffbauerdam in Berlin, where Brecht's *The Threepenny Opera* had already been received by enthusiastic audiences.[4] And like Kafka's work, Brecht's too, including the Mahagonny songs, drew the attention of Benjamin who, in the wake of their gradually developing friendship, also became one of Brecht's first serious critics as well. This chapter will therefore examine "The Great Theater of Oklahama" and "The God in Mahagonny Play" in an explicit Benjaminian context, even if Benjamin himself does not point out any explicit connections, neither between them nor with America.

Kafka's and Brecht's imagined theatres and performances located in America are both variations on some of Freud's concerns in his 1930 book *Das Unbehagen in der Kultur*, drawing attention to the "discomfort" of culture, even if the book is usually translated as the "discontents" of civilization. It was written in 1929, in the same historical context within which Brecht and Benjamin were writing, and in this respect Kafka was more of a prophet. Freud's final paragraph is particularly relevant in this context:

> The fateful question for the human species seems to me to be whether and to what extent their cultural development will succeed in mastering the disturbance of their communal life by the human instinct of aggression and self-destruction. It may be that in this respect the present time deserves a special interest. Men have gained control over the forces of nature to such an extent that with their help they would have no difficulty in exterminating one another to the last man. They know this, and hence comes a large part of their current unrest, their unhappiness and their mood of anxiety. And now it is expected that the other of the two "Heavenly Powers", eternal Eros, will make an effort to assert himself in the struggle with his equally immortal adversary. But who can foresee with what success and with what result.
>
> (Freud: 92)[5]

In the shadow of the destructive forces of technology, and the anxiety this has caused even for Freud, the "Heavenly Powers" are significant, even if they are personified by Eros. Both Kafka and Brecht situated their fictional worlds in an extreme form of *Unbehagen*, a capitalistic, almost surreal vision of America governed by forces that emphasize the insignificance of the individual. Brecht later repeated this "move" to America in other plays, like, for example, *The Resistible Rise of Arturo Ui* from 1941. Furthermore, the fictional realities of these works from the pre-Nazi era depict very similar fantasy versions of theatre and theatrical experiences in America, both containing strong supernatural and metaphysical characteristics.

The European fascination with the "New World" has a long and complex history where fantasy, dream, and utopian longings have been combined with critical views of economic exploitation, imperialism, social injustices, and the fear of devastation. At a time when Hollywood was gradually becoming the dream-factory of the world, these two European writers were projecting universal claims of salvation through a combination of a ritual and theatrical experience in America. The imaginary theatres of Kafka's "Oklahama" and Brecht's "Mahagonny" are situated far away from "home", in extreme states of physical and spiritual exile. Both were expressions of the universal life-drama, depicting in particular the individual's confrontation with death. The theatres of "Oklahama" and "Mahagonny" – both four-syllabic names with open vowels – constitute an extreme form of existential, exilic performance and they are both also closely connected to the "experience" and aesthetic representation of death.

The "American" theatres of Kafka and Brecht, thanks to a large extent to Benjamin, who at least indirectly brought them together in different ways, also serves as a basis for considering theoretical concepts related to the theatre, and in particular to the theatrical image. In both instances the notion of the "American theatre" also functions as a "figure of thought" – a *Denkbild* – through which the aesthetic, metaphysical as well as the social concerns of Kafka as well as Brecht, and of course of Benjamin himself in discussing their work, are expressed in images which also have overt philosophical implications. The *Denkbild* (thought-picture/thought-image), with its implicit performative qualities, is a form of writing, usually in prose, bringing out an abstract, philosophical idea through a short narrative or a description that has a distinct emblematic quality. It was practiced by a vaguely defined group of writers like Walter Benjamin, Franz Kafka, Bertolt Brecht, Ernst Bloch, Sigfried Kracauer, and Robert Musil and after the Second World War, also Theodor Adorno.[6] The *Denkbild* frequently also has a distinct dramatic quality, and both of the imaginary American theatres – Kafka's depicted in lyrical prose and Brecht's through the short play-within-the-play as part of the extremely theatrical social life of Mahagonny – bring out performative aspects that are closely related to the genre of the *Denkbild*.

In conjunction with their deep sense of alienation and aimlessness these examples laid the basis for an American performativity that is both provocative and insubordinate. This American performativity is at the same time also a metaphor for the anxieties awakened in the shadow of modernity and its hopes for creating new opportunities on the basis of technological inventions and economic growth, as well as a theatricalized strategy for coping with exile and alienation in such situations. And both in Kafka's and Brecht's versions of this form of performativity, the final stages of the life-drama of the exiled individual are acted out as theatre in a multileveled social web where exile, social injustices, exploitation, theatre, and performativity intersect. Mahagonny, in the words of Begbick in Brecht's play, talking about the newly founded city in the opening scene as a network, a worldwide web:

> Darum laßt uns hier eine Stadt gründen
> Und sie nennen Mahagonny
> Das heißt: Netzestadt!
> Sie sein wie ein Netz
> Das für eßbaren Vögel gestellt wird.[7]

Which can be translated approximately as: "Therefore let us establish a city here / and call it Mahagonny / That means the net-city / It will be like a net / Cast out to snare edible birds." And this web does not only serve as a net for catching birds, but inevitably includes the performativity of a metaphysical theatre as well.

*   *   *

The section in his Kafka essay where Benjamin analyses the "Great Theater of Oklahama" is called "A Childhood Photograph" and it begins with a presentation of an early photograph of Kafka, whose "immensely sad eyes dominate the landscape arranged for them [the eyes]" while he seems to be carefully listening to the sounds coming from this landscape (1999a: 800). After describing this "portrait" of Kafka as a child, Benjamin goes on to say that "The ardent 'Wish to be a Red Indian' [Wunsch, Indianer zu werden] may have consumed this great sadness at some point." (800) and then Benjamin quotes Kafka's short, fragmented and fragmenting narrative about the wish to be an Indian:

> If one were only an Indian, instantly alert, and on a racing horse, leaning against the wind, kept on quivering jerkily over the quivering ground, until one sheds one's spurs, for there needed no spurs, threw away the reins, for there needed no reins, and hardly saw that the land before one was smoothly shorn heath when the horse's neck and head would be already gone.
>
> (Kafka: 390)

After quoting this enigmatic narrative about the disintegrating, disappearing horse – which, because of the wish to be a "Red Indian", is obviously also about America – Benjamin summarizes: "A great deal is contained in this wish", and immediately continues that, "Its fulfillment, which he finds in America, yields up its secret" (quoted in Benjamin 1999a: 800). These "American" performances ultimately reveal some aspect of the secret contained in such a wish; a wish which, paradoxically, is at least partly fulfilled by the act of wishing itself. This secret, with its extreme theatricality, is for Kafka, but also partly for Brecht, who ended his *Threepenny Opera* (1928) with a riding Deus ex Machina, connected to the riding of a horse. If for Freud the dream is the fulfillment of a wish, for Kafka and Brecht their American performances express a wish for integration and redemption in a world governed by forces that are much more powerful than the individual. The wish is a gesture through which the wishing in itself, regardless of its fulfillment, or even the possibility that it will ever be fulfilled, is performative. This is a much more complex procedure of performativity than Austin and Searle were able to produce, relying on sincerity and felicity, and it brings out the forms of theatricality that are ominously present in the American theatres of Kafka and Brecht.

Immediately following the quotation about wishing to be a Red Indian, Benjamin connects the experience of riding on the dissolving horse with "The Great Theater of Oklahama". The hiring of the actors for this theatre, as well as some of its theatrical activities, actually takes place on a racetrack:

> On a street corner Karl saw a poster with the following announcement: "Today, from 6 A.M. until midnight, at Clayton Racetrack, the Oklahoma [sic!] Theatre will be hiring members for its company. The great Theater of Oklahoma [sic!] calls you! The one and only call is today! If you miss your chance now, you miss it forever! If you think of your future, you belong with us! Everyone is welcome! If you want to be an artist, come forward! Our theater can use everyone, and find the right place for everyone! If you decide to join us we congratulate you here and now! But hurry, so that you get in before midnight! At twelve o'clock the doors will be shut and never opened again! A curse on those who do not believe in us! Set out for Clayton!"
>
> (quoted in Benjamin 1999a: 800)

After this quotation – the opening section of the fragment in Kafka's novel about the great Oklahoma Theater – Benjamin remarks that even if a racetrack is the only place on which Karl Rossman attains his object of desire, "This racetrack is at the same time a theater, and this poses a puzzle" (1999a: 801) However, Benjamin infers, the enigmatic mysteriousness of the place is fully congruous with the total transparency of the main character himself, who never hides anything from himself, at least of what he knows. And this opposition between racetrack and theatre, Benjamin concludes, brings out a performative modality which actually stems from the Chinese theatre, adding that "One of the most significant functions of this theater is to dissolve events into their gestural components" (801) Such a gestural analysis, based on the image of the racetrack with its running horses, has the same basic structural characteristics as the well-known Muybridge photographs of galloping horses from the late 1880s, paradoxically presenting the movement of the animal at what is at the same time a standstill,[8] catching each of its multiple gestural components separately. Benjamin thus introduces an opposition between the gradually disintegrating horse from "Wish to be a Red Indian" and the perception of the distinct gestural components of the running horse.

To Karl Rossman's question why the recruiting to the "Great Theatre of Oklahama" takes place in a race course, Fanny, whom he obviously already knows from before – who takes part on a huge live altar and is dressed as an angel and is playing the trumpet – just like the trumpet that is heard in "My Destination", the Kafka-story I quoted as an epigraph to this chapter – answers that "we make the largest accommodations for the greatest crowds. There's lots of room on a racetrack. And wherever the bets are usually taken, the hiring offices are set up."[9] The fact that the bets are made and the actors are hired in the same place is no doubt significant, referring to the metaphorical spillover of both of these activities. And somewhat later, as he has finally been employed by the theatre, Karl:

> remained standing and looked across the large racetrack that reached on every side into the distant forests. He suddenly wanted to see a horserace, he hadn't yet had an opportunity for that in America. In Europe he had once been taken along to a race, but could remember nothing other than not wanting to be torn away from his mother in the middle of all the people he was being pulled through. He had actually not seen a race yet.[10]

The fact that Karl has not seen a race yet, for fear of being "torn away from his mother" when he had an opportunity, probably means that he also does not know what the theatre really is. And the "Great Nature Theater of Oklahoma" is obviously not a conventional theatre. It is the core of life.

The strange fusion of the huge human altar-piece of which Fanny is a part, on the one hand, and the race track, on the other, infuses this theatre with a unique, even uncanny atmosphere. Benjamin, for whom the fact that this "racetrack is at the same time a theatre, and this poses a puzzle" (Benjamin 1999a: 801) finds a resolution to this paradox by interpreting many of Kafka's stories as theatrical stagings:

> One can go even further and say that a good number of Kafka's shorter studies and stories are seen in their full light only when they are, so to speak, put on as acts in the "Nature Theater of Oklahoma [sic!]." Only then will one come to the certain realization that Kafka's entire work constitutes a code of gestures which surely had no definite symbolic meaning for the author from the outset; rather, the author tried to derive such a meaning from them in ever-changing contexts

and experimental groupings. The theater is the logical place for such groupings.

(801)

Kafka's own stories about horses are perhaps the most natural candidates for such a strategy of theatrical stagings.

Besides presenting Kafka's "Wish to be a Red Indian", Benjamin has also included a discussion of another of Kafka's short fragmentary stories about riding, "The next village" ("Das nächste Dorf"), in his Kafka essay:

> My grandfather used to say: "Life is astonishingly short. Now, in my memory, it is so compressed that I can hardly understand, for example, how a young person can decide to ride to the next village without being afraid that – apart from accidents – even the time allotted to a normal, happy life is far too short for such a journey."[11]

This unattainable village could even be "The Great Theatre of Oklahama". But beyond its allegorical dimension this story indirectly also serves as a bridge to Brecht's understanding of the gesture (*Gestus*), which is quite different from the dialectics developed by Benjamin on the basis of his reading of Kafka.

*   *   *

In the early summer of 1934 Walter Benjamin traveled from Paris to Skovsbostrand, a village just outside the small town of Svendborg on the shore of the small Danish island of Fyn, to visit Bertolt Brecht who had at that time already been living there with his entourage for more than a year. On 5 August 1934 Benjamin wrote in his diary, posthumously published as "Notes from Svendborg", that "three weeks ago I gave Brecht my essay on Kafka to read. He doubtless read it, but did not allude to it on his own accord; and on the two occasions when I brought the subject up, he responded evasively" (Benjamin 1999b: 785). But in order to test their respective views on Kafka, Benjamin noted, they decided to discuss one particular Kafka text, "Das nächste Dorf". A few weeks later, on 31 August, there is a long entry reporting that "The day before yesterday, a long, heated debate about my Kafka" (787) This is how Benjamin summarized their respective readings of Kafka's text:

> Brecht said it was a companion piece to the story of Achilles and the tortoise. A rider can never reach the next village if he divides

the journey up into its smallest components – even aside from any incidents en route. Because life is too short for such a journey. But the error lies in the concept of "a rider." For you have to divide up the traveler, as well as the journey. And since in this you abolish the unity of life, you likewise do away with its brevity. However short it may be. This doesn't matter, because the man who started out on his journey is different from the man who arrives. – For my part, I proposed the following interpretation: the true measure of life is memory. Looking back, it runs through life like lightning. The speed with which you can turn back a few pages is the same as the speed with which memory flies from the next village back to the place from which the rider decided to leave. Whoever, like the Ancients, has seen his life transformed into writing, let him read this writing backward. Only in this way – in full flight from the present – will he be able to understand it.

(1999b: 788)

Benjamin's interpretation of Kafka's story is consistent with his under-standing of history presented in several other contexts, culminating in his essay "On the Concept of History". The journey to the next village is for Benjamin a journey backwards through memory to the time/place – a Bakhtinian "chronotopos" – where the journey began – its origin (*Ursprung*) – and where it will inevitably end, like in Karl Rossman's case.

On the other hand, according to Brecht, as Benjamin reports in his diary entry, the Kafka text is a story of survival, showing that there is an error in considering life to be too short for the rider to complete the journey. This error "lies in the concept of 'a rider' ". Not only the journey but also the traveler himself must be divided up into its smallest units, and added Brecht, "the man who started out on his journey is different from the man who arrives." This transformation of the subject is closely connected to the Brechtian notion of *Verfremdung*, based on different methods for fragmenting the performance which in turn leads to fractured characters in constant transformation as a form of accommodation. The idea that it is a different person who arrives than the one who set out on the journey also introduces the possibility of a moral assessment of the journey. These ideas can perhaps be most clearly distinguished in *Mother Courage and her Children*, but it can already be found in some of his earlier texts, including *The Rise and Fall of the City of Mahagonny*.

Brecht begun writing *Mother Courage and her Children* during his stay in Denmark, more or less in conjunction with his meeting with Benjamin there, and he decided to open his renewed theatre career in Berlin, in

January 1949, a few months after his return there (as a changed person after long travel to this radically changed "village") with a production of this play. When in the opening scene the "wagon is rolled forward against the movement of the revolving stage" (Brecht 1972: 340) as Brecht prescribed in his "Modell-Buch" for the play, two opposite circular movements were superimposed on each other. The revolving stage turned clockwise while the wagon, from the point of view of the spectators, moved counter-clockwise. This superimposition made the spectators see a double circular movement in opposing directions through which the wagon actually remained in one and the same place, at a total standstill. This clearly shows in concrete terms how the dynamics of the standstill function. The war is based on the same capitalistic forces that govern his earlier play about Mahagonny and it leads to nothing but loss and despair. Mother Courage, who unknowingly from the very beginning has been caught in a *perpetuum mobile*-impasse of a destructive treadmill, neither sees nor is able really to express the tragic significance of the events. And she ends her journey with her wagon, which in the opening of the play was drawn by her two sons instead of by horses, quite a different person from who she had been in the triumphant beginning of the performance. Now she is alone with her carriage, silently in quest for a village where she can find rest.

In his "Commentary on Poems by Brecht," (published in April 1939) Benjamin had already clearly recognized the principles of transformation through which nothing really changes, expressed in Brecht's work, drawing attention to how the "men of Mahagonny" constantly accommodate themselves to the sudden and sometimes cruel changes around them. They are "saying yes to everything God tells them", at the same time as Benjamin saw their situation as a complement to the major characteristics of the exilic situation, but quite differently from his understanding of Kafka. Kafka's figures are given "absolutes" confronting another "absolute", usually a metaphysical reality; while Brecht's characters, just like the rider in the Kafka-story which he and Benjamin had discussed, constantly change their positions and attitudes with a glance or with a raised eyebrow.

> The "men of Mahagonny" form a troupe of eccentrics. Only men are eccentrics. Only subjects endowed by nature with male potency can be used to demonstrate conclusively how far the natural reflexes of human beings have been blunted by life in present-day society. The eccentric is simply a washed-up average man. Brecht has brought together several of them to form a troupe. Their reactions are as

nondescript as can be, and even these they can muster only as a collective. To be able to react at all, they have to feel like a "compact mass" – and here, too, they mirror the average man, alias the petty bourgeois. The "men of Mahagonny" exchange glances before they express an opinion. The resulting opinion follows the line of least resistance. The "men of Mahagonny" limit themselves to saying yes to everything God tells them, asks them, or imposes on them. This, according to Brecht, is no doubt how a collective which accepts God must be constituted. Moreover, their God is himself a reduced version.

(Benjamin 2003: 221)

The poem Benjamin is commenting on is "Mahagonny Song no 3", that is, the song passage from scene 19, "The Execution of Jimmy Gallagher (Paul Ackerman)". After Jim says to his (former) friends who are going to administer the death sentence that "Ihr wißt wohl nicht, daß es einen Gott gibt?" (Brecht 1963: 73; 1994: 230)[12] – to which they answer by putting on the play *"God comes to Mahagonny"*, a performance which, at the same time as it concretely presents the possible immanence of the metaphysical, establishes different levels of distancing ironies to such a metaphysical reality.

It is obvious that God, if he exists at all, usually does not come to places like Mahagonny, and that is the reason why it is necessary to perform his appearance through a theatrical Deus ex Machina substitution, just like in the ending Brecht had already given to his *Threepenny Opera* where Mackie is saved by the messenger of the king riding on a horse. In *Mahagonny*, however, there is no white horse and the traditional appearance of the metaphysical is played out through the song which begins with the refrain, repeated again after each verse:

> One morning when the sky was grey
> During the whisky
> God came to Mahagonny:
> During the whisky
> We recognized God in Mahagonny.
>
> (Brecht 1994: 230)

And at the end of the song, "Moses, who plays the role of God, detaches himself from the others, steps forward and covers his face with his hat" (230), hiding, as if he was apparently ashamed by what he has done. We are witnessing an anti-pageant, presented as a play-within-the-play, which ends when the men of Mahagonny claim that they have actually been in hell all along. Here, just like in *Hamlet*, the "play's the thing", and just as in Shakespeare's play, here too the performance does not prove anything except that playing and performing are one of the ways to confront the presence of death. At the end of the performance, Jenny shouts in the megaphone that the people of Mahagonny actually claim that they have not seen God at all. Such a denial creates the kind of distancing irony Brecht activates not only in this opera, but in many of his other plays as well.

Also Jim's (Paul's) song that Brecht placed in scene 11 in the final version of the play, with its more psychological as well as existential message, originally belonged to this extended meta-theatrical scene:

> Dreams have all one ending:
> To wake and be coldly sure
> To see the dark descending
> To hear the wind portending
> A night that shall endure.
> (1994: 198)

Had this remained in the play-within-the-play scene it would have added an additional dimension of despair to the Deus ex Machina pageant. These five lines even point forward to the ending of another play in the "tradition" of American performativity, which even if it does not specify where it takes place geographically is closely related both to Kafka's "The Great Theatre of Oklahama" and Brecht's Mahagonny: Samuel Beckett's *Endgame*. In his last monologue, which is the end of ends, Hamm with obvious metaphysical implications says: "You prayed. You CRIED for night; it comes – it FALLS: now cry in darkness. You cried for night; it falls: now cry in darkness. Nicely put that. And now? Moments for nothing, now as always, time was never and time is over, reckoning closed and story ended" (Beckett: 133).[13]

In his "Notes on the Opera," an essay published in 1930, which is his first full statement of his ideas about the Epic theatre, Brecht claimed that:

> The opera *Mahagonny* pays conscious tribute to the senselessness of the operatic form. The irrationality of opera lies in the fact that rational elements are employed, solid reality is aimed at, but at the same time it is all washed out by the music. A dying man is real. If at the same time he sings we are translated to the sphere of the irrational.
> (1964: 35–6)

Even if nobody is really supposed to die on the stage – except if it takes place as an "accident", like for Molière – the theatre as an art form, because of the live presence of the actor on the stage, is based on the "resistance" of the real to the forms of aesthetic transformation this reality is subjected to. Even those who die in their roles will take the final bow after the performance. The opera, on the other hand, is the genre where a dying man is singing on the stage, openly subverting this resistance by willingly submitting to the aesthetic transformations, just like Karl Rossman has to join the "The Great Theatre of Oklahama" in order to be transposed into the eternal life of the dead and of heavenly trumpet music. In the interface between theatre and opera, Brecht argues, the irrational sphere begins to take form. This is exactly where, as it is expressed in his play: "We caught sight of God in Mahagonny". For Karl Rossman, however, even the possibility to imagine such an event, as seeing god, even wishing for it, is impossible. This is the difference between the life-drama depicted by Kafka in prose as opposed to Brecht's theatricality and *Verfremdung* taking place on the stage. And for both, America is a metaphor for the strange combination of utopian longings and exilic alienation that does not necessarily have to take place on that particular continent, even if it has to take place "Away-From-Here". Rather, this projection on America stems from their common fascination with theatre as such, and as Benjamin also recognized, it expresses their common desire to depict the moment when the theatre and the highly theatrical become necessary as a form of expression reflecting on itself, on art in general, and the confrontation with death.

Notes

1. In *Parables and Paradoxes*: http://www.kafka.org/index.php?id=162,172,0,0,1,0 (accessed 3 July 2008).
2. I will refer to it as *Amerika* here, as Benjamin did in his essay.
3. The fact that Brecht himself also spent six years, 1941–47, on this continent, will not be dealt with here. See, e.g., James F. Lyon, *Bertolt Brecht in America*, Princeton, NJ: Princeton University Press, 1980. For an illuminating comparison between these works by Kafka and Brecht, see Heinz Brüggemann, "Kafkas Theater von Oklahoma und Brechts Netzestadt Mahagonny: Urbane Visionsräume der Moderne", in *Brecht Jahrbuch* 29 (2004): 113–25.
4. 1920/21: Brecht began working on the "Mahagonny-Gesänge" for the poetry collection *Hauspostille*. 1927: Weill approached Brecht with the idea of adapting five of these poems into a short opera for the festival of chamber music in Baden-Baden. *Mahagonny Songspiel* premiered 17 July 1927. 1929: first version of *Rise and Fall of the city of Mahagonny* was completed in October and published by Universal Edition in Vienna. 1930: Premiere with revisions at

the Neues Theater in Leipzig on 9 March 1930. 1930: Second version published in *Versuche* (Heft 2, 1930). Here the names of the lumberjacks are less American-sounding. 1931: December, Berlin premiere.

5. The last sentence was added in 1931.
6. According to Klaus L. Berghahn, ("A View through the Red Window: Ernst Bloch's *Spuren*", in *Not Yet: Reconsidering Ernst Bloch*, ed. Jamie Owen Daniel and Tom Moylan, London and New York: Verso, 1997, pp. 202–14), this "genre" includes among other texts: Walter Benjamin, *Einbahnstrasse* (*One-Way Street*, 1928); Siegfried Kracauer, *Die Angestellten* (*The salaried masses: Duty and distraction in Weimar Germany*, 1930); Ernst Bloch, *Spuren* (*Traces*, 1930); Bertolt Brecht, *Geschichten von Herrn Keuner* (*Stories of Mr Keuner*, 1926–34); Robert Musil, *Nachlass to Lebzeiten* (*Posthumous papers of a living author*, 1936); and Theodor W. Adorno, *Minima Moralia*, (1944), here p. 202.
7. Bertolt Brecht, *Aufsteig und Fall der Stadt Mahagonny*, Berlin: Edition Suhrkamp, 1963, p. 8.
8. I am using the term "standstill" to refer to this form of image creation on the basis of Benjamin's own formulation in the *Arcades Project*: "It is not that what is past casts its light at what is present, or what is present on what is past; rather, image is that wherein what has been comes together in a flash with the now to form a constellation. In other words, **image is dialectics at a standstill**. For while the relation of the present to the past is a purely temporal one, the relation of what-has-been to the now is dialectical: is not progression but image, suddenly emergent. – Only dialectical images are genuine images (that is, not archaic); and where one encounters them is language" (1999c, [N2a,3] p. 462 my emphasis).
9. http://www.kafka.org/index.php?missingfragments (accessed 7 July 2008).
10. http://www.kafka.org/index.php?missingfragments (accessed 7 July 2008)
11. Quoted from: http://bmj.bmjjournals.com/cgi/content/full/319/7225/1617/a. Kafka's story was first published in *Ein Landartzt: Kleine Erzählungen*, Munich and Leipzig: Kurt Wolff Verlag, 1919, pp. 88–9. In German: "Mein Großvater pflegte zu sagen: Das Leben ist erstaunlich kurz. Jetzt in Erinnerung drängt es sich mir so zusammen, daß ich zum Beispiel kaum begreife, wie ein junger Mensch sich entschließen kann, ins nächste Dorf zu reiten, ohne zu fürchten, daß – von unglücklichen Zufällen ganz abgesehen – schon die Zeit des gewöhnlichen, glücklich ablaufenden Lebens für einen solchen Ritt bei weitem nicht hinreicht."
12. Bertolt Brecht, *Aufstieg und Fall der Stadt Mahagonny*, 1963, p. 73. ("You don't seem to know that there's a God", Brecht, *The Rise and Fall of the City of Mahagonny*, 1994, p. 230. After the subsequent quotations the page numbers are given in parenthesis in the text.
13. I have omitted the stage directions in this passage without indicating this by brackets.

Works cited

Beck, Evelyn. *Kafka and the Yiddish Theatre*. Madison: University Wisconsin Press, 1971.

Beckett, Samuel. *Endgame*. In *The Complete Dramatic Works*. London: Faber & Faber, 1986, pp. 89–134.

Benjamin, Walter. "Commentary on Poems by Brecht". *Selected Writings*, vol. 4. Cambridge, MA, and London: Harvard University Press, 2003, pp. 215–50.

———. "Franz Kafka: On the Tenth Anniversary of His Death". In *Selected Writings*, vol. 2. Cambridge, MA, and London: Harvard University Press, 1999a, pp. 794–818.

———. "Notes from Svendborg, Summer 1934". In *Selected Writings*, vol. 2: 1927–34. Cambridge, MA: The Belknap Press of Harvard University Press, 1999b, pp. 783–91.

———. *Arcades Project*. Trans. Howard Eiland and Kevin McLaughlin. Cambridge, MA, and London: Harvard University Press, 1999c.

Berghahn, Klaus L. "A View through the Red Window: Ernst Bloch's *Spuren*". In *Not Yet: Reconsidering Ernst Bloch*. Ed. Jamie Owen Daniel and Tom Moylan. London and New York: Verso, 1997, pp. 202–14.

Brecht, Bertolt. *The Rise and Fall of the City of Mahagonny*. In *Collected Plays*, vol. 2. Trans. W. H. Auden and Chester Kallman. London: Methuen, 1994, pp. 171–235.

———. *Mother Courage and Her Children*. In *Collected Plays*, vol. 5. Trans. Ralph Mannheim. New York: Vintage Books, 1972, pp. 133–210.

———. *Brecht on Theatre: The Development of an Aesthetic*. Ed. and trans. John Willet. New York: Hill & Wang, 1964.

———. *Aufsteig und Fall der Stadt Mahagonny*. Berlin: Edition Suhrkamp, 1963.

Freud, Sigmund. *Civilization and its Discontents*. Trans. James Strachey. New York: W. W. Norton, 1961.

Kafka, Franz. *The Complete Stories*. New York: Schocken Books, 1971.

Lyon, James F. *Bertolt Brecht in America*. Princeton, NJ: Princeton University Press, 1980.

6

America Relocated: Karel Čapek's Robots between Prague, Berlin, and New York

Veronika Ambros
University of Toronto

> *Thou shalt not make unto thee any graven image, or any likeness of any thing that is in heaven above, or that is in the earth beneath, or that is in the water under the earth.*
>
> Exodus 20: 4–6, King James Bible

The fascination with new technology and science at the beginning of the last century revived old dreams of an artificial human being, an automaton in modern theatre and cinema. The actor and film director Paul Wegener,[1] for instance, in *Golem, How he Came into the World*[2] (*Der Golem, wie er in die Welt kam*, 1920) visualized the story of a golem on screen.[3] As in numerous tales and plays, Wegener also shows the revered Rabbi Loew, the "Jewish Faust",[4] who conjured up an assistant to protect the Jewish Ghetto in seventeenth-century Prague.[5] Wegener's Golem is a man made out of clay, brought to life as a hybrid creature with human facial expressions and features, and the movements of a statue.

In contrast to this "hybrid fictional world" (Doležel), Karel Čapek's *R.U.R. (Rossum's Universal Robots)*, "an utopistic and collective drama in three acts with an introductory comedy",[6] written also in 1920 and produced in 1921, is not based on a confrontation between the natural and the supernatural world. The play focuses on the clash of different views on progress, profit, and science presented as a conflict between human beings and their human-like products. This dramatic text mixes Utopia and dystopia, drama and comedy, as well as the fantasies of the Old World, with the nightmares and dreams of the New World.

That *RUR* is often mentioned among the most important examples of expressionist drama "as a nightmarish fantasy of the future" (Holman: 215) shows the classical exilic experience of a group of people on an island, whose commitment to their belief in progress, technology, and science leads to extermination of mankind. Čapek explores the ethical issues of modern times and pays tribute to Jamesian moral ideas and what he calls "'gaya scienza', the philosophy of pragmatic optimism"[7] (2000: 59). Using *R.U.R* (1921) as a point of departure, this chapter discusses the imaginary 'America' in the dramatic text and on stage when performed in the early 1920s in Prague, Berlin, and New York.

Pedestrian America

> Surely Americans don't travel in slow trains; they go with the express, and even then it's not fast enough for them, the trains are quicker in America they say, with much bigger carriages, and a white-coated waiter brings you iced water and ice-creams, don't you know? [...] Good Lord! That's life in America, you know: it's no use trying to tell you.
>
> (Čapek 1990a: 11)

This interior monologue opens Čapek's novel Hordubal (1933), in which the eponymous hero returns home from America to his village in Carpathian Ukraine, one of the poorest spots in interwar Czechoslovakia (1918–38).[8] Hordubal, who left eight years before and worked in the mines to support his wife and daughter, considers himself an American. His image of the foreign land, however, is composed of random objects like a flashlight, a piece of fabric, various pictures cut out of the newspapers. These pieces, as much as the few English words he learned signify the incomprehensible world of his journey, mark his allegiance to his America and his distance from home.

Ironically, however, his home underwent changes similar to those he experienced abroad. Forced to leave America after he was fired from his job, he finds that there is no work waiting for him at home, which had turned into a prosperous farm managed by his wife and a young farmhand. Akin to his experience in America, Hordubal is silenced by the speed, and hostility of his surrounding, and eventually not only robbed of his money but also most certainly of his life. His enigmatic death turns him into the hero of a mystery story which one might expect to happen in America rather than in Czechoslovakia. Yet, Čapek frustrates the expectation of his readers even further by breaking the conventions of this genre, confronting them with different points of view on the death of the protagonist and leaving it up to them to solve the possible crime novel.

Hordubal's thoughts about America reflect a fictional first-hand experience, which Čapek did not have. His own conjectures about the United States were mediated through literature[9] (Walt Whitman, Edgar Allan Poe, Henry James), philosophy (William James) and his talks with T. G. Masaryk, the president (1918–35) of the first Czechoslovak republic (1918–38), who traveled through the States and whose wife was American.[10] Masaryk, respected America, and was not afraid of the Americanization of Europe, which he considered fair given the European influence in America. He foresaw both continents developing towards each other (Čapek 1937: 172)

In May 1926, Čapek compared America with Europe in his letter to the *New York Times Sunday Magazine*: "Europe was in very little haste when she made her cathedrals and her philosophic systems. A man who wants to think out something does not hurry, watch in hand" (1996: 143). He was not inquiring whether the American demand for speed, efficiency, and success was good for America. But he insisted that it was not good for Europe (Bridges 2003: 97–107). In view of this statement, it will come as no surprise that the speed, success, and greed that characterize both Hordubal's Europe and America, are also at the core of *RUR*, where they motivate the fictional end of mankind. Čapek "thinks the Tubes are terrible – the quintessence of Robotism" (Šolić 2008). When describing the traffic in London he speaks about his childlike anxiety in this metropolis in which people, and vehicles alike are producing noises that accompany their constant movements (Čapek 1980: 72–3.). The mechanization of everyday life, the speed, and haste alongside success and quantity are among the important features of Čapek's imagined America, mentioned in his letter to the *New York Times* and expressed in his play, albeit relocated to a distant island. By constructing a new man and a new society, he theatricalizes the deterritorialization of the fictional America and her traditional perception of authority and meaning.[11]

The America of Speed, Success, Profit, and Dreams of the New World

The fact that most dictionaries today include the word *robot* indicates the worldwide success of *RUR*.[12] Coined by Karel Čapek's brother Josef (1887–1945), a painter, journalist, and writer himself, the word evokes the Czech word robota, which refers to toil, drudgery, and corvée (forced labour of the serfs[13]). This neologism in Czech relates to the initial intention of the old Rossum, the fictional originator of the robots, to free people from their hard work. His successors, however, were interested in cost efficient products, with limited needs, which would liberate man from labour altogether.

The sudden popularity of robots was also due to the fact that the theme of transformation or metamorphosis was topical across the genres (cf. Kafka, Shaw, Leivick, Meyerink), as was the "problem of progress and of man's relation to machines" (Wellek: 50). Although conceived as biochemical products, the robots soon became the epitome of man's mechanical creations, even machines. But Čapek objected to this interpretation:

> If the author was thinking of any of the marvels of the human spirit during their creation, it was not of technology, but of science. With outright horror, he refuses any responsibility for the thought that machines could take the place of people, or that anything like life, love, or rebellion could ever awaken in their cogwheels. He would regard this somber vision as an unforgivable overvaluation of mechanics or as a severe insult to life. The author of the robots appeals to the fact that he must know the most about it: and therefore he pronounces that his robots were created quite differently – that is, by a chemical path. The author was thinking about modern chemistry, which in various emulsions (or whatever they are called) has located substances and forms that in some ways behave like living matter.
>
> (1996: 143)

Hence, Čapek's creatures, though industrially produced, unable to reproduce themselves, and at first unable to express any emotions, are closer to the results of contemporary scientific experiments, like cloning and genetic manipulation, than to the mechanical monsters of pulp-fiction and B-movies (e.g., John Wyndham's "Lost Machine", Steven Spielberg's *Artificial Intelligence*). The serial production of robots, however, corresponds with modern industrialization's mass production and reproduction (Benjamin) which, though not necessarily exclusively American, is associated with Ford and other American symbols of so-called technological progress. As will be discussed here other devices of the dramatic text, including title, set design, props, characters, and dialogues, support this association.

In 1920, the hitherto unknown robots[14] appeared as a part of the title ("Rossum's Universal Robots") concealed by the acronym *RUR*. The name of the old Rossum is a distorted form of the Czech word *rozum* (i.e., reason, intellect, or ratio), which hints at the Americanized source of the robots as a product of human mind. Although the title refers to the robots, they represent only one type of a collective hero (cf. the subtitle), albeit one equally close to the German expressionist nightmares of the new man, as to the American dream of technological and scientific progress, which will remodel the existing world into a truly New World. The other collective of the play, however, consisting of six men, is responsible for this transformation. They deal with their dreams in the Utopia of the prologue and encounter the nightmares of the dystopia in the three acts that follow. Consequently, as William Harkins notes:

> What is new in Čapek's play is the complex meaning of the symbol of the robot, which represents not only the machine and its power to free man from toil but, at the same time, symbolizes man himself, dehumanized by his own technology.
>
> (85)

Similarly to the chronotope of the island that marks the deterritorialization in time and space, the robots help to address and question the issue of the Other both group represent for each other. The label *universal* stresses the multipurpose and supranational nature of the robots, as well as the contemporary trend of naming big companies such as Universal Film Studios in Hollywood.[15] The abbreviation of the title emulates the jargon of the business world, as does the English plural ending, which taunts the tendency to Anglicize even domestic products for marketing purposes. At the same time, the foreign spelling defamiliarizes the ordinary Czech words and ridicules the readiness of Czechs to imitate the foreign elements as the price of losing their own identity. In fact, the title mocks anyone and everyone.

While the title emphasizes the exotic and ubiquitous nature of the artificially produced human-like beings, the subtitle refers to a collective hero, while the attribute utopian defines not only the time in which the action is set, but also its fictionality. The narrated time, however, begins in the present, in the year in which the play was written, when the old Rossum[16] set out for the distant island on which the action takes place. His discovery of the matter close to the living substance happened 440 years after the discovery of America. As a result the date 1492 is used as the beginning of a new era, and timetable. Thus, the first spectators were confronted with the attitudes of their own time[17] and their consequences, and saw the island, its inhabitants, and the action in which they were involved as a metonymy of their own possible future.

The play, consisting of an "initial comedy and three acts", opens with the arrival of the young, idealistic, and beautiful Helena Glory, who visits the island as the representative of the League for Humanity to fight for the rights of the robots. Harry Domin, the director of the factory, receives her first as just another visitor, by giving her a brief and obviously memorized presentation about the history of robots and their production. True to his name, he dominates their exchange, interrupts Helena, or finishes her sentences for her. The ensuing dialogue results in repartees (stichomythia)[18] that indicate the speed and the distribution of power between the interlocutors. In this regard, however, Domin's discourse is also close to the robots and their mechanized speech.[19] This attitude changes, however, when Helena removes her veil. He is first lost for words, later, when he finds his speech again, he proposes to her. This brief comedy of manners continues when Helena, introduced to Domin's colleagues, mistakes them for robots thus exposing the likeness of the robots and their producers. As the names of the two robots Marius and Sulla betray, the technocrats and robots alike are creatures "without history" (1979: 307), the robots, however, have a large memory capacity and no past to remember. True products of Rossum's reason, they lack emotions, have no 'soul'.

The first act takes place ten years after Helena's arrival, when the robots had become more irritable and launch war against man to prove their superiority. Helena, now Domin's wife, and her nanny Nána (the name connotes a Czech nitwit and an English nanny[20]), the "voice of the people" ("hlas lidu", 1990a: 84) and memory ("thousand years"),[21] blame the scientists for making the robots without emotions and empathy. The men, however, continue their dreams about the enhancement of robots, their national and racial differentiation while the robots strive to take power over man. The attempts to humanize robots in the second act end up in their mutiny and eventually in a massacre, which annihilates the human beings. In the third act, the only man saved is Alquist, the director of the construction department, who the robots consider akin to themselves, since he too works with his hands.[22] They expect him to restore the formula of the old Rossum for their reproduction, destroyed by Helena, who desperately tried to stop the mass production of robots and restore the order of the human world, in which children would be born again. In spite of the fact that people lost their ability to procreate, and the last man cannot recover the instruction of how to produce robots, life on Earth might return through a couple of robots, who discover their affection for each other. Quoting the Bible, Alquist concludes the play with an apotheosis of love, therefore suggesting a new evolutionary cycle.

By juxtaposing the humanist point of view of Helena, Nána, and Alquist[23] with their awareness of history and belief in the future, progress, speed, and profit represented by Domin and his companions the play evokes the opposition between reason (rozum) and intuition, which might be considered either Bergsonian or Jamesian (Čapek 1937: 216). Eventually, the intuition seems to prevail and avert the imminent end of the world.[24]

As the stage directions specify, there is a difference between the human-likeness of the robots in the prologue and their uniform appearance in the play proper. Compared with Golem, who is a unique servant and whose statuesque quality is foregrounded, the faces of the robots are first described as motionless and therefore close to masks; later, however, they are almost interchangeable with their human counterparts except for their uniforms. They seem to prefigure workers employed in huge factories, presented in the classic film of German expressionism, Fritz Lang's *Metropolis* (1927), which also evokes the American model of big corporations and mechanization of human beings by confronting the human Maria, with her artificial double. In *RUR,* however, the similarity between *homo sapiens* and their products defamiliarizes the human beings and questions their uniqueness. This is alluded to when Domin interrupts Helena's question, because "Everyone asks the same thing" (Čapek 1990a: 36).[25]

The group of men appear as predecessors of an American think tank, an exilic collective of uprooted expatriates of different backgrounds, which demonstrates American equality in contrast to European hierarchy.[26] Congruent with its expressionist bent, the text does not list the men as individuals but differentiates them through their names, professions, appearance, and origin.[27] Furthermore, each of them represents different attitudes toward the philosophical underpinnings of the mass production of robots, and signifies a separate voice, which (as in Hordubal) results in a polyphonic discourse at times close to an antic chorus.

The head of the human team is Harry Domin (the robots are later led by Damon[28]), whose first name points to his Anglo-Saxon origin while his surname indicates his position not necessarily in this group,[29] but as the representative of the human race. The alliteration of the first name 'Harry' with 'Helena' shows a certain kinship of the characters, confirmed by their initial exchange, which becomes "a complex and sophisticated game" (Mukařovský 1964: 136):

DOMIN: Miss Glory, it is an unusual honour for us to –
HELENA: – to be unable to show you the door.

(Čapek 1985: 5)[30]

Disguised in the modern garb of an emancipated, witty, young, and presumably American lady, Helena carries the legacy of her namesake, the mythological Helen of Troy, of igniting passions and eventually even a war. Her last name Glory supports both her American connection and her exceptional position (she is the daughter of an unspecified president). As the author himself suggests, in his view, everybody is right, man (woman), and robots alike,[31] hence it is up to the spectators to build their opinion. This approach produces ambiguity, provokes an individual reaction, which seems to emulate the democratic principles of American society as much as the European fears of her laissez-faire attitude.

The characters are presented not as individuals but the embodiment of certain types. In fact, they could be considered representatives of vices or virtues coming straight from both the medieval and modern tradition (commedia dell'arte,[32] as well as mystery plays, and expressionist drama[33]). Hence, in *RUR* as in *Hordubal* Čapek experiments with several literary conventions; in addition to those already mentioned, he introduces fantasy based on scientific discoveries and projected into the future as another genre popular at the beginning of the twentieth century, for example, H. G. Wells, and his dialogues are reminiscent of conversation comedies by G. B. Shaw or Oscar Wilde. Furthermore, *RUR* is often used as an example of science fiction,[34] even though this designation was coined long after its opening night.[35] In fact, Čapek's work helped to define this category which expanded and challenged the conventions of its predecessors, such as fairy tales, gothic novel, and horror stories. Čapek's dramatic text, however, is unique because it presented utopia and dystopia as comedy and drama on stage.[36] Moreover, Čapek's robots also extend the contemporary focus on objects typical of modern fine arts, while props such as maps and posters advertising the robots as merchandise, an American desk, and a typewriter are signs of a modern efficient enterprise. Unlike Hordubal's American keepsakes, however, these objects are pieces of a collage that captures not an individual past (Hordubal's) but a projected Americanized collective future. Similarly metonymic are the windows and the phone, which suggest the connection of the office with the outside world. While the windows emphasize the insular character of the headquarters situated at the centre of a factory complex, the phone as a modern version of a messenger report or teichoscopy signifies the new technology that helps to expand the fictional world beyond the limits of the action space. Čapek introduces the fact that the transcontinental service begun in 1915, a few years before the play was completed to stress the paradigm of the "exilic" experience, which at first shows specialists of various disciplines who share the goal of progress and profit deemed as American. In the play proper the exile appears in the theme of isolation, of confrontation between the minority and majority, where the democratic rules apply to the communication within the group but do not respond to the demands of their 'serfs', the robots. Although they can be seen as allusions to the recent American history and the treatment of slaves, Čapek eschews any unequivocal reading.

The demise of mankind appears in this fictional world of the imaginary American exiles as a consequence of adhering to the present values without ever questioning them or considering them in the historical context (cf. above, the ignorance of history is exemplified in naming the female robot after a Roman general). As a result, the dramatic text theatricalizes the utopia and dystopia, and provides a "frame-relevant view of the working of the world" (Goffman: 563).

The Stage Revolts in Prague, New York, and Berlin

Animating American Statues in Prague

The play has [...] considerable theatrical qualities: the men-automatons moving stiffly like dolls, the tension of the great revolt, the striking types of men – all this testifies to Čapek's lively sense of the stage.

(Wellek: 50–1)

The theatricality of Čapek's text tested the performance tradition, challenged the stage conventions, and, by confronting man and object, questioned the dichotomy inherent in the notion of the Other. J. L. Styan claims that "the mechanical gestures and movements of the actors playing the robots provided a norm of stylized performance which impressed audiences everywhere" (55).[37] Styan's observation implies that the text required a specific style of acting, which might have served as a model for future staging of robots and similar characters. Similarly, František Černý, a Czech theatre historian, notes that from "the point of view of theatre history, the presentation of the robots was most interesting because the professional actors were facing the task of creating such a stage figure for the first time" (99).[38] The novel performance style, however, draws upon several tendencies of modern theatre at the turn of the twentieth century, such as the use of puppets (Craig, Jarry), objects, masks, and statues that confront realistic theatre tradition.[39] Following these models, while performing robots the actors tried to reduce their facial expressions to approximate a mask and appear as objects by moving like a statue.[40] In this regard, the robots foreground (actualize) the tension between the dynamic and static features of the actor on stage as described by Mukařovský:

> The immobility of a statue and the mobility of a live person is a constant antinomy between the poles of which the dramatic figure oscillates on stage. Craig – [...] drew attention to this hidden but always present antinomy of the art of acting. What is usually called a "pose" is clearly a sculptural effect. [...] the transition between the immobility of a solid mask and the make-up of a modern actor is quite continuous [...].
>
> (206)

Another novelty was noted by Otokar Fischer, one of the most prominent Czech theatre critics, after the opening night of *RUR* on 25 January 1921 at the National Theatre[41] in Prague: he saw the play as a culmination of Čapek's "Americanism", which is allegedly present in the title, setting, and in the structure that reminds him of an American film. What Fischer also considered American was the camaraderie of the men, their joyfulness, their heroism, and gentlemanly behavior (gentlemanství) towards a woman, as well as the swift conquest of her heart. He suggested, however, that the point of departure and the solution of this "human tragedy target another elsewhere than a definite centre of human civilisation: they both target a universal human sphere [...]" (Čapek 1966: 121). His colleague Jindřich Vodák, also mentions the American appearance of the men in the play. Although he admires the colorful set, he tries to find rhyme and reason for the use of colors and different patterns (Čapek 1966: 118). Vodák's reaction bears witness to the fact that the first staging of *RUR* was heavily influenced by contemporary fine arts, and more specifically by Karel's brother Josef, who designed the costumes. He also partially accepted the suggestions of Bedřich Feuerstein, a hitherto unknown architect. Feuerstein, who was inspired by Asian art and American architecture, highlighted the fictionality of the space, which was playful, colorful, and evocative of modern visual arts. His image of the future and therefore of the imaginary America is less driven by technology than by a certain naiveté and opulence. Judging by the reaction of the critics, Feuerstein successfully relocated the America of those who, according to Čapek, America might consider "idlers", such as William James and Walt Whitman (Čapek 1991: 123), and who counterpoint the America of speed, profit, and the success of the text.

Robots between America and Europe – transfer of cultures: the "Czecho-Slovakian Frankenstein" in New York[42]

> [T]he text is much more than a series of words: grafted on it are ideological, ethnological and cultural dimensions.
>
> (Pavis 1992: 6, 155)

According to Patrice Pavis the appropriation of culture "[...] sufficiently indicates that the adapter and the receptor take possession of the source culture according to their own perspectives [...]" (16).[43]

In this context, the Czech translation theorist Jiří Levý notes that the translation of a play has to consider the theatre and acting tradition of the particular country. He uses the example of the American audience which is less prone to accept stylization than, let's say, its French counterpart. He thinks that American drama is based on realistic details (cf. below Scholes) and shows the tendency to explain characters and past events.

Since many translations (and stagings) are the result of a confrontation between two different cultures, a text and its reception can serve as a source of information about a particular target culture. Thus we can ask how and what do *robots* relate to the audience when they speak, for instance, in American English? As a matter of fact, however, the language of American production came from England, where the translator Paul Selver co-operated with the playwright Nigel Playfair. Moreover, they altered the dramatic structure of the original and consequently might have deprived the dramatic text of its complexity.[44]

It is the shift in the segmentation of the text, however, that deserves more attention. In Selver's rendition, the comedy of the prologue was marked as the first act, while the third act was transformed into an epilogue. Čapek's instructions regarding the intermission after the prologue and second act are not listed in the Oxford edition, so that the "caesura" after the prologue is missing, and the contrast between the comedy of the prologue and the drama proper is obfuscated. Turning the third act into an epilogue separates this act from the rest of the play rather than presenting it as a culmination point.

Selver also "Anglicized" the text by making Helena the daughter of an Oxbridge professor, and sanitized it by omitting all the additional description of characters, such as the remark about Busman's Jewish origin. Consequently, the American reader or spectator was not confronted with his own prejudices and stereotypes, which Čapek mocks when he typecasts his vision of the future based on present clichés thus demonstrating a polyphonic display of attitudes.

A more subtle modification concerns a shift in the sentence structure. Often the dashes were replaced by conventional punctuation that substitutes the incomplete thoughts with finished units, thus eliminating the tension between the interlocutors, and suggesting a more conventional relationship between the genders. In their book on science fiction the American authors Scholes and Rabkin state that the America of the twenties and thirties: "was still relatively isolated from the rest of the world and innocent of political development abroad" (26). European science fiction was written by acclaimed authors while their American colleagues:

> [...] were still trying to master the techniques of realism. [...] The spread of public education [...] had given a great body of readers rudimentary reading skills but no interest in the more esoteric reaches of literature.
>
> (36)

As a result, science fiction and anything resembling it was considered pulp. Similarly, instead of using the American tongue, the robots had to adjust to the style of "the American Academy of Dramatic Arts" that, as Spencer Tracy "discovered, was an Oxford accent".[45]

Both Čapeks were popular as playwrights in New York for one season.[46] The success of the almost simultaneous performances of *RUR* and the play by Karel and Josef *Ze života hmyzu* (*From the Life of Insects*) in New York in the fall of 1922 was never to be repeated. As a list of plays produced that year illustrates, their appeal was not primarily due to their exoticism. *Ze života hmyzu*, for instance, had an opening night the same day as Pirandello's *Six Characters in Search of an Author*. In spite of the American propensity toward realistic plays (Levý, Scholes), dramas by Gerhart Hauptman, John Galsworthy, and Luigi Pirandello were also part of the repertoire (Hughes 1951: 386). While for the staging as well as for the reception of the play in Prague, America served as a model of a future society (Černý: 84), the first North American production of *RUR* did not reveal this connection. The Theatre Guild in New York (9 October 1922), a theatre company known for its staging of European and experimental dramas, opened its fifth season with this European novelty. They were even "bold enough" to accept G. B. Shaw's challenge of a management which was:

> clever enough to know that the alternative to pleasing the audience for two hours is to put the utmost strain upon their attention for three, and send them home exhausted but impressed.
>
> (Eaton: 49)[47]

Shaw's concept of defamiliarization obviously fit the bill of the well-educated young theatre enthusiasts willing to stage a play by an unknown, relatively young (32) playwright from a newly founded, virtually unknown country. Directed by Philip Moeller with Lee Simonson's set designs, "hauntingly suggestive costumes and make-up for the Robots" (Eaton: 66), *RUR* had a remarkably long run of 184 performances. Most of the contemporary journals included reviews of the play (Čapek 1966: 142) that surprised many by its originality.

The images of the performance at the Theatre Guild, show that the director and the set designer followed the author's directions regarding the windows, which both separate and unify both worlds. This is congruent with the technique of "double reflection" from within and from outside, a device which produces ambiguity that, according to Mukařovský, is typical of Čapek's work in general. The costumes by Simonson, however, apparently reduced the similarity between man and robot, since the robots appeared as ogres, thus turning them into fantasy figures which subsequently served as visual models of many contemporary film and TV man-made characters of monsters, aliens, and futuristic creatures.[48] They range from the giant robot Gort, who comes from another planet on a peace mission in *The Day the Earth Stood Still* (1951), directed by Robert Wise, to the character of Data in the made for television series *Star Trek* who, like Čapek's creatures at the beginning of the play, has an analytic mind and no notion of emotions. Correspondingly, his facial expressions are close to a mask. His performance, in fact, is reminiscent of that of Spencer Tracy, who in the first production of *RUR* "was to move mechanically and keep a poker face" (Swindell: 33). Moreover, even Stephen Spielberg's *Artificial Intelligence* (2001), considered in a BBC poll in 2003[49] the second worst film after *Titanic* (1997), seems to have been somewhat inspired by Čapek's work, even though it lacks its ambiguity, theatricality, and philosophical dimension. The latter, however, was what Brooks Atkinson noted about *RUR*, namely that it "provided a philosophical scandal that most people relished" (19).

John Corbin suggested a parallel between the robots and modern monsters by labeling the robots the "Czecho-Slovak Frankenstein" (1922): "Having been worn threadbare in the country of its origin, the Frankenstein metaphor has reached Czechoslovakia and has there achieved a social consciousness – has become, in fact, class conscious." Corbin's reading seems to substitute the creatures of the future with Gothic narrative and a monster from the previous century. He does not recognize in the fictional beings the potential results of the present development in what was considered the "most advanced state" (Černý: 84), that is, in his own country. In fact, by mentioning the "social consciousness" he draws attention to the geographic and ideological proximity of the newly emerged Czechoslovakia and the revolutionary Russia. This notion, however, locates the play in the realm of a European fantasy instead of showing a projection of an American future, and the tragic end of the human exiles.

Corbin mocked the ending as well. To him the fact that the couple of robots find a cottage with a cat and a dog seems utterly ridiculous. Yet this ending demonstrates the humanization of robots as opposed to the mechanization (Bergson) of man presented in the prologue. Moreover, the human qualities of the two robots introduce the human world again, and pay tribute to Jamesian optimism. In fact, it almost appears as a translation of Čapek's views on James' "trust in the perseverance of the goodness in humans such trust that is not given but is gained in a process that culminates in a picturesque image of the world" (Čapek 2000: 58–9.).

From the fair-booth in Vienna to the highbrow art salons in New York

The performance of *RUR* in Prague coincided with the reactions to the new state, and expectation of a bright future. At the same time, more or less unscathed by the war New York begun to take interest in European culture. Berlin, however, was exposed to turmoil after the war, where the defeat, the inflation, the crushed socialist uprising, political murders, and cultural experiments clashed and the future was altogether uncertain. For many, America played either the role of a promised land, to be approximated, or the epitome of capitalist oppression.

In this atmosphere the staging of *WUR* (the German title)[50] performed first in Berlin at the Theater am Kurfûrstendamm on 29 March 1923 and later in Vienna on 19 October 1923 at the Neue Wiener Bühne. It became a milestone of modern theatre history due to the work of a young

Viennese architect, Friedrich Kiesler, whose set design turned Čapek's drama into a remarkable intermedial event: "[...] Kiesler's 'electrome-chanical' set was a huge montage, compiled from the most diverse appa-ratuses and machine parts (megaphone, seismograph, *tanagra* device, iris diagram, light bulbs) [...]" (Lesak: 40). He used loudspeakers that dis-torted the speech of the characters, while a complex system of mirrors produced miniature images of the actors in a mechanized fictional world. To achieve this particular effect he applied the technology known from the fairgrounds as *tanagra*.[51]

In retrospect, Kiesler describes his creation:

> This *RUR* play was my occasion to use for the first time in a theatre a motion picture [a small cinema projection was also incorporated in the set] instead of a painted backdrop, and also television[52] in the sense that I had a big, square panel window in the middle of the stage drop which could be opened by remote control. When the director of the human factory in the play pushed a button at his desk, the panel opened and the audience saw two human beings [...] a foot-and-a-half tall, casually moving and talking, heard through a hidden loudspeaker. It was quite an illusion, because a minute later you saw the same actors appear on stage full size.
>
> (Kiesler (1961: 109), qtd in Pringle 2004)

The projected film, as Barbara Lesak notes, might have expanded the function of the windows as a device to watch the outside world.[53] His montage technique, however, also shifted the spatial distribution of the play. Instead of the two sets of rooms divided along gender lines that represented the core opposition between reason and intuition, Kiesler's design which, as in a cubist painting, appeared fragmented, divided into several units, defamiliarized the familiar settings (office, sitting room),. This spatial solution, however, corresponds with the segmentation of the text by dashes noted by Mukařovský.

Kiesler turned the stage itself into a moving mechanism, thus expand-ing the notion, "that not only can a person be an actor but so can a wooden puppet or a machine" (Honzl 75). In fact, using modern technol-ogy Kiesler foregrounded the visual effects, illustrated the utopian quality of the text, and supported the stage illusion of a future mechanized uni-verse rather than breaking it. In contrast to Čapek, his fictional world embraced the America of speed, noise, and machines. By applying mod-ern technology, however, he showed that the robots do not only fulfill old dreams, but also signify new nightmares connected with the modern trend of people turned into masses that occlude their individuality, as described by Walter Benjamin:

> In big parades and monster rallies, in sports events, and in war, all of which nowadays are captured by camera and sound recording, the masses are brought face to face with themselves. [...] This means that mass movements, including war, constitute a form of human behavior, which particularly favors mechanical equipment.[54]

Kiesler's concept was certainly one of the models of modern theatrical practice, including the acclaimed Magic Lantern.[55] Yet, the set design reinforced the unequivocal understanding of robots as machines (as did later Fritz Lang in *Metropolis* with his distribution between good and evil). Consequently, the biological quality of the robots was lost. Instead, comparable to Craig's *Übermarionette* or to the man of clay, they were more like an animated statue, or the evil mechanical robot Maria in *Metropolis*, which served as the model for many horror and science fiction movies.

Kiesler's radical concept, however, revealed the abstract nature of the text. It also relocated the America of technological progress, speed, and efficiency to the stage in Berlin, where the fair-booth tricks turned into technological miracles. They drew the immediate attention of experts who asked him to organize the first international exhibit of set design in Vienna in 1924, an honor which made Kiesler into a leading figure of international theatre. What followed was an invitation to work in the United States where he:

> was through the 1920s, 30s, 40s and 50s among the more venturesome thinkers, a conduit in the United States for the very latest of European artistic ideas. [...] Mr. Kiesler "proposed nothing less than a total reformulation of art that would liberate it from the confines of the isolated aesthetic object" for his contribution in spreading the gospel of European modernism and for adding his own idiosyncratic and rather spiritualistic interpretation to it, Mr. Kiesler earned himself a place in the history of American art.
>
> (Kimmelman 1989)

As a result, while Čapek's America helped Kiesler to relocate and find his niche in American high culture, Čapek himself, though a respected modern European writer for another decade or two, is mentioned mostly in literature on science fiction, and not as a source of inspiration and innovation for modern drama in Europe and America. *RUR* became in

America "a standard high school text in the thirties and established the word 'robot' as a name for mechanical creatures" (Scholes and Rabkin: 29).

This reaction of the American critics might be connected to the fact that "America was relatively isolated from the rest of the world and innocent of political development abroad" (Scholes and Rabkin: 26). In addition: "The science fiction written in Europe in the twenties and thirties was both more dignified and more durable than that produced in the United States." In contrast the American writers "were still trying to master the techniques of realism [...]" (35). Expressionism, however, challenged the realistic tendency typical of American literature, where science fiction and anything resembling it was considered pulp. Thus, the reviewers label the mixed genre of comedy and drama as melodrama, while the horror story replaces the expressionist anxiety and modern questions of human responsibility. The conflation of the known and foreign, Frankenstein and Czechoslovakia also place the drama elsewhere, outside America. Hence, instead of recognizing America's own legacy of slavery among the sources of Čapek's drama, "it was suspected of being a Communist propaganda" (Atkinson: 19) and thus relocated back to Europe, not causing any philosophical or aesthetic discomfort.

Čapek's play relocated America from page to stage, thus visualizing and defamiliarizing it. While that image oscillated between two types of creativity, the "idlers" on the one hand and the exilic community on the other, in Berlin the robots were integrated among the cultural symbols that marked American culture like jazz, boxing and Chaplin. In America, however, *RUR* introduced new icons of American culture, a new type of monster that joined Golem as a creature produced by human acumen, which expands the limits of human existence. Čapek's America was relocated mostly into a familiar and therefore safe universe of fantasy. While Kiesler, provided the bridge between European and American modern art, Čapek deterritorialized the fantasies of the Old World and the (science) fiction of the New World, thus projecting modernist excitement as utopian and the concurrent fear of either fictional or real exilic experience, technology, and the new distribution of power that generates a dystopian vision of the transformation American values of speed, progress, and success might produce.

Notes

1. A prominent actor in Max Reinhardt's theatre.
2. The third and only preserved film of his Golem trilogy

3. Golem is the protagonist of numerous tales and some plays written in the first decades of the twentieth century, e.g., Arthur Holitscher, *The Golem*, 1908; H. Leivick, *The Golem*, 1920.
4. Paul Leppin, "Die Golemsage in der deutschen Literatur", *Prager Presse*, Jg. 14, No. 335, v. 7.121(934): S.4
5. The sets of architect Hans Poelzig were inspired by the medieval Jewish ghetto of Prague. The cinematography of Karl Freund, in collaboration with Poelzig and Wegener, is cited among the most outstanding examples of German Expressionism.
6. The subtitle varied: the published text denotes "collective drama", the German translation by Otto Pick uses "utopian collective drama" and the poster for the National theatre introduces the word "utopistic".
7. Čapek studied philosophy and devoted a chapter of his dissertation on pragmatism to William James (Čapek 2000).
8. Carpathian Ukraine or Ruthenia was discovered by Czech writers of the thirties who set some of their works in this forsaken part of the country whose inhabitants could just barely make a living and were forced to leave, e.g., Andy Warhol's family came from there. *Hordubal* (1933) is part of a truly remarkable trilogy about different journeys. The other two novels are *Meteor* (1934) and *Ordinary life* (1935).
9. On Čapek's knowledge of English and American literature, cf. Vočadlo, 1995.
10. *Hovory s T. G. Masarykem* (*Conversations with T. G. Masaryk*) 1928–35 (Čapek 1937).
11. Deleuze and Guattari derived the term from Čapek's contemporary, Franz Kafka, and his diary entry about the small literature. The word "minor" does not correspond with the "klein" of the original, which means small. Gilles Deleuze and Félix Guattari, "What is a Minor Literature?", in *Reading Kafka: Prague, Politics and the Fin de Siècle*, ed. Mark Anderson, New York: Schocken, 1989, pp. 259–62.
12. "[T]he play was translated and performed in most of the countries of Europe, as well as in the United States and Japan. Čapek's name (in various mispronounced and even misspelled forms) became a household word, along with the term 'robot' itself" (Harkins: 84).
13. *Pace* Christopher Goulding, who found an early mention of the word *robota* in English: "The peasantry, called Robota, were not all in an equal degree of slavery." While *robota* can be found in a slightly modified form in other Slavic languages, where it denotes work, the word *robot* is still a neologism coined by Josef Čapek (Goulding: 380–1(2)).
14. Today the meaning rejected by Čapek is the established one: A robot is described as "a machine in the form of a human being that performs mechanical functions of a human being but lacks sensitivity" (Senn and Johnson: 465).
15. Morton Klass sees their universality connected with their versatility with respect to their industrial tasks (Klass 1983: 174).
16. V. Majakowskij later uses a similar technique for instance in his *Klop* (*Bedbug*), 1929.
17. The reverse focus is present in *Věc Makropulos* (*The Macropulos Case*), 1922, in which the past, the passage of time, and immortality are the main subject.

18. The Czech literary scholar Jan Mukařovský based one of the most insightful studies on stage dialogue on this exchange, showing the importance of punctuation, mainly dashes. The English version does not reveal that the article is an obituary for Čapek (Mukařovský 1964: 133–49).
19. Max Brod noted a general proximity of people and robots. (Černý: 100).
20. In his translation to English Paul Selver changed her name to Emma, thus depriving his reader of this connotation.
21. Abrash sees Nána's comments as "dogmatic singlemindedness", but the function of this character is that of a *raisoneur*, a commentator who represents traditional values (Abrash: 188)
22. Here the origins of the word *robot* are foregrounded.
23. Except for Alquist's attitude the conflict between reason and intuition is mostly presented as a clash between female and male values, supported also by the distribution of the places in which the action is set (office and laboratory in the prologue and third act, and Helena's private rooms in the first and second act).
24. Kamila Kinyon discusses Kant and Hegel in her article on "Phenomenology of Robots", yet Bergson also offered Čapek important philosophical ideas (cf. Heftrich).
25. Cf. their similarity with *Masse Mensch* (*mass man*) Ernst Toller's eponymous play of 1921. The translation used here is that by Claudia Novack Jones, since she follows the text segmentation of the original. Neither Selver nor Majer, or Porter preserve this division.
26. Cf. Berger's chart mentioned in Berger (1–9).
27. *Domin* alludes to *dominus*, which meant in ancient Rome, "master" or "owner", particularly of slaves (http://www.britannica.com/EBchecked/topic/168799/dominus). He and Helena are the only characters with first names: the name of the technical director Fabry evokes the Bergsonian category of *homo faber* (the man producing tools) as much as fabric and the Czech word for factory *fabrika*; the physician Gall might just allude to the English word *gall*, but also to the name Galen, since in *Bílá nemoc* (*The White Sickness*), 1937, the protagonist, a doctor, is Dr Galen, evoking Claudius Galen (*c*.ad 129–*c*.216), a famous Greek physician. Busman confirms the stereotypes about Jews as businessmen. Incidentally, the reference to Busman as a Jew is left out in most English versions, which disregard the function of this reference, namely to underline the multinational character of the group (cf. below). Philmus does consider it a literary device typical of expressionism but speaks about a "whiff of anti-semitism" (27). Alquist might point to an inquiring mind, a person questions everything.
28. He is missing in Selver's translation. Cf. Kinyon's discussion of Damon recalling the Hellenist and Platonic tradition of transitory beings.
29. Cf. Hallemeier, who addresses him not as a boss but with the familiar "you rogue" ("Ty kluku") (Čapek 1966: 72).
30. Mukařovský suggests that a similar device acquires a different function in the second act: "The sentence is [...] taken over by the other person not in order to 'cut him off,' but in order to divide the lyrical part in the manner of a litany [...]" (1964: 137).

31. In his reaction to a public debate in London in 1923, in which G. B. Shaw and G. K. Chesterton discussed the robots, Čapek explained each of the characters from the point of view of the comedy of truth (Harkins: 91).
32. Karel and his brother Josef were among the first Czech playwrights to play with the tradition of commedia dell'arte in their first one act play *Lásky hra osudná* (*Fateful Game of Love*), 1910.
33. In fact, *RUR* is often used as a prime example of an Expressionist drama. In William Harkin's view Čapek "blended expressionism with realism". Harkins considers only "the robot itself [...] expressionistic; otherwise Čapek's treatment is conventional and realistic" (86). This opinion, however, does not pay attention to the characters of the team as types, the episodic structure of the play, and its language.
34. Isaac Asimov defined it as "that branch of literature which is concerned with the impact of scientific advance upon human beings" (*Modern Science Fiction*, 1953).
35. Cf. more on this topic: Andrew Milner (242–52).
36. Harkins questions the uniqueness of the play by pointing to Léo Delibes's ballet *Coppélia* and Offenbach's opera *The Tales of Hoffmann* (1881) both based on E. T. A. Hoffman's story *Der Sandman* (*The Sandman*, 1816), which introduced the automaton Olympia.
37. Unfortunately, Styan does not reveal, which performance lead him to this observation.
38. Černý: 99. All translations from Czech to English are mine unless indicated otherwise.
39. This topic will be the subject of a separate study.
40. Herein they differ from Wegener's Golem, whose facial expressions were that of a human being.
41. An amateur performance of the play in Hradec Králové on 2 and 3 January 1921, however, preceded this event. In his aforementioned insightful article on the play, Milner gives the date of this staging as that of the first night in Prague.
42. John Corbin, "The Play": "Having been worn threadbare in the country of its origin, the Frankenstein metaphor has reached Czechoslovakia and has there achieved a social consciousness – has become, in fact, class conscious." *New York Times*, 10 October 1922: 24.
43. Jacqueline Lo and Helen Gilbert offer very useful criticism of Pavis's model, especially of his somewhat one-directional notion of the hour-glass. See Jacqueline Lo and Helen Gilbert, "Toward a Topography of Cross-Cultural Theatre Praxis", *The Drama Review* 46.3 (T175), Fall 2002, New York University and the Massachusetts Institute of Technology, 2002.
44. Philmus: 7–32. Cf. the character of Damon was deleted or collapsed into one with Radius; Nána, the nanny, turned into a maid; this list could go on.
45. Swindell: 33.
46. Of a production in 1948 in New York, the reviewer states: "what seems to have struck another generation as powerfully interesting theatre, as profound wisdom and searching analysis now seems only interesting" (Atkinson: 3).
47. "[...] the taste of the Guild directors was European [...]." The Guild was the first American stage to produce a play by G. B. Shaw (Eaton: 42).

48. According to the *FANTASTIC CINEMA SUBJECT GUIDE* (Senn: 465–76), there were around 80 movies about robots listed until 1992. For a detailed discussion of some of these aspects, cf. Milner.
49. http://news.bbc.co.uk/1/hi/entertainment/film/3242607.stm (accessed 20 November 2008).
50. Otto Pick defamiliarized the German word *Verstand* in a similar way as Čapek did with its Czech equivalent, thus changing the title to *WUR* (Werstand's *UR*). This form was also used in one of the Russian editions (Čapek 1966: 204). Milner and Philmus claim that this translation targeted the Sudeten Germans. Yet the fact that the play was staged in Berlin in 1922 shows that Czech literature was successfully promoted by Pick, Brod, and others outside of Czechoslovakia. Vočadlo mentions several of the Čapek–Selver collaborations; this work is listed in Philmus's article, but not examined (Philmus: 7–32).
51. "Tanagra Theatres existed in many European cities in the years 1910–1920 (Viefhaus-Mildenberger, 1965: 27–30). The name comes from the figures excavated at Tanagra in the 1890s whose name became synonymous with perfect living miniatures, particularly female. The sideshow illusion consisted of a miniature stage where living actors appeared as real but tiny figures, through an arrangement of plain and concave mirrors. Its development as a sideshow attraction came about as a by-product of research into optical instruments, which could better sustain the perception of depth (von Rohr 1920). The use of concave mirrors has a long history in magic but for the Tanagra the stronger light of electricity was essential" (Pringle 2004).
52. "It was only television in the sense of suggesting control over remote spaces. No screen is involved in a Tanagra, the images are viewed in a concave mirror" (Pringle).
53. Unfortunately, there is no information about the nature of the film. In any case, Kiesler's use of projection on stage counts among the very first attempts to combine film and theatre. The most detailed account about both productions can be found in (Lesák 1988)
54. http://web.bentley.edu/empl/c/rcrooks/toolbox/common_knowledge/general_communication/benjamin.html (accessed 6 December 2008), in German footnote 63. Note that the English translation uses the word *reproduction*, Benjamin, however uses *Reproduzierbarkeit*, i.e., reproducibility.
55. The work of the director Alfred Radok, in which film projection and stage action are intertwined, was introduced at the World Exhibition in Brussels in 1958 (cf. (Stehlíková 2007).

Works cited

Abrash, Merritt. "'R.U.R.' Restored and Reconsidered", *Extrapolation* 32.2 (1991): 184–92.

Atkinson, Brooks and Hirschfeld, Albert. *The Lively Years, 1920–1973*. New York: New York Association Press, 1973.

Benjamin, Walter. "The Work of Art in the Age of Mechanical Reproduction": http://web.bentley.edu/empl/c/rcrooks/toolbox/common_knowledge/general_communication/benjamin.html (accessed 6 December 2008).

————. *Das Kunstwerk im Zeitalter seiner technischen Reproduzierbarkeit*. Frankfurt am Main: Suhrkamp,1970.

Berger, Arthur. "Sign, self and society". In *Semiotic Bridge: Trends from California*. Irmengard Rauch and Gerald F. Carr (eds). Berlin: Mouton de Gruyter, 1989, pp. 1–9.

Bridges, Peter. "Playwrights, Presidents, and Prague". *The Virginia Quarterly Review* (Winter 2003): 97–107.

Čapek, Karel. *Pragmatismus čili filosofie praktického života* (*Pragmatism, or the Philosophy of the Practical Life*). Praha: Votobia. 2000.

————. "The Author of the Robots Defends Himself", *Science-Fiction Studies* (1996): 143.

————. "O amerikanismu". In *Spisy XXI. Kritika slov o věcech obecných čili zóon politikon*, Prague: Československý spisovatel, 1991, pp. 120–4.

————. *Three Novels*. Highland Park, NJ: Catbird Press, 1990a.

————. *Toward the Radical Center: A Karel Čapek Reader*. Ed. Peter Kussi. Highland Park: Catbird Press, 1990b.

————. *RUR and The Insect Play*. Trans Paul Selver. Oxford, Oxford University Press, 1985.

————. *Spisy. Cestopisy* I, Praha: Československý spisovatel, 1980.

————. *RUR*. Prague: Československý spisovatel, 1966.

————. *Hovory s T. G. Masarykem 1928–1935* (*Conversations with T. G. Masaryk. 1928–35*). Praha: Borový, 1937.

Černý, František. *Premiéry bratří Čapků*. (*Premieres of the Čapek Brothers*). Prague: Hynek, 2000.

Corbin, John. "A Czecho-Slovak Frankenstein", *New York Times*, 10 October 1922, p. 24.

Doležel, Lubomir. "Karel Čapek-a Modern Storyteller." In *On Karel Čapek*. Michael Makin and Jindřich Toman (eds). Ann Arbor: University of Michigan Press, 1992, pp. 15–28.

dominus. Encyclopædia Britannica. 2008. Encyclopædia Britannica Online. Dominus. http://www.britannica.com/EBchecked/topic/168799/dominus (accessed 2 December 2008).

Eaton, Walter Prichard. *The Theatre Guild: The First Ten Years*. New York: Brentano's, 1929.

Goffman, Erving. *Frame Analysis: An Essay on the Organization of Experience*. Boston: Northwestern University Press, 1986 [1974].

Goulding, Christopher. "Robot: Antedating the Entry in The Oxford English Dictionary", *Notes and Queries* 52.3 (September 2005): 380–1

Harkins, William E. *Karel Čapek*. New York: Columbia University Press, 1962.

Heftrich, Urs. "Karel Čapeks Auseinandersetzung mit Henri Bergson" ("Karel Čapek's Critique of Henri Bergson"), *Zeitschrift für Slavische Philologie* 50.2 (1990): 354–87.

Holman C. Hugh. *A Handbook to Literature*. New York: Macmillan,1972.

Honzl, Jindřich. "Dynamics of Sign in the Theater". In *Semiotics of Art: Prague School Contributions*. Ladislav Matejka and Irwin R. Titunik (eds). Cambridge, MA : MIT Press, 1976, pp. 75–94.

Hughes Glenn. *History of the American Theatre 1700–1950*. Binghamton, NY: Vail-Balloui Press, 1951.

Kiesler, Frederick. "Interview", *Progressive Architecture* XLII (July 1961), p. 109 quoted in Patricia Pringle, *Scan Journal* 1.2 (June 2004): http://scan.net.au/scan/journal/print.php?journal_id=34&j_id=2#_edn20 (accessed 6 December 2008).

Kimmelman, Michael. "An Architect's Dreams And What He Built", *New York Times*, 27 January 1989: http://query.nytimes.com/gst/fullpage.html?res=950DE6DC153DF934A15752C0A96F948260 (accessed 7 December 2008)

Kinyon, Kamila. "The Phenomenology of Robots: Confrontations with Death in Karel Čapek's *R.U.R.*", *Science-Fiction Studies* 26 (1999): 379–400.

Klass Morton, "The Artificial Alien: Transformations of the Robot in Science Fiction", *The ANNALS of the American Academy of Political and Social Science* 470 (1983): 171–9.

Leppin, Paul. "Die Golemsage in der deutschen Literatur", *Prager Presse* Jg. 14, Nr. 335, v. 7.12 (1934): S.4.

Lesák, Barbara. "Visionary of the European Theater". In *Frederick Kiesler*. Ed. Lisa Phillips. New York: Whitney Museum of American Art, in association with W. W. Norton, 1989, pp. 37–45.

———. *Die Kulisse explodiert: Friedrich Kieslers Theaterexperimente und Architektprojekte, 1923–1925*. Wien: Locker Verlag, 1988.

Levý, Jiří. *Umění překladu* (*The Art of Translation*). Praha: Panorama, 1983.

Lo, Jacqueline and Helen Gilbert. "Toward a Topography of Cross-Cultural Theatre Praxis". *The Drama Review* 46.3 (T175), Fall 2002. New York University and the Massachusetts Institute of Technology, 2002).

Milner, Andrew. *Literature, Culture and Society*. New York: Routledge, 1996.

Montrose, J. Moses. *Dramas of Modernism and their Forerunners*. Boston: Little, Brown, 1936.

Mukařovský, Jan. "On the Current State of the Theory of Theater". In *The Prague School: Selected Writings, 1929–1946*. Ed. Peter Steiner. Austin: University of Texas Press, 1982, pp. 201–19.

———. "K. Čapek's Prose as Lyrical Melody and As Dialogue". In *A Prague School Reader*. Ed. Paul Garvin. Washington, D.C: Georgetown University Press 1964, pp. 133–49.

Pavis, Patrice. *Theatre At The Crossroads Of Culture*. New York: Routledge, 1992.

Philmus, Robert. "Matters of Translation: Karel Čapek and Paul Selver", *Science-Fiction Studies* 28, Pt 1 (2001): 7–32.

Pringle, Patricia "Seeing Impossible Bodies: Fascination as a Spatial Experience", *Scan Journal* 1.2 (June 2004): http://scan.net.au/scan/journal/print.php?journal_id=34&j_id=2#_edn2 (accessed 6 December 2008).

Robot. http://www.wordsources.info/words-mod-robots.html (accessed 6 December 2008).

Scholes, Robert. and Rabkin, E. S. (eds). *Science Fiction : History, Science, Vision*. New York: Oxford University Press, 1977.

Senn, Bryan and Johnson, John. *Fantastic Cinema Subject Guide: A Topical Index to 2500 Horror, Science Fiction, and Fantasy Films*. Jefferson, NC: McFarland, 1992.

Šolić, Mirna. *Karel Čapek's Travels: Adventures of a New Vision*, doctoral thesis, 2008.

Stehlíková, Eva (ed.). *Alfréd Radok mezi filmem a divadlem*. Praha: Akademie múzických umění – Národní filmový archiv, 2007.

Styan J. L. *Expressionism and Epic Theatre*. Cambridge, Cambridge University Press, 1981.

Swindell, Larry. *Spencer Tracy*. New York: NAL, 1969, p. 33.
Suvin, Darko. *Metamorphoses of Science Fiction: On the Poetics and History of a Literary Genre*. New Haven: Yale University Press, 1979.
Viefhaus-Mildenberger, Marianne. *Film und Projektion auf der Bühne*. Emsdetten Westf: Lechte, 1965.
Večadlo, Otakar. *Anglické listy K.Čapka*: Praha: JAN, 1995.
Wellek, René. "Karel Čapek ". In *Essays on Czech Literature*. Introduction by Peter Demetz. Slavistic printings and reprintings, 43. The Hague: Mouton, 1963, pp. 46–61.

7

At Home in Exile: Finding America in *Casablanca* and *Camino Real*

Alan Ackerman
University of Toronto

> *American social space invites a mobility that becomes nearly cost free.*
> *Ultimately, wherever one moves will be enough the same to feel very*
> *quickly "like home." It is an interesting American invention, both*
> *semantic and literal, to live not "at home" but in a place that feels*
> *"like home."*
>
> Philip Fisher, "Democratic Social Space: Whitman,
> Melville, and the Promise of American Transparency"

> *Continent, city, country, society:*
> *The choice is never wide and never free.*
> *And here, or there … No. Should we have stayed at home,*
> *Wherever that may be?*
>
> From Elizabeth Bishop, "Questions of Travel"

It is well known that the institutionalization of American Studies began in the 1940s with a concerted effort by the US government in combination with American universities, often through ostensibly private funding organizations such as the Ford Foundation. With the founding of the journal *American Quarterly* in 1949 and the American Studies Association in 1951, the work of American Studies aimed to promote the study of American culture and "the strengthening of relations among persons and institutions in this country and abroad devoted to such studies, and the broadening of knowledge among the general public about American culture in all its diversity and complexity".[1] This project was integral to Cold War, and largely covert, American foreign policy, a campaign of cultural persuasion, in which American intellectuals and artists enlisted knowingly and unknowingly, responding to a Soviet campaign, run through the Communist Information Bureau (Cominform), to shape Western opinion and convince Europeans that America was a culturally barren wasteland. American scholars drawing on historian Frederic Jackson Turner's "frontier thesis" and Perry Miller's *Errand into the Wilderness*, sought to understand a distinctive "American Mind" and its "location in the New World" (Wise: 306). Representative works of the generation of scholars of American literary culture that came of age in the 1940s and 1950s, such as Henry Nash Smith's *Virgin Land*, R. W. B. Lewis's *American Adam*, and Leo Marx's *Machine in the Garden*, discovered central myths of America and drew heavily on pastoral imagery and its critique, reaching back to the first theatrical representation of this "brave new world" as a space simultaneously of exile and of self-government, a state of nature and of culture in *The Tempest*. But, even in 1940, Smith, while arguing for American exceptionalism – "an irruption of novelty in history" – contested the tendency in Turner and in the agrarian tradition of American literary and social criticism that "made it difficult for Americans to think of themselves as members of a world community" (260). If entering the world community was the imperative of the early 1940s, shaping it became the project of the post-war era, the dark reflection of which was no longer isolationism but imperialism. America would be not a utopia, or no place, but an infinitely reproducible way of life, every place.

The *idea* of America that emerged in the works of intellectuals and artists, many of them former communists themselves, was thus inextricably linked to a war-torn Europe characterized by flight and fragmentation, by exile and return, and to a humanistic culture and "struggle for men's minds" that centered paradoxically on the mobility or freedom of the individual. In the context of this international cultural mission, I wish to turn to the classic Hollywood film *Casablanca* (1943) and Tennessee Williams's response to the movie in his play *Camino Real* (1953), which I read as a commentary on the movie, and specifically on the themes of American cultural identity, isolationism and exile, internationalism and geopolitical determinism. Both epitomize the project of locating a paradigmatic American in a "real" yet self-reflexively figurative site, but their differences and their dialogical relationship also speak to the narrative arc that describes America's emergence as a global superpower. In key ways, *Casablanca* represents the literary-historical project that attempted to *ground* the figure of the exiled American in what Henry Luce called, in ungrounded terms, the "American century".[2] Ironically, the putative American of the film is grounded ultimately not in the Western Hemisphere, but in Africa – a map of which is the movie's final image. This map does not so much repudiate the humanism of Cold War American Studies approaches as, like the movie as a whole, it more generally suggests that humanists, "rank sentimentalists", and exiles, such as Rick Blaine, are implicated in making the maps from which they appear to be disaffected. It is not to the United States but to "the freedom of the Americas" (the shooting script reads "the New World"[3]) that many eyes turned with the coming of the Second World War, as we are told by the narrator's voice that intones at the film's opening over images, first, of a turning globe that appears with the mention of turning eyes – indicating the subjectivity of an ostensibly objective geopolitical reality – and, then, of a map, which fades in and out with newsreels of displaced persons on the march.

When *Casablanca* was first released, the relatively unknown and penniless Tennessee Williams spent months watching the movie while patrolling the aisles of the theater, an experience he recounts at length in his *Memoirs*:

> A friend was employed in 1943 at the old Strand Theatre on Broadway as an usher, and, knowing that I was between profitable engagements, he told me that the Strand was in need of a new usher and that I might get the job provided I fitted the uniform of my predecessor. Luckily it happened that this former usher was about my height and of similar build. I was put on the job. The attraction at the Strand was that World War II classic, *Casablanca*, which was an early starring vehicle for Ingrid Bergman and Humphrey Bogart, both hot as blazes; the cast also included Peter Lorre and Paul Henreid, and there was Dooley Wilson playing and singing that immortal oldie, "As Time Goes By." In those days, with an attraction like that, the movie houses of Broadway were literally mobbed and the aisles had to be roped off by the ushers to restrain the patrons till they could be seated. It was my job, at first, to guard the entrances to one of these aisles, and at an evening performance an enormously fat lady broke through the velvet rope and started to charge down the aisle, evidently intending to occupy a seat on the screen, and when I attempted to restrain her, she struck me over the head with a handbag that seemed to contain gold bricks. The next thing I remember I was still employed at the Strand but I was now situated near the entrance, in a spot of light, and directing traffic with white-gloved hands. "This way, ladies and gentlemen, this way please," and "There will be a short wait for all seats." And somehow, during the several months run of

Casablanca, I was always able to catch Dooley Wilson and "As Time Goes By."

(2006 : 75–6)

This amazingly rich reminiscence is full of what today we recognize as typical Williams motifs: the heat imagery that characterizes sexual attraction and the violent fat lady who, like Big Mama, cannot be restrained but bursts into the Apollonian space of illusion. Ungovernable and lacking self-government, she is a figure of appetitive capital – swinging her bag of gold – or of capitalism, a figure for America. She now wishes to take her place not before but *on* the screen, itself not a literal space but an illusion of three dimensions. As a variation on the many women who have stood for America in literature and art, Williams's fat lady represents a new aggressiveness, a refusal to keep in her place, a transgression of boundaries or borders inseparable from the seductive power of American culture. If the fat lady knocks the usher/author into a state first of oblivion and then of docility, altering his consciousness, she also renders him complicit, a benign, unquestioning traffic cop with white gloved hands who pockets his pay and maintains order – ultimately a world order – over which glows inexorably (as time goes by in the American Century) the silver images not only of Bogart and Bergman but also of the globe and map.

When Williams became an usher at the Strand Theatre, his motive was simple: profit. The job's single requirement was simple too: uniformity. Fitting the uniform of the former usher, Williams was put to work. But Williams's account of his first day and the months that followed at the Strand – his relationship to the audiences, the theatre space, the screen, the music, the actors and characters, and the world of Broadway in 1943 – is dense and complex, suggesting in the retrospective vision of the 1972 memoir that the work of the artist is not only immortal but also rooted in its time and place. The Strand Theatre itself is a particular, *real* place, but it is also a representative democratic space. It is open to the newcomer. In it difference is erased. Theatres just like it are in every city, and therefore it is infinitely reproducible. *Casablanca* has appeared in any number of other "movie houses" in America and, of course, the world.

The democratic logic of leveling diversity is invoked in the movie itself by the character Rick Blaine, American, age 37 (as his papers read), when he speculates that, while he sits in Morocco, in America everyone sleeps: "I bet they're asleep in New York. I bet they're asleep all over America." Of course, that was in December 1941, the moment in which the movie was set, when America slept and the Japanese attacked Pearl Harbor. Rick, previously a mysterious, isolated, and cynical figure, wakes up to a sense of responsibility in the world not only by facing a past disappointment in love but also by embracing the fight against fascism (and its totalizing aims) when it confronts him in personal terms. Now, for America to awake, as Rick is awakening, is to become aware of difference and seemingly to engage in conflict. Spaces may be uniform, but people are not: "Of all the gin joints in all the towns in all the world, she walks into mine", he famously complains. However, the plot of *Casablanca* depends on the resolution of this rather ordinary conflict, resolving itself, as everyone knows, in the peculiarly overdetermined homosocial relationship of the American abroad, Rick (Humphrey Bogart), the American, and Captain Renault (Claude Rains), representative of the Vichy government in what will be, they decide, the beginning of a "beautiful [often read colonial] friendship", anticipating the similar alliance between Nellie Forbush and Emile de Becque in Rodgers and Hammerstein's *South Pacific* (1949). In *Casablanca* Renault suggests that he and Rick visit a French garrison in Brazzaville, a location that was to have further significance after 1944, when Brazzaville hosted a meeting of the Free French forces and representatives of France's African colonies, leading to the Brazzaville Declaration that redefined the relationship between France and its African colonies after the war.

If *Casablanca* is the quintessential pre-war (pro-war) movie, Williams's play *Camino Real*, the first draft of which was written in 1949, is a distinctly post-war and Cold War work; as such, it deliberately and directly responds to the former, critiquing its peculiar model of the American in exile, not only in geopolitical but also in theatrical terms, and in doing so represents a severely damaged democratic social space, like the woman charging down the aisle. *Camino Real* is a self-reflexively dramatic text that can illuminate the value of theatre, not just as a metaphor, but also as a cultural form that suggests ways of structuring and challenging modes of perceiving what we take to be America and American selves in relation to it. Williams said, "it was the first time on Broadway of which I know when actors ran down the aisles and went out into the audience" (2006: 166). It is also a problematic work, a failure in the box office, largely disparaged by critics, and regarded with ambivalence even by the author, who wrote of the 1953 opening, "I remember thinking that, although it may have been flawed, it surpassed its flaws" (167). I won't offer an apology for Williams's play, but, in reading Williams's Cold War work as an overt and detailed critique of and homage to the movie *Casablanca*, of the figure of the American in exile, of the Myth-and-Symbol school that, in the same decade, produced analogous mappings of the American landscape, and of the possibilities of theatrically re-imagining artistic and geopolitical borders, I argue that what have been read as the play's flaws and its ambivalence about literature (and literary characters) *in the world* also perform the cultural work prevalent in the late 1940s and early 1950s of trying to locate an American Mind simultaneously in a New World and in a global community. "More than any other work that I have done", Williams wrote, "this play has seemed to me like the construction of another world, a separate existence. Of course, it is nothing more nor less than my conception of the time and world that I live in" (2000a: 743). Like the Myth-and-Symbol school, Williams expresses his conception of his time and place through attempts to construct other worlds and other places. This quasi-exilic imagination is another version of the US nationalism of the era.

Many of the scholars of the generation that brought American Studies to its maturity in the 1940s and 1950s sought to discover a prior state of American experience whose importance was defined by the fact that it was lost, like Blanche Dubois's Belle Reve in *A Streetcar Named Desire*, a central and almost always pastoral myth of America – the vanished Eden or Virgin Land. At the same time, these scholars themselves felt increasingly exiled (in academia) from the burgeoning materialistic culture around them; hence the appeal of writers such as Henry James and Tennessee Williams, who also expressed forms of alienation from capitalism and the materialism that characterized both America and, increasingly, the world. In short, the disappointment of myth by fact, the failure of reality to live up to the ways in which it had been imagined came to dominate the way American literature was taught in universities. To *place* Williams in relation to the Myth-and-Symbol school of American Studies, while acknowledging his penchant for flight, for travel, even for exile, is to recognize that even while separate, he is also in the Cold War American scene.

A crucial and curiously neglected figure in the history of defining this field has been that of theatre. Henry James, whose imagination particularly appealed to critics of Williams's generation, imagined theatre and, by extension, America, as a "practice" in *The American Scene*, his autobiographical account of homecoming and exile, of coming to a home that was no longer a home.[4] Theatrical models are vital to understanding America. Dramatic metaphors pervade the discourse not only of but also about American Studies, from Gene Wise's "'Paradigm Dramas' in American Studies" to Nina Baym's "Melodramas of Beset Manhood".[5] There are numerous examples of the ready adoption of a theatrical vocabulary to render a sense of both unease and delight in the experience of national, continental, and social displacement from the Cold War period. To select one, the poet Elizabeth Bishop spent her life in the United States, in Canada, and, for 18 years (1951–69) in Brazil. The poem "Questions of Travel", from which I quote above, was written in Brazil, to which it makes specific reference, as other poems in her book of the same title make reference to Nova Scotia, to Venus, and to Mars. Bishop registers a sense of cosmic alienation that she derives in part from Pascal, yet she also articulates a different, more existential exilic condition (*"Or could Pascal have been not entirely right / about just sitting quietly in one's room?"*) that she describes as being at home in exile and in exile at home, and for which the hemispheric or geopolitical model is profoundly inadequate. Theatre, in this poem, becomes an operative metaphor for a liberal American subject, distinguished not by geographical location as such, but by existential quandary, ethical situation, and spectatorial vantage. "Should we have stayed at home and thought of here?" she writes. "Where should we be today? / Is it right to be watching strangers in a play / in this strangest of theatres?" Hers is a portable theatre, an ethically problematic and distinctly American way of establishing relations in worlds that are hers and yet not hers. She makes this point in the line "*Continent, city, country, society*", for society is not a *place* like continents, cities, or countries, though it is commonly hypostatized. I do not mean to suggest that America has not promoted forms of imperialism or produced imperial, as well as imperialized, subjects, but Bishop's honest sense of difference suggests the untidiness of explicitly theatrical spaces that we find often in twentieth-century American texts. Bishop critiques the tendency to romanticize the idea of the American in exile or, perhaps more accurately, she offers a vivid instance of the fact that the romance of exile in America is always already challenged. Like those of Williams and James, Bishop's attitudes toward the American in exile are often an ambivalent mixture, romantic and realistic. For her, the exiled subject is never free and unbounded, for (as James too recognized) she is always shaped, as spectator or actor, by the spatializing assumptions of community and difference.

*   *   *

Don Quixote, a key figure in, and the dreamer of, the play *Camino Real*, enters from the audience and breaches the proscenium, like the fat lady at the Strand.[6] In the play, he embodies the tension between the American mind and the world, Old World and New, myth and reality, which preoccupied the critics of Williams's generation. The setting of the play is almost exactly the same as that of the movie, a walled "tropical seaport" that is also paradoxically in the desert, an external space called in the play "Terra Incognita". In both, the city is the temporary abode of a bevy of international (and in Williams's case literary) refugees, waiting desperately for the plane (called in Williams, "The Fugitivo") that periodically lands, takes, off, and zooms overhead, but can hardly fit all of the exiles competing for a seat in order to depart. As Williams wrote in his Foreword, he and Elia Kazan "kept saying the word 'flight' to each other as if the play were merely an abstraction of the impulse to fly" (2000a: 744). Rick, the figure of the exile in *Casablanca*, must overcome his isolationism ("I stick my neck out for nobody") and commit himself to a cause; as the Fat Man says, "In these times, my dear Rick, isolationism is no longer an advisable foreign policy." Williams's "normal American", Kilroy, a former boxing champion, now a "fugitive Patsy" (780), finds a temporary traveling companion in Jacques Casanova, and, like Casanova, is now completely emasculated (his oversized heart precludes sex). He becomes literally a clown, with fright wig and a big crimson nose that lights up.

As the curtain goes up on the stage for *Camino Real*, down a central aisle of the theatre, bathed in blue light, comes Don Quixote de la Mancha, dressed like a "desert rat": "*As he enters the aisle he shouts, 'Hola!', in a cracked old voice*", and, in his progress down the aisle, he "*jostles the elbow of an aisle-sitter as he staggers with fatigue; he mumbles an apology*" (2000a: 749–50). He arrives at the foot of the steps to the forestage where he is greeted by guards, who "*lower black and white striped barrier gates as if the proscenium marked a frontier*". "Vien acquí", says the guard, paradoxically marking another kind of barrier or difference (linguistic and cultural) while announcing, even creating, presence – a temporal and spatial *here*. But papers are demanded which, unlike the identity papers in *Casablanca*, may serve as a reminder that Don Quixote is himself a meta-fictional construct exiled from his "home" text, and that he, the deluded reader of tales of knights errant, exists nowhere but in writing. His companion Sancho, however, announces "I know this place", for he has a map; it is the map of Cold War American Studies, demarcating the mythic landscape from the real, and it has writing on it, instructions like those the white-gloved author/usher offered in the Strand: "Look, it says here: 'Continue until you come to the square of a walled town which is the end of the Camino Real and the beginning of the Camino Real" (751). The question of pronunciation in a foreign language (and of the name of a non-domestic space) marks the space in which the native speaker becomes the linguistically amputated exile, but it also marks the ability to distort, shift the emphasis of pronunciation, as one of the peculiar powers of the exile. On 16 July 1945, the "real" Camino Real de Tierra Adentro (the Royal Road of the Interior), a *double entendre* the dream play implicitly exploits, was illuminated by the first atomic bomb which was detonated 35 miles away, and this historical event is incorporated into Williams's scene: "*Above the ancient wall that backs the set and the perimeter of mountains visible above the wall, are flickers of a white radiance as though daybreak were a white bird caught in a net and struggling to rise*" (749); it is not the last time the white radiance appears.

Beyond countless superficial references and allusions, the play revises significant details of the movie. For instance, the central role of the "Fat Man", clearly modeled on Sidney Greenstreet's character Ferrari in *Casablanca* (though named Gutman after Greenstreet's role in *The Maltese Falcon*) with his parrot Aurora (the name on the window of the Fat Man's establishment, "The Blue Parrot", in *Casablanca*), becomes the master of ceremonies in Williams's play. ("Fat Man" was also, as Williams and his audiences would have known, the code name of the atomic bomb dropped on Nagasaki.) Of course, in *The Maltese Falcon*, Greenstreet's fat Gutman is after the precious thing that stands for relationships between powerful countries and their colonies too, a pursuit that deeply corrupts Bogart's Sam Spade as well, as is rendered most vividly when, gazing at the falcon, his face distorts with greed. Williams is less interested in the appetite for the falcon – the imperial gaze – than in desire, the material appetite that cannot be transcended because it is all there ever is. Unlike the fat lady in the movie theatre, Williams's Fat Man is not an opportunistic capitalist but a fascist sympathizer, demiurge, and Mephistopheles, and his theatrical machinations are central to the corruption of the democratic social space symbolized by the open plaza whose well has run dry. David Savran reads the play as encouraging the creation of real, historical "sites of resistance", of which the theatre itself is to be the prime instance, a fulfillment of Williams's "utopian pledge" (174), and he incites us "to redeem the promise of Mr. Gutman in *Camino Real*: 'Revolution only needs good dreamers who remember their dreams'" (174). But this reading takes Gutman's line out of context. The character is not ecstatic but cynical. This "lordly fat man wearing a white linen suit" (Williams 2000a: 750), director of public diversions, imposer of martial law, and heartless owner of the Siete Mares – a hotel inhabited by transients – does not utter a promise. Rather, he has telephoned the Palace, and, speaking hurriedly into the receiver, he warns the Generalissimo, whom he calls "sweetheart", that dreams can cause harm to the state: "Revolution only needs good dreamers who remember their dreams, and the love of the people belongs safely only to you – their Generalissimo!" (761). This drama could take place in any port, as Williams is at pains to suggest: "The plaza [...] belongs to a tropical seaport that bears a confusing, but somehow harmonious, resemblance to such widely scattered ports as Tangiers, Havana, Vera Cruz, Casablanca, Shanghai, New Orleans" (749). *Camino Real* is certainly Williams's most *overtly* political play, but it is an anti-propagandistic politics of myths and symbols, its characters embodying the paradox of immortality, or timelessness "as time goes by", in a space that is both specific and universal. Literary figures, plucked from their home texts in which they are immortal, speak to a time and place that both are and are not "real". They are contingent and transcendent.

The representation of borders in *Camino Real* is best understood not in reference to Brechtian alienation-effects, but in relation to the visual realism of the movies, as depicted in the usher's account and the desire to transcend an oppositional structure that it prompts in the naïve spectator who plans to take a seat on the screen, as well as its basis in an economy of such violence that to resist consumption (of the film) is to receive a blow to the head from a pocketbook filled with gold. The fat lady hovers behind this play like the a-bomb whose glow lights the stage. In short, Williams offers a critique not exactly of totalitarianism – though Gutman supports the otherwise invisible totalitarian apparatus – but of a certain model of democratic social space and of American exceptionalism, the special essence that, ironically, can become universal, leveling difference, the emblem of which is the Gypsy's Daughter, Esmeralda, whom her mother sells each night but who regains her virginity with the moonrise.

The mechanical reproduction of virginity, like the redemption of former communists effaces the possibility of an original or true source of innocence. The literal heart of the play, the soldier Kilroy's *heart*, is compared to a baby's head, a core of innocence, but it is ultimately removed in a surgical operation. After it is discovered to be pure gold, it is tossed like a football and claimed as property of the State. Kilroy, the model American, like Don Quixote, is a dreamer, who through enacting the dialectical relationship between mind and reality, idealism and history, becomes another figure for a tradition of knight-errantry and, I want to argue, of American Studies, which became preoccupied with the disappointment of myth by the world and with a narrative of history in decline. As the Gypsy's loudspeaker knowingly blares in the play:

Do you feel yourself to be spiritually unprepared for the age of exploding atoms? Do you distrust the newspapers? Are you suspicious of governments? Have you arrived at the point on the Camino Real where the walls converge not in the distance but right under your nose? Does further progress appear impossible to you? Are you afraid of anything at all? Afraid of your heartbeat? Or the eyes of strangers! Afraid of breathing? Afraid of not breathing? Do you wish that things could be straight and simple again as they were in your childhood? Would you like to go back to Kindy Garten?

(Williams 2000a: 766–7)

This parodic description of typical post-war American anxieties suggests a position apart from either Marxian socialism or Cold War liberalism, but, as Kilroy listens, a prostitute picks his pocket, and he discovers that he needs some cash. Having explored the dangers of cynicism, the play expresses a desire to rescue the individual from the collective abstractions of the Left and of the Right. Although the sacrifice of Kilroy's heart in the end allows the dry fountain in the square to flow again and violets to bloom through the rocks, his departure with Don Quixote may remind us of Rick's with Captain Renault, who calls himself "just a corrupt French official". But Williams does not endorse *Casablanca*'s closure any more than he instantiates Savran's utopian liberationism, though it may be more accurate to say that he embraces both with the characteristic ambivalence of his Southern Episcopalian upbringing. Here too we can hear echoes of Bishop's poem, "must we dream our dreams and have them, too?" Dreaming and having are distinct, converging only in death, but they are also invariably related.

In Rodgers and Hammerstein's *South Pacific*, Americans dream of another kind of imaginary colonial place, Bali Hai, "their own special island", only to discover when they get there that it cannot be quite their own and that its being special is a feature of possessive projections that have been cultivated by indigenous people who are, themselves, not disinterested. A place that promises the fulfillment of desire, it beckons to the exiled sailors, who long, like the refugees on the Camino Real, to commandeer a boat and depart. But Bali Hai is also, like the Camino Real, an economic space, where an enterprising mother may sell her daughter to a handsome American soldier. If the prostitution is less overt in *South Pacific* than in *Camino Real*, it does not disguise the commodification of the young woman. Liat, who speaks no English, mimes "happy talk" with "traditional gestures" (337) in attracting Joe Cable ("You like? You buy?" her mother Bloody Mary urges the lieutenant), while in Williams's play, Esmeralda, the virginal whore, surprised by Kilroy's desire for talk as a standard feature of foreplay, discusses (incoherently) the power of the Yankee dollar and her complacency about "the class struggle" (2000a: 822). The dialogue between Esmeralda and Kilroy does not lead to revolution but highlights the pervasiveness of market forces and avoids the either/or choice between pragmatism and Marxism (e.g., "Oh, the Bolsheviskies, those nasty old things with whiskers!"), cultural and real politics, private and public affairs, capitalism and democracy, as well as reason and desire. The Camino Real is a space of passage, not a separate world of authenticity and personal freedom, as the contingency of the fictional, stage world and the commercial space of the audience, from which actors breach the fourth wall, also indicates.

Williams was not alone in imagining exile, the separation of self from home/land/country, as the necessary condition of *poetics* or *making*. This post-lapsarian vision of innocence contributed to a "positive and original sense of tragedy", as R. W. B. Lewis argued in 1955. "A century ago", writes Lewis, "the challenge to debate was an expressed belief in achieved human perfection, a return to primal perfection. Today the challenge comes rather from the expressed belief in achieved hopelessness" (9–10). Attention to theatrical genres and modes of performance is vital to understanding America, but theatre/performance studies also needs to attend to the rich tradition of literary-critical representations of America so as not to oversimplify this contentious and over-mapped field. American fiction and film of the post-war period continually represents the experience of trying to come home only to discover, as James Baldwin writes in *Giovanni's Room* (1956) "that home is not home anymore" (315). As the character Lord Byron says in Williams's play: "*Make voyages! – Attempt them!* – there's nothing else" (2000a: 797). Understood in this context, the exilic condition that Williams dramatizes can serve as a more expansive artistic paradigm than the inclusion-exclusion model that continues to characterize progressive historiography and, specifically, American theatre history.

*   *   *

Finally, I want to challenge hemispheric conceptions of US power by situating Williams's dramatization of exile, of America, and of theatricality in relation to post-colonial developments in North Africa and another figure of exile in *Camino Real*, the son of the Gypsy, Abdullah. In spite of the eclectic menagerie of the play's exiles, figures from literature (Don Quixote, Lord Byron, Marguerite), from film (Gutman), from history (Casanova), and generic exiles (the Gypsy), there is a peculiar sense of strangeness in the figure of the Muslim youth in a site that is supposedly not North African but North American.[7] (The Camino Real, which still exists, was first blazed in its entirety in 1598 by the Spanish in search of a direct route to the *tierra nueva* in the far north, and for 200 years would serve as the only link between New Mexico and the outside world.[8]) Although Williams's imaginative mappings of America represent his sense of proximity to Latin America, derived, as his *Memoirs* illustrate, from his own trips along the Camino Real across the border to Mexico, his many holidays in Cuba, and his home in Key West, his symbolic geographies suggest the inadequacy of a hemispheric way of imagining America and his place in it.

In *Cat on a Hot Tin Roof,* which was produced two years after *Camino Real* and set on the Mississippi Delta, Big Daddy, the Delta's biggest cotton planter, repeatedly positions his 28,000 acres in relation to the Valley Nile, references that resonate, in the context of Cold War history, with the United States promise in 1954 of 56 million dollars to aid in financing the construction of the Aswan High Dam in Egypt (to dam the Nile and prevent flooding of the valley), Gamal Abdul Nasser's Pan-Arab Nationalism, and the subsequent nationalization of the Suez Canal. The United States, Egypt, and the World Bank aimed at the protection of just those rich acres of farmland bordering the Valley Nile with which Big Daddy considers his plantation to be continuous. His conflation of the Valley Nile and his plantation on the Mississippi Delta subverts the geographical mythos of America prevalent in the 1940s and 1950s, specifically Smith's *Virgin Land*, Lewis's *American Adam*, and Marx's idea of American pastoral. In *Camino Real*, Esmeralda, Abdullah's sister, though prostituted by her Gypsy mother and her brother every night, becomes a virgin again and again. Williams's site-specific yet highly symbolic representations of America in *Camino Real* (1953), *Cat on A Hot Tin Roof* (1955), and his 1956 screenplay *Baby Doll* implicitly critique the myths of America propagated by New England-based scholars in American Studies in those years and also suggest (via the myth of the ever-new virgin) that United Stated exceptionalism and global colonial exploitation in fact draw on a common fund of justificatory symbols.

Williams's idiosyncratic regionalism, his rejection of Southern agrarianism in characters like Blanche Dubois and Big Daddy Pollitt, and his simultaneous subversion of Cold War strategies of global consolidation and containment gain clarity if considered in relation to his references to North Africa, which is not analogous to, but contiguous with, an American landscape, mapping America, in Elizabeth Bishop's terms, not only as a country, a continent, or a hemisphere, but also as a society. It is just after referring to his possession of "twenty-eight thousand acres of the richest land this side of the valley Nile" (2000b: 929) in act two, that Big Daddy asserts his humanity in a recollection of travel, exoticism, sex, and homecoming, and then learns from his son about the terminal illness that marks homecoming of any kind as false or at least impermanent:

> And then in Morocco, them Arabs, why, prostitution begins at four or five, that's no exaggeration, why, I remember one day in Marrakech, that old walled Arab city, I sat on a broken-down wall to have a cigar, it was fearful hot there and this Arab woman stood in the road and looked at me till I was embarrassed. [...] She had a naked child with her, a little naked girl with her, barely able to toddle, and after a while she set this child on the ground and give her a push and whispered something to her. [...] Jesus, it makes you sick t' remember a thing like this! It stuck out its hand and tried to unbutton my trousers!
>
> That child was not yet five! Can you believe me? Or do you think that I am making this up? I wint back to the hotel and said to Big Mama. Git packed! We're clearing out of this country [...].
>
> (930)

Big Daddy is embarrassed by very little. So it may seem a signal case of depravity that sends the Americans packing, but the play subverts this orientalist logic by representing Big Daddy's plantation as continuous with, not distinct from, the Valley Nile. Big Daddy's desire to believe that some boundary exists between the prostitution of a Moroccan child and forms of exploitation more familiar to him thus seems disingenuous. Dramatizing foreign affairs Williams recognizes a queer, destabilizing subtext that supplements the seductive and overtly masculine Cold War "doctrine of containment", associated with diplomat George F. Kennan's 1946 "Long Telegram" and 1947 "X-Article". The language of "containment", which Kennan intended to serve a specific, limited diplomatic purpose vis-à-vis Soviet power, was subsequently disseminated in ways that proved uncontainable, for example, connected with the Truman Doctrine that Kennan repudiated. "If, then, I was the author of a 'doctrine' of containment", Kennan later wrote, "I emphatically deny the paternity of any efforts to invoke that doctrine today in situations to which it has, and can have, no proper relevance" (387).

For Williams, sex is a global phenomenon that respects no borders. In bed one can be at home, though in exile. Out of bed, one may be exiled in one's own house, as Brick and Maggie find in *Cat*. Kilroy's exile in *Camino Real*, too, originates in his departure from the bed of his wife with whom he can no longer have sex. To go to bed with foreigners, with children, and particularly with foreign children, is to register a sense that one has all along been in exile and to renew, not only in *Camino Real* but also in most of his work, a paradoxically fallen virginity or corrupt innocence. Big Daddy's grandchildren, the "no neck monsters", and the Moroccan child prostitute are hardly emblems of innocence. As Stella shows in *Streetcar*, to fall is fortunate because desire is the essence of life. In *Baby Doll*, the foreigner Silva Vacarro crawls into Baby Doll's crib, implying that infant depravity must be acknowledged and even exploited. The "voluptuous" Baby Doll is one of many troubling (and troubled) figures of virginity.

In 1973 Williams traveled to Tangier where he was befriended by a Moroccan writer, Mohamed Choukri, who had traveled little but read much and to whom Williams appeared like a brother from another planet. Choukri's diary-like account of their brief relationship, translated from Arabic by their mutual friend Paul Bowles, devotes considerable space to the challenge of making Williams at home, finding him a place to live, and a boy to sleep with. In his record of their conversation, after Williams has asked his Moroccan friends to find him a handsome boy, Choukri says, "prostitution here still starts at the age of four, as Brick's father tells him" (36), identifying Williams's encounters with child prostitutes with Big Daddy's and subverting what seems the key assertion that grants Big Daddy moral status (his opposition to child prostitution). In this light it appears not only as the self-righteous indignation of paternalism and privilege but also of nationalist retreat ("Git packed! We're clearing out of this country"). The prospect of young Moroccans causes Williams to pack his bags not to depart but to come.

Williams's imagination is shaped by the notion of original sin, like that of the somewhat older Southern writers, Allen Tate and Robert Penn Warren. Unlike Tate and Warren, Williams never sought to achieve a coherent political position or even to be politically active. While he claimed an allegiance to socialism in his *Memoirs* and letters, he hardly lived his life by socialist tenets. Yet Williams's brand of humanism would be unfairly characterized as a quixotic retreat from political engagement. In 1950 he attended a Congress of Cultural Freedom conference in West Berlin (he and other delegates had to be transported across the Soviet blockade by American military aircraft), and his plays were produced in Europe as part of the American cultural offensive. Yet, like many dissidents of the 1940s and 1950s, Williams manifested an aversion to collective abstractions and messianic ideologies. His work is preoccupied with the (often unsuccessful) rescue of the individual, drawing on the tattered legacy of classical humanism which had come to resemble Don Quixote in rags. The energy of his plays arises from the tensions and contradictions of his time: democratic–elitist, national–international, optimistic–pessimistic, Old World–New World, rooted–exilic. Although he dramatized vivid local cultures, his artistic project often parodied the notion of innocence as a naïve form of regionalism, and he eschewed a vulgar literary nationalism. If the Mississippi is continuous with the Nile, he shows, America has never been a virgin land.

Like Robert Penn Warren, Williams saw that corruption was inseparable from the legacy of slavery, a legacy that also links the Mississippi with Africa. At the center of *Casablanca* is the black singer, Sam.[9] When the Fat Man asks Rick what he'll take for him. Rick says he doesn't "buy or sell human beings". Of course, as in *Casablanca*, in *Camino Real*, human beings are the "leading commodity", and those willing to traffic in them can make a fortune on the "Black Market". In the play's final moments the old European courtesan Marguerite, drawn from Dumas's *La Dame aux Camelias*, screams for Abdullah. He does not appear, indicating a new unresponsiveness to the European master. In ways that Williams could not have foreseen, the prospects of Abdullah – severely compromised by selling his sister for a "Yankee dollar" – would expand, or at least change, in the post-colonial 1950s, as they would for his historical counterparts in the *Valley Nile*, with the coming of a new world order that Frantz Fanon would characterize as inescapably interdependent, poverty-stricken, and violent: "The poets of negritude will not stop at the limits of the [African] continent. From America, black voices will take up the hymn with fuller unison" (213).[10]

Williams was not an activist, and, though he referred to himself as a "revolutionary", his revolutionary aims, "the discovery of a new social system" (2006: 94), were never clear and always attenuated. However, he both represents and implicitly questions the spatial and temporal assumptions of Cold War American Studies, drawn from the realm of international politics in which the United States was understood as an autonomous, circumscribed territory with a liberatory national history (Pease and Wiegman: 14). At the end of *Camino Real*, when Kilroy, whose regicidal name suggests his revolutionary heritage, walks off the stage arm in arm with Don Quixote, we may think back to Rick Blaine's exit with the *soi-disant* corrupt French official. Cold War Americans are in exile in the world, always already banished from Eden, where innocence was lost, sex was discovered, and there is no turning back to Kindy Garten.

Notes

1. Constitution and Bylaws of the American Studies Association: http://www
   .georgetown.edu / crossroads/AmericanStudiesAssn/about/asaconst2000.htm
   #article-1. The idea that the nation can serve as a unifying subject of study
   has been severely critiqued, and the institutionalization and funding of the
   emergent field of American Studies in the Cold War, as Paul Giles has shown,
   were inextricably related to state-sponsored "patriotic empire-building". The
   Displaced Persons Act of 25 June 1948 was the first expression of the US policy
   for admitting persons fleeing persecution.
2. See Edwards 2003: 70.
3. See *Casablanca (1942): The Shooting Script*. American Films Scripts Online.
4. James returned to America in 1904, after 23 years in Europe. In his chapter,
   "The Bowery and Thereabouts", he vividly records his sense of being out
   of place in the context of American theatricality: "There they all sat, the
   representatives of the races we have nothing 'in common' with, as naturally,
   as comfortably, as munchingly as if the theatre were their constant practice"
   (196).
5. By "paradigm dramas", Wise means that historical ideas should be understood "not as 'enveloped' by their surrounding climates, but rather as a
   sequence of dramatic acts – acts which play on wider cultural scenes, or historical stages" (296). Recent reassessments of Wise's thesis have emphasized
   the utopian (Mechling) and heterotopian (Pease and Wiegman) dimensions
   of his work. As Pease and Wiegman write, "The American studies in which
   Wise received his training named the academic site where the disciplines [...]
   were assigned the task of both studying and understanding the United States'
   geopolitical boundaries. Often referred to today as 'exceptionalist' in its conceptual orientation, the field operated by spatializing assumptions drawn
   from the realm of international politics in which the United States was
   represented as a circumscribed territory" (15–16).
6. Don Quixote was resurrected ten years later in the meta-theatrical *Man of La
   Mancha* and is a figure richly deserving of further attention in this historical
   and formal theatrical context.
7. Abdul, a figure in the film *Casablanca*, is the only named Muslim in the
   movie; he is the character who guards the door to Rick's private room. José
   Martí also wrote a patriotic verse drama titled *Abdala* in 1869 about a North
   African slave revolt and a "sincere" man who gives his life for his country,
   but Williams's Spanish was not strong, and it is doubtful that he knew the
   play, though many drafts were in circulation and he could have.
8. For a history of the Royal Road, see Douglas Preston and José Antonio
   Esquibel, *The Royal Road: El Camino Real from Mexico City to Santa Fe*,
   Albuquerque: University of New Mexico Press, 1998.
9. This figure is much discussed in the voluminous critical literature on the
   movie. See, in particular, Robert B. Ray's comparison of Rick and Sam to
   Huck and Jim in "The Culmination of the Hollywood Classic: *Casablanca*",
   in *A Certain Tendency of the Hollywood Cinema, 1930–1980*, Princeton, NJ:
   Princeton University Press, 1985, pp. 89–112.
10. Also see Brian T. Edwards, "Fanon's *al-Jaz"ir*, or Algeria translated", *Parallax*
    8.2 (April–June 2002): 99–115, which examines Fanon's Algerian writings and

the ways in which Fanon incorporates Arabic words and etymologies into his French prose, and "performs the disappearance of the local; and which underlines his more explicit argument about revolutionary communication". Edwards's discussion of what he calls the "globalization of language" pertains also to Williams's mode of employing particular forms of polylingualism in his plays, including the demarcating of the stage space and communication problems in *Camino Real* with English, Spanish, French, and Italian.

Works cited

American Studies Association. Constitution and Bylaws: http://www.georgetown .edu/crossroads/AmericanStudiesAssn/about/asaconst2000.htm.

Baldwin, James. *Giovanni's Room. Early Novels and Stories*. New York: The Library of America, 1999.

Baym, Nina. "Melodramas of Beset Manhood: How Theories of American fiction Exclude Women Authors", *American Quarterly* 33.2 (1981): 123–39.

Bishop, Elizabeth. *Questions of Travel*. New York: Farrar, Straus & Giroux, 1965.

Choukri, Mohamed. *Tennessee Williams in Tangier*. Trans. Paul Bowles. Santa Barbara, CA: Cadmus, 1979.

Edwards, Brian T. "Preposterous Encounters: Interrupting American Studies with (Post)Colonial, or *Casablanca* in the American Century", *Comparative Studies of South Asia, Africa and the Middle East* 23.1–2 (2003): 70–86.

———. "Fanon's *al-Jaza'ir*, or Algeria translated", *Parallax* 8.2 (April–June 2002): 99–115.

Epstein, Julius J. and Epstein, Philip G. *Casablanca (1942): The Shooting Script*. American Films Scripts Online. http://www.alexanderstreet4.com/cgi-bin/asp/ afso/getvolume.pl?FS000561-1# FS000561-1-1.

Fanon, Frantz. *The Wretched of the Earth*. Trans. Constance Farrington. New York: Grove, 1963.

Fisher, Philip. "Democratic Social Space: Whitman, Melville, and the Promise of American Transparency". In *The New American Studies: Essays from Representations*. Berkeley: University of California Press, 1991, pp. vi–xxii.

Giles, Paul. "Reconstructing American Studies: Transnational Paradoxes, Comparative Perspectives", *Journal of American Studies* 28 (December 1994): 335–58.

James, Henry. *The American Scene*. Bloomington: Indiana University Press, 1968.

Kennan, George F. *Memoirs, 1925–1950*. New York: Bantam Books, 1967.

Lewis, R. W. B. *The American Adam: Innocence, Tragedy, and Tradition in the Nineteenth Century*. Chicago: The University of Chicago Press, 1955.

Mechling, Jay. "Commentary". In *Locating American Studies: The Evolution of a Discipline*. Ed. Lucy Maddox. Baltimore, MD: Johns Hopkins University Press, 1999, pp. 211–14.

Pease, Donald E. and Wiegman, Robyn. "Futures". In *The Futures of American Studies*. Durham, NC: Duke University Press, 2002, pp. 1–42.

Rodgers, Richard and Hammerstein, Oscar II. In *South Pacific. Six Plays by Rodgers and Hammerstein*. New York: Random House, 1955, pp. 268–366.

Savran, David. *Communists, Cowboys, and Queers: The Politics of Masculinity in the Works of Arthur Miller and Tennessee Williams*. Minneapolis: University of Minnesota Press, 1992.

Smith, Henry Nash. 1950. *Virgin Land: The American West as Symbol and Myth.* Rpt. Cambridge, MA: Harvard University Press, 1978.

Williams, Tennessee. *Memoirs.* 1972. Rpt. New York: New Directions, 2006.

———. *Camino Real.* In *Plays 1937–1955.* New York: The Library of America, 2000a, pp. 741–844.

———. *Cat on a Hot Tin Roof.* In *Plays 1937–1955.* New York: The Library of America, 2000b, pp. 873–1008.

Wise, Gene. "'Paradigm Dramas' of American Studies: A Cultural and Institutional History of the Movement", *American Quarterly* 31.3 (1979): 293–337. http://www.jstor.org/sici?sici=00030678(1979)31% 3A3% 3C293% 3A% 22DIASA% 3E2.0.CO;2-U.

Part 3
America and the Other: From Representation to Intervention

8
Deterritorializing Voices: Staging the Middle East in American Theatre

Erith Jaffe-Berg
University of California, Riverside

> *How could movements of deterritorialization and processes of reter-*
> *ritorialization not be relative, always connected, caught up in one*
> *another? The orchid deterritorializes by forming an image, a tracing*
> *of a wasp; but the wasp reterritorializes on that image. The wasp is*
> *nevertheless deterritorialized, becoming a piece in the orchid's repro-*
> *ductive apparatus. But it reterritorializes the orchid by transporting its*
> *pollen. Wasp and orchid, as heterogeneous elements, form a rhizome.*
> Gilles Deleuze and Félix Guattari[1]

In their book *A Thousand Plateaus: Capitalism & Schizophrenia*, Gilles Deleuze and Félix Guattari describe a network of interlinking and mutual unfolding in which two entities, in their metaphor, the orchid and the wasp, define each other, reflecting their interconnectedness and mutual dependence. Deleuze and Guattari use the terms "deterritorialization" and "reterritorialization" within a complex continuum of relationality. The wasp and orchid suggest a nexus that has meaning only when wasp and orchid are considered in their rhizomatic relation to one another. On the one hand, the rhizome constitutes the dynamics between deterrito-rialization and reterritorialization in which orchid and wasp deceptively appear to form a hybrid. On the other hand, the terms used by Deleuze and Guattari, in relation to "territory", suggest conquest and coloniza-tion, which rule out hybridity as a possibility. A relational approach to cultural studies and an emphasis on hybridity in identity and culture gained currency in the 1990s initiated by Homi Bhabha, who argued for the connection between globalization and cultural hybridization.[2]

Writing along lines similar to Bhabha, theorists such as Seyla Benhabib, whose ideas gained ascendancy in scholarly circles and perhaps within

progressive circles of American broader culture in the 1990s, emphasize hybridization of culture and language as concomitant with the rise
of globalization.[3] Benhabib proposes that "cultures are formed through
complex dialogues and interactions with other cultures; that the boundaries of cultures are fluid, porous, and contested" (184). Rather than
singular, Benhabib suggests, culture is itself internally contested and
hybridic. She locates this contestation in various public spheres which
are themselves flexible and mobile, be they transnational contexts or
virtual spaces.

Benhabib's articulation of culture as internally riven cannot be further
from the stable notion of territory and the aggressive and imposing act
of deterritorializing through violence and war suggested in the terms of
Deleuze and Guattari's relational model. Whereas the ideas of a delib-
erative democracy (Benhabib) and cultural hybridity may have been
more salient in academic and intellectual circles as well as within critical media, post-9/11 these discourses have been challenged both in the
mainstream media and through the creation of protective and potentially putative government sectors, such as Homeland Security. Although
hybridity had in some ways appeared to supplant the discourse of deterritorialization in the 1990s (at least in progressive circles), the post-9/11
world and recent events suggests otherwise: a war in Iraq in 1990, 9/11, a
second war in Iraq in 2003, and even more recent wars in the Middle East
(Israel–Hezbollah, summer 2006; Israel–Hamas, winter 2008–09) bring
the notion of *territory* back to the fore. The trauma created by the immediate post-9/11 period challenged even progressive circles in the United
States. For example, the theorist Susan Buck-Morss argues for laying to
rest once and for all the discourse of territory which re-emerges in the
broader media as well as within academic institutions and intellectual
circles post-9/11.[4] Buck-Morss, among other intellectuals in the United
States, attempts to reconstitute a global public composed of Western and
Islamist thinkers in order to rethink cultural domination in all its forms.

Language figures in both Buck-Morss's conceptualization of a post-
9/11 public sphere as well as in Benhabib's understanding of the hybridic
and internally riven nature of culture. The enactment and performance
of language and multilingualism within culture indicates the dialogic
contestation of culture(s) in a very direct way. The primacy of language may be one reason why theatre has become an important site
to create a discursive forum around questions of territorialization in
the American context. The duration of a performance is relatively long
and continuous, allowing for a more sustained engagement with issues.

Theatre also creates a fleeting, but tangible, sense of community, if only for a few hours, whose temporary purpose is a collective engagement with issues.[5] Finally, the staging of language and multilingualism is one of the key devices in probing issues of both hybridity and territoriality in the context of America's response to the Middle Eastern conflicts.

In the most basic way, multilingualism in the theatre recreates real life situations in which different languages are spoken in a given context. In his exploration of theatrical multilingualism, Marvin Carlson points out: "A character speaking an alien language is a particularly clear example of this ongoing struggle in theatre between verisimilitude, the actual or apparent utilization of the real, and artistic convention, which adjusts and qualifies reality in the interests of consensual strategies of reception" (12).[6]

The theatre additionally deliberates the linguistic contestation inherent in these situations by amplifying the way in which contestation occurs and by questioning assumptions we make about the language speakers. In that way, multilingualism in theatre does more than merely reflect a given reality, it plays with the language, as well as with the interweaving of languages and the use of translation as elements of the performance. Carlson details the many ways in which multilingualism or heteroglossia, a term he borrows from Bakhtin, functions historically from the ancient to the post-colonial theatre. While multilingualism is often used in order to realistically reflect polyglot contexts, Carlson also demonstrates other uses it has, most notably, the theatre's incorporation of many languages to reflect on cultural outsiders. In this way, multilingual theatre reproduces the cultural dynamic in which some people are left outside of dominant cultural and global context. As Carlson reflects: "Surely nothing so immediately marks an outsider as representing another culture than the fact that he speaks an alien language, and the alien voice of the outsider has always been a major contributor to the heteroglossia in the theatre" (21). At the same time by using languages that the audience may not understand, multilingual theatre scathingly critiques cultural domination by challenging monolingual audiences or those who do not speak in the languages incorporated within the performance. In addition, multilingual plays foreground cultural translation and adaptation, key issues in post-colonial theatre:

It is doubtless a mark of the growing preoccupation with the functions of language and also of the more frequent and complex linguistic encounters in modern times that characters serving as translators are

> more often encountered on contemporary than on historical stages.
> Even more significant [...] is the attention often given to the opera-
> tions of translation, to its inadequacies, its compromises, and thus to
> its functioning as yet another voice in the play.
>
> (Carlson: 183)

Finally, Carlson indicates the connection between hybridity and heteroglossia as parallel strategies in addressing cultural diversity, where
heteroglossia "stages" the other in a variety of ways, ranging from cultural stereotyping to embodied deterritorialization and hybridity (110).

The American theatre has responded to the Middle Eastern conflicts in
a number of plays which create a discursive forum for audiences, playwrights, and production teams alike. However, within the context of
American theatre the audience is not homogenous; nor are the writers, directors, actors, designers, or technicians necessarily of the same
religious or linguistic background. How one "stages" the Middle East
is a question that literally begins with how one represents the bodies
and voices of its peoples as much as how one's own stance influences
the process. My use of the term "staging" suggests both representation
and "putting on", and the theatre exploits both. Depending on the
mis-en-scène and what language the actors are using, what gestures they
are incorporating and their use of *gestus* on stage, any expression can be
"staged" within a spectrum that ranges from the supposed "real" to the
"put on". The "put on" emphasizes both the artificiality of the gesture
and the construction based on cultural assumptions.[7] Unsurprisingly,
the very materiality of this staging of bodies and languages are central
issues in contemporary American representations of the Middle East.

In this chapter, I will study three plays that emerged in the years pre-
ceding 9/11, during 2001/2, and a few years afterwards, written largely
for American audiences. Historians caution that a full perspective on an
event can only be gained a couple of decades later, and clearly our perspective on this event will only broaden and sharpen with time. Yet,
the theatre itself is a response to the community and a vehicle for con-
structive engagement with current events. As such, there are compelling
aspects that are part of the dramaturgy of these three plays that already
raise questions about how 9/11 has influenced American theatre making.

The plays I will study all represent the cultures, conflicts, and politics of the Middle East and the Arab world. However, even to make that
statement involves ambiguities of category and meaning. The dictionary
provides an exact delineation of the geographical Middle East as: "the
countries of SW Asia and N Africa – usu. considered as including the

countries extending from Libya on the W to Afghanistan on the E".[8] However, the term "Middle East" is often generalized inaccurately and applied in a variety of ways, either in general reference to Arabic-speaking countries or to Muslim countries or even more simply to Arab countries. In addition, the "Arab World" is either narrowly defined as the "Semitic peoples of the Arabian Peninsula" or more broadly defined as the "Arabic speaking peoples".[9] Both phrases – "Middle East" as well as "the Arab World" – indicate the generalities through which the many peoples, religions, languages, and cultures of the region are filtered by others who do not live in the region, specifically by the West (an equally reductive term). Both terms, "Middle East" and "Arab World", globalize a vast region and its many peoples into a single, "apparently cohesive, imagined whole".[10] In this chapter, notwithstanding the obvious generalizing implicit in the continuously contested term "Middle East", I will myself occasionally fall into this usage as a shorthand reference to the region.[11]

The plays I will study: Karen Hartman's *Gum* (1999), Naomi Wallace's *In the Heart of America* (1996), and Kushner's *Homebody/Kabul* (2001, 2002, and 2004) are written from an American, non-Arab perspective and reflect a gamut of generational outlooks.[12] All of the playwrights make use of a similar "staging" strategy that in itself says much about how the theatre represents the cultures, conflicts, and politics of the Middle East and the Arab world. The playwrights use female characters who are either Middle Eastern or Arab-American. Interestingly, even in the cases when these plays do include Middle Eastern male characters, the central action still unfolds through the women's narratives. In all three plays, the women are the catalysts for the action, albeit to somewhat different ideological ends. In *Gum*, women's stories are the basis of the play, where male characters' perspectives are marginalized by the plot. However, the effect of the play's highlighting of Arab or Middle Eastern female characters inadvertently re-engages a colonizing configuration of the "other" as female and presents a largely reactionary politic.[13] In the play, the victimization of the female characters by their Arab and Muslim context reinscribes habitual ways of stereotyping the Arab and Muslim world as male-dominant, territorializing, and oppressive to its female inhabitants.

Both *In the Heart of America* and *Homebody/Kabul* develop different ways of breaking down the territorialization/deterritorialization binary by presenting attempts to figuratively "dwell" in the interstices of hybrid and exiled existences. In *In the Heart of America*, women's narratives and reconstituted events structure the play. Wallace's interweaving of two female narratives of war and loss suggests parallels between the contexts of Vietnam and the Middle East. The function of this inter-weaving underscores a commonality of experience shared by the female characters, but not by any of the men in the play. The dialogue forged between the two women unfolds a critique of territoriality and a commonality in their exilic and diasporic conditions. In *Homebody/Kabul* the Homebody's disappearance in Afghanistan occasions her daughter and husband's arrival in Kabul and her eventual surrogating by a Middle Eastern woman. The Middle Eastern character's cultural hybridity presents one of the more salient elements in the play because her expressions are largely multilingual.

In all three US-based stagings of the Middle East that I discuss here, language plays a central role in the dramaturgy. The monolingualism of *Gum* reverberates in its representation of the binarism of deterritorialization and reterritorialization. The multilingualism of the other two plays suggests a different rendering of the represented cultural dilemmas. In these two plays hybridity and exile become states of being in and of themselves and are enacted with multilingual expression. Hybridity more fully expresses the interstices between states of deterritorialization and reterritorialization, which are often marked by multiple "languagescapes" that contain English, Arabic, and other idioms. In the plays, cultural barriers are manifested in the barrier of language. In order to penetrate, challenge, or escape this barrier, the female characters often challenge language itself by their use of an explosive language and by multilingualism. This chapter will focus on how the three plays in question explore the binaries of deterritorialization and reterritorialization, and how these binaries relate to the notion of hybridity. To what extent do the plays reconfirm or challenge the binary and to what degree do they re-evoke, problematize, and/or redefine the notion of hybridity? And last but not least, how do linguistic choices from monolingualism to heteroglossia serve as devices to embody the ambiguities of deterritorialization and hybridity?

A monolingual viewing in *Gum*

Karen Hartman's *Gum* (1999) is an entirely monolingual text. The linguistic nature of *Gum* suggests the very different politics of the play which casts the Middle East in oppressive terms. At the same time, the play is quite internationalist in its implicit message of the interconnection of all women.[14] In that sense, though part of a discourse on the Middle East, *Gum* is also equally invested in a critique of female marginalization in society. Hartman claims to have been inspired to write the play after reading a newspaper article about Egypt, where purportedly a ban was placed on gum when it was suspected of being "laced" with drugs by some other country. As recounted by Todd London in the introduction to published versions of *Gum* (2003) and Hartman's one-act, *The Mother of Modern Censorship* (first performed in 1996 but published in the same 2003 edition as *Gum*):

> *Mother*, written first, was inspired by a *New York Times* article Karen brought to a workshop led by British playwright David Edgar at the Yale School of Drama in the mid-1990s. She had recently returned from a year of living in Jerusalem and traveling the Middle East, experiences that informed both the choice of newspaper clipping and the play that emerged. Accompanying the article was a picture of three veiled women, listening to Western pop music on headphones, searching for smut. Another article (also from Egypt) in the same paper nearly a year later, resulted in *Gum*. The story had a photo too: a pack of (allegedly aphrodisiac) gum with a picture of a (Spanish) fly on the box – "Splay" gum.
>
> (London: xiii)

In the play, gum has been forbidden in the "faraway" country in which two sisters, Rahmi and Lina, live. However, the sisters cannot resist the seduction of gum, as much as they cannot resist other "Western" exports they indulge in – music and the allure of sex. Predictably, the sisters succumb to the temptation and disobey the laws prohibiting gum chewing. They find sensual pleasure in the act: "I like the square bits of polished stone, [...]. The first bite cracks the coating and your mouth goes sweet and liquid all at once. You can hold it down and suck" (Hartman: 10).[15] This indulgence does not stop a perfume merchant, Inayat, from falling in love with Rahmi, whom he literally wins in negotiations with Rahmi's father, a figure who remains unseen on stage. Auntie brokers the marriage and suggests to us Rahmi is lucky to get any man willing to marry her because her wild proclivities are too much for the repressed society in which they live. However, Rahmi's fate is sealed when a young man appears and reveals Rahmi is no longer a virgin. The punishment is genital mutilation, complications from which lead to Rahmi's death.

As a consequence, Lina escapes from the "fictitious faraway country" in which the play is set is to a "new place", presumably in the West, by the end of the play. The "faraway country" which Hartman is careful to disguise, is nonetheless clearly an Islamic one, since the sisters wear a veil. And so, quite deliberately, Hartman has engaged the binarism of "East" and "West" in which "Islam" figures as an oppressive context as opposed to the "West" which is a liberating one. With this ending, the internationalism which, as I remarked earlier, initially inspires the play deteriorates into a Eurocentric, albeit feminist, critique of the Islamic world that reinstates the binarism of deterritorialization and reterritorialization. In the words of the critic Alisa Solomon in a review for the *Village Voice*: "Hartman's 'fictitious' country is patently Muslim – and, unfortunately, in the most Orientalist of ways. Every woman-suppressing aspect of any part of the East takes place in her primitive fantasy land: full veiling, genital mutilation as punishment, chattel marriages" (Solomon, "Heady": 2). This theatrical representation contrasts starkly with Islamist feminist contestations regarding Muslim women's political and social status. In the words of the feminist theorist Zillah Eisenstein: "The politicization of Muslim women in their struggle for rights is 'on their own terms, from their own understandings of what Islam means. They do not need "the" west for an assist' " (Buck-Morss: 49).

In the introduction to the published version of *Gum*, Todd London associates the fictional women with real women living in Afghanistan or Pakistan, although he knows that the initial inspiration was Egyptian women. This displacement of the action is symptomatic of how other critics locate the setting. For example, David Bogoslaw reviews the play assuming the reference is to Iran (Bogoslaw: 1). Where the play clearly plays with not having an absolute, clear reference, the assumptions made by critics and commentators reflect how little differentiation there is regarding "Arab" or "Islamic states". London, writing the introduction to the printed edition of the play post-9/11, in 2003, easily groups various Islamic states together when he writes:

> And so we are in faraway countries that fuse the fictitious and the real, the fabled and the factual. Time, though – and a publication date that nearly coincides with the first anniversary of the World Trade Center and Pentagon attacks, and the subsequent war on Afghanistan's Taliban regime – has tilted them back toward their newspaper roots. When I read *Gum* now, I can't help thinking of stadium executions of women in Afghanistan and the fatal penalties imposed on rape victims (or of rape used as a tribal penalty) in Pakistan. The image of veiled women with headphones now seems less like a humorous invention than an ironic discovery. Plays that two years ago had an air of exoticism about them now feel almost journalistic.
>
> (xiii–xiv).

For London, the obscurity of reference is not a problem. From his perspective, the women can be Afghani, Pakistani, or Egyptian, all are equally oppressed by the Islamic state, be it the Taliban regime, or the Pakistani government. In a post-9/11 world, the play reinforces these perceptions by representing the "Islamic world" as a site of oppression, without making clear delineations among different states and their treatment of women or about how class and religious subgroup affect the treatment of women.

Gum is dedicated to Maria Irene Fornès, and many of its scenes seem to recall aspects of Fornès's dramaturgy. Thus, Fornès's contrasting of long, monologue sequences with spurts of dialogue in which characters speak to each other in disjointed conversations is emulated in Hartman's writing. For example, in scene four Rahmi is seen reading a biology book in a way which recalls segments in which whole passages from Dante or from botanical texts are read in Fornès's *Abingdon Square*.

> RAHMI (*Reading*): A group of cells is like a group of men. They live collaboratively for the community. When a cell senses it is no longer of use to its larger organism, it kills itself. Programmed cell death, or apoptosis, is characteristic of healthy bodies. In this way each organism stays clean and alive.
> (*Imagining*)
> I am a fish swimming in tea.
> Bird flying over the fire.
> Turtle crawl out of the pot.
> With no sister at all.
>
> (22)

Hartman's play with free association here recalls Fornès's linguistic stylization in the way both use language metaphorically to signal the insipience of oppression to the point that it affects everything the characters say and do. However, within the cultural context of *Gum*, Hartman's choice of purposefully stilted language: "Bird flying over the fire/Turtle crawl out of the pot", orientalizes Rahmi's words. The orientalizing is further underscored by the monolingualism of the text. The stilted speech enacts the kind of "stage speech" that, as Carlson indicates, has been traditionally the way theatre has represented cultural other:

> The force of verisimilitude encourages the use of actual foreign languages on stage, while the necessity of adopting the raw material of life to the theatrical and social conventions of a particular public,

here including the language they speak, has resulted in a variety of
substitutions for or supplements to actual foreign speech.

(13)

The reproduction of the foreign speech in English indicates Hartman's
attempt to reflect the Middle Eastern context. But by using monolingualism, Hartman inadvertently filters the language through her own
assumptions about the represented culture and audience. To incorporate a monolingual scheme in a play about the Middle East written for a
US-based, contemporary audience is to ignore the probable heteroglossic
context of the production team and audience.

Gum is steeped in the assumptions of orientalism, not only in language but also through its setting, notably the description of an inner
courtyard, bathed by the light of the moon. In *Orientalism*, Edward Said
famously critiqued the false and romanticized view of the so-called Arab
East held by the West, exposing this image as a justification for Western colonialism and imperialism.[16] In this regard, the inability of the
play *Gum* to negotiate an internationalist call for feminist resistance to
oppression with a more nuanced and fair view of the Middle East is one
of its main faults. Or, in the words of the theatre critic David Bogoslaw:
"While we may be tempted to accept Ms. Hartman's view of women's
sexual desires as more or less universal, there are cultural nuances we
sense have been left out."[17] *Gum* was written for an audience whose
hyper-attention to the Middle East was still arguably nascent before 9/11.
However, as noted by Todd London in the introduction to the play, since
the play's publication in 2003, one cannot help but see it now through a
post-9/11 frame of reference. From this perspective, London accepts the
play's visions of women in the Middle East (confirming the conservative turn Buck-Morss rails against), whereas critics viewing its New York
premier in 1999 were far less forgiving. Ultimately, Hartman stages the
women in *Gum* as unfortunate Others who are either sacrificed in the East
or saved by the West. Hartman offers no critique that disturbs the reproduction of a cultural stereotype and a colonialist dynamic, confirming for
her audience the patronizing gaze of the West at the female inhabitants
of the "faraway" world depicted.

Decentered bodies: *In the Heart of America*

In contrast, Naomi Wallace's *In the Heart of America* offers an ambivalent
view of the "East" and "West" whose very distinction as good and bad
is contested in the play. By juxtaposing timeframes and fluidly weaving

between histories of war in Iraq and Vietnam, Wallace reveals generalities of war while attempting to avoid cultural generalizations about either context. Despite the fact that Wallace's work has had a history of uneasy reception in the United States,[18] that may be changing, as indicated by a number of productions of *In the Heart of America* projected for upcoming seasons.[19] One reason for this resurgent interest in the play has to do with the fact that though the play was about the Gulf War, it speaks equally to the current US war in Iraq.

The play constantly disrupts expectations as to what is center and "here" and what is peripheral by exchanging places fluidly throughout the sequence of events. The play follows the journey of Fairouz in search of her brother and her meeting with Craver, whom she believes to have been her brother's lover during the war. This plotline is non-linearly interspersed with flashbacks to her brother's own journey of self-discovery in the Middle East. Another parallel plot line is introduced by Lue Ming, the spirit of a Vietnamese woman whose daughter was killed in the War in Vietnam. Lue Ming's haunting search for her daughter's murderer literally "looms" over the play and is paralleled by Fairouz's search for her brother's missing body. Initially, it may seem that the play simply pits the American soldier as a White, Christian "oppressor". In fact, Fairouz's brother Remzi, the American soldier fighting in Iraq is a Palestinian-American whose patriotism remains unquestionable throughout the play. The play shows different approaches to the war within Palestinian-American communities through Remzi's sister, Fairouz, who opposes the war, and through Remzi, who remains steadfast in his alignment with the war effort, a central aspect of his determination to associate with America. The conflicting opinions about the tactics often associated with the Palestinian struggle are implicit in Remzi's confrontation with Fairouz which challenges her convictions while asserting his own struggles:

> Oh, martyrdom! Why don't you get out of the house and throw a few stones around here! You've got a big mouth, Fairouz, but your world is this small. I'm sick of being a hyphen: the Palestinian, the gap between Arab-American. There's room for me here. Where I have my friends.
>
> (Wallace: 95)

Remzi yearns for a definitive, non-hybridic identity, not a scattered one, as he says later in the play, but rooted, clearly associated with cause, flag, and country. Brother and sister find themselves ideologically at odds.

But the play proposes a conflicted while nuanced identification that is neither one nor the other. Considering that both Remzi and Fairouz are challenged by their circumstances – Fairouz has a limp and endures this disability amidst insults and abuse and Remzi is a gay, Arab-American man in the military – they offer complex versions of Palestinian-Americans. Arguably, Remzi and Fairouz reside in rhizomatic spaces between identities, to borrow from Deleuze and Guattari; they are neither stereotypical "Americans" nor "one kind" of Palestinians. Although the characters exemplify hybridity, as Palestinian-Americans living within two cultures and languages, their experience of hybridity is less than ideal. They are, to borrow from Remzi, "the gap between Arab-American". Since they cannot repatriate to Palestine, they are exilic by default – their hybrid identity is perhaps more a mark of where they cannot belong than a celebration of "rhizomatic nomadism". While the play offers a critique of hybridity, seen through Remzi's yearning not to be hyphenated, it never solves this dilemma for him. In similar ways, Fairouz challenges Remzi's deafness to his Palestinian cultural origin, but never fully resolves for herself (and for the audience) how she sees herself as a Palestinian-American whose exilic state prohibits her repatriation in Palestine.

Benhabib's articulation of culture as internally contested and the understanding of transnationalism as evoking complexity rather than binarism is rehearsed continuously in *In the Heart of America*. In writing about transnationalisms in the Middle Eastern context, the cultural theorist Ella Shohat has addressed the very complexity this play speaks to:

> Rather than pit a rotating chain of resisting communities against a Western dominant (a strategy that privileges the "West," if only as constant antagonist), we argue for stressing the horizontal and vertical links threading communities and histories together in a conflictual network.
>
> (133)[20]

In Wallace's play various "Americas" are reflected: there is the horrific scepter of "White America" personified by the killer Boxler, but equally, there is Craver, who yearns for and finds love with Remzi. There is also Fairouz and Remzi, as Palestinian-Americans in a deterritorialized world, engaged in a struggle to reclaim their identity (reterritorialize) in a changing dynamic that is sometimes painful.

Furthermore, for Wallace, chronology and history are much more interlaced than linear – war has no beginning or end, leaving people permanently wounded as it does. For that reason, Wallace enfolds a Vietnamese character, Lue Ming (who lost her daughter during the war in Vietnam), within the reality of the 1990s. In this way Wallace colludes different chronotopes, or time space realities, to borrow a Bakhtinian term. The Palestinian-American and the Vietnamese woman are both searching in the heart of America, where the play takes place: in the Kentucky motels where Fairouz comes looking for her brother, seeking information from Craver, and where Lue Ming appears looking for the soldier who murdered her daughter. War's "theatre" may be in the Middle East, but we bring it home, Wallace makes clear. Her writing is anchored in her own Kentucky backyard to which the world inadvertently comes. The juxtapositioning of Fairouz and Lue-Ming's search creates a theatrical chronotope that functions to link the journeys of the women, and their historic, cultural struggles. As much as this connectedness functions as a "utopian performative", the chronotope uniting the two women also suggests the disruptiveness and transience that is part of the transnational experience. Furthermore, since American soldiers appear both in the Vietnamese and in the Middle Eastern chronotopes of the play, Wallace suggests that hybridity also involves a degree of complicity – the American element within the hybridic unit in this case signals militarized force rather than the notion of intercultural community. In that sense hybridity is not simplistically celebrated in the play but deeply problematized, pointing out that hybrid or transnational identities and communities often emerge out of violence and rupture.

The thematic interweaving of characters and timeframes extends into the actual movement of the piece; there are many moments in which the bodies and gestures of one character are echoed by another character living a different reality. For instance, in the opening sequence Fairouz tells us that Remzi has a difficulty achieving balance, a metaphor for his biculturalism. Later, Remzi foresees his own death and makes Craver practice the fateful walk Remzi knows Craver will have to make towards his dead body. "Let's say I'm lying over there, dead as can be, and then you see it's me, from a distance. But you still have to walk over to my body to check it out. So, how would you walk?" (88). Wallace ends this scene with Remzi and Craver arm in arm, practicing walking. Their physical touch presents tremendous intimacy in the presence of the bodies together, at the same time foreshadowing the walk Craver will eventually have to make to Remzi's dead body. The final image of the men hand in hand is juxtaposed with the next image the audience senses in the fluidity Wallace creates between moments in her plays. In this linked scene Fairouz and Lue Ming are on stage together, connected, although their bodies do not touch.

> *Fairouz is also practicing a walk, in a similar, but different, motel room*
> FAIROUZ: Keep your chin in the air at all times. As though your chin has a string attached to it that is pulling it up.
> *(Lue Ming appears and walks in unison behind her, Fairouz doesn't notice her.)*
> No, a hook is better, a hook in your chin like a fish. Beauty lessons number seven: walking with grace.
> LUE MING: It's all a matter of balance.
>
> (90)

Their linking is symbolic, metaphoric and their co-presence on stage marks a theatricalized use of two different chronotopes in order to draw connection between the two places and times the characters live in.

In an article on Wallace's plays, Shannon Baley relates the Brechtian notion of *gestus* (through Elin Diamond's feminist explication) and Jill Dolan's idea of the utopian performative to Wallace's work:

> The utopian performative, as defined by Dolan, is not only something that happens on stage, propelled forcefully into being by the virtuosity of actors and directors, playwrights and dramaturges, designers and technicians, but a collaborative, "intersubjective," and affective event occurring among all present at a performance [...] Dolan notes that, contained in the collective effort of the utopian performative is a sense of "relief," a respite shared between performer and audience, cueing which "gestic moments of clarity" can occur.
>
> (239).[21]

Lue Ming's interjection, "It's all a matter of balance", which recalls Remzi's articulation of balance, can be seen as such a moment of the utopian performative. The poignancy of the previous walk taken by the two male lovers, one of whom is about to die, is relived in Fairouz's walk, while Lue Ming's move to partner with Fairouz, who would otherwise be alone, offers some sense of appeasement and balance.

Fairouz and Lue Ming's bodies and the gesture of walking metaphorically enact an image of the impossibility of living through adversity. These women's co-presence on stage also combines different chronotopes in a way which suggests Dolan's utopian performative, as explicated by Baley. The two bodies, though distinct, are nevertheless interrelated, and their struggles are given greater meaning when they echo in one and other. Rarely in the play do we ever see a body alone on stage. Usually, we have at least two and sometimes three bodies, inter-connecting, mutually defining each other's belonging with or exiled relation to another body. Thus, at every juncture of the performance, the fluidity of the bodies' movement – from distinct identities into ones which mirror, echo, or actually touch one another – suggests not only community but a global interconnection. In Baley's explanation: "Like Dolan's utopian performative, Wallace's bodies are anything but static: the body, a site of unmaking or remaking, is a place where, Wallace observes, 'it's possible to make a new vision' of oneself as well as a 'new vision of desire'" (241). In Baley's words the process of "unmaking or remaking" occasioned by the bodies' presence on stage corresponds to a kind of performative *gestus* that refers to the process of deterritorializing and reterritorializing in itself. Each character affects the other by hearing their story, allowing the character's remembrance of their past through a physical re-membering. All the while, the audience's relation to the characters, too, shifts from "us" and "them" to deep empathy for the stories unfolding on stage.

Another way in which Wallace explores the continuum of deterritori-alization and reterritorialization and the issue of hybridity is in language. Wallace's text is deeply dialogic and infused with Arabic as well as Vietnamese and English. Arguably, the use of more than one language within the play diminishes the total dominance of English and reinforces a sense of the author being implicit and complicit in the represented cul-tural dynamic. Rather than looking at the Other from a safe linguistic distance, as Hartman does, Wallace implicates herself in her staging of Vietnamese and Middle Eastern characters by inserting text in a language that is not her own, and over which she does not have full authorial control (some of the words are transliterated and others are left to the production team to devise). Although Vietnamese does not at first seem an obvious choice in a play about the war in the Middle East, the pres-ence of Vietnamese within the play's soundscape broadens the discourse beyond one specific war and shows the global reverberations and after-shocks of conflict. Wallace incorporates other languages in two salient ways – by either offering transliterations of Arabic within the text or by indicating, in stage directions, that Arabic or Vietnamese are to be used. For example, Wallace indicates in a stage direction that a *lullaby is to be sung in Vietnamese*, or *words are to be spoken in Arabic*. Such is the case when "*Lue Ming calls*: 'where are you/' *in Vietnamese*" and "*begins to sing a Vietnamese lullaby*" between scenes six and seven of act one (103).

The fact that Wallace does not always give the exact translation through transliterated text makes it necessary for the production to actually be active in addressing the languages in the text. The process of performance is thereby exploratory in the most fundamental way. The cast, director, and dramaturge will need to translate the text and in so doing they will come up with a translation unique to their production, since the translation process is not a one-to-one exact science. This is a struggle completely occluded from monolingual performative contexts such as *Gum*. Ambiguities of language, the inexactitudes of translation and the fact that there are certain words which exist differently in different languages surface through this process. Experientially, for the cast, the process of exploring another language can be in itself transformative, and it seems to me, Wallace is aware of this when she chooses to provide some text in transliteration and coaxes the production team to create some of the text on its own.

Like Vietnamese, Arabic is invoked throughout the text, as when Fairouz "(*Speaks in Arabic and then translates*). 'They'll kill him. The Yankees will kill him.' Silly old woman. She's all mixed up" (106). In this example, Fairouz recalls her mother's words, which we know to be prophetic. Since Fairouz first imitates her mother in Arabic and then translates for the audience, the audience finds truth located in the Arabic narrative. Here, Wallace is clearly shifting the exilic voice and creating audience identification with the Arabic voice. The audience also follows Remzi's journey from deterritorialization to a struggle for reterritorialization in his linguistic experience of Palestinian Arabic. At first Remzi rejects Arabic:

> REMZI: You're going to blame me that no one wants to marry a girl with a gimpy foot.
> FAIROUZ: My foot is deformed, but my cunt works just fine!
> REMZI: You have a mouth full of dirt, Sister. What is it you want from me?
> FAIROUZ: What I want? (*She speaks some angry lines to him in Arabic*)
> REMZI: Gibberish, Fairouz. Save it for the relatives.
> *(Fairouz speak another line of Arabic to him.)*
> I'm not a refugee. It's always somewhere else with you, always once removed. I am not scattered.
>
> (95)

Remzi is deaf to Arabic in this recollection of a conversation between brother and sister before Remzi enlisted. His deafness is like a cultural refusal of his Palestinian "scattered", exilic state. Arabic to him is the language of a refugee "always once removed", English is the language of the present. Bodily, physically, Fairouz almost succeeds in cajoling him gently into learning Arabic in a moment in which she recalls their mother:

> FAIROUZ: In the stores, for years, she'd lift me in her arms, and whisper in my ear: "Chubbes."
> REMZI: "Chubbes."
> FAIROUZ: And I would say: "Bread." "Halib," and I would say: "Milk."
> REMZI: "Halib."
>
> (94)

But the spell of this hypnotic, soothing recitation is broken. Only away from home, in the Saudi desert where Remzi should feel exiled from his American life is Remzi able to retrieve the language he was closed to. After returning from a visit to his father's village Al-Dawayima, near Hebron, where Remzi recounts he found only flattened earth, he visited a Palestinian refugee camp where he was greeted with food and language:

> REMZI: Tabun, Mawid. Zbib, trab ahmar, dibs
> *(Carver enters. He listens to Remzi a while.)*
> Maya, zir, foron.
> CRAVER: Sounds like you had a good leave.
> REMZI: Zbib, trab ahmar, dibs. Raisins. Red soil. Molasses.
>
> (106)

These words, which are at first opaque, are quickly translated: for instance, *"Zbib"*, for raisins, is repeated until the audience starts to become familiar with the sound. Just as Remzi is moving toward an exploration of his background, the audience is warming to the language. Craver, too, begins to feel his way around new sounds. When Remzi offers him a fig from the Palestinian camp, Craver responds, "Nice you remembered I existed. I think of the three, I'm the white fig variety. How do you say it?" Remzi responds: "Abiyad." "Yeah. Abiyad. (*Tastes a fig*) These are nasty" (107). Remzi responds:

> Eating is like walking. My sister taught me that. There's a balance involved. You have to eat the fig gently. As though it were made of the finest paper. (*Puts a fig in his own hand*) Look. I'll put the fig in my hand, and, without touching my hand, you pick it up. Gently.

(Craver starts to use his fingers, Remzi stops his hand.)
With your mouth. (*Beat*) Go on. See if you can do it.
(Craver leans down to Remzi's open hand and very carefully and very slowly lifts the fig from Remzi's hand. Craver holds the fig between his lips.)
Now take it into your mouth. Slowly.
(Remzi helps the fig inside Craver's mouth.)
Slowly. There ... Well. How does it taste now?

(Wallace: 107–8)

Significantly, the trust and desire implicit in the *gestus* of feeding Craver the fig references both nourishing the body and communicating through speech. The mouth is used in both taking in and letting out food and language. What begins as Craver embodying Remzi's language by mouthing the word *Abiyad* transforms into Craver letting that fig into his body. Language becomes transformative, as another experience Remzi had in the Palestinian camp reveals. There, he was greeted by a Palestinian woman who called him "'Yankee Palestina'" (107). In the exilic space of a refugee camp Remzi finds words to describe his state. What at first seems a bizarre hybrid, "Yankee Palestina", that could be taken as offensive, is actually profoundly true of Remzi. He is an American and a Palestinian, but somehow the term *Yankee*, conjuring an almost mythic image of the desired self rather than *American*, the reality, is appropriate here.

Although Wallace's plays sometimes receive mixed critical responses in the United States, this play has been published and certainly has received a number of stagings.[22] The resurgence of interest is due both to the open-ended nature of the writing, the playing with chronotopes, and the topicality of the play, given that the United States is still engaged in a war in Iraq. Yet, perhaps it is also the optimism the play ultimately provides for audiences and production teams alike. After all, when Fairouz speaks to Remzi in Arabic and he angrily retorts: "Gibberish, Fairouz. Save it for the relatives", we see this is only temporary. Just as for Remzi, what was gibberish soon turns into a language he not only remembers with but also connects himself to the present through, by using it with his lover, so Wallace seems to suggest, the audience's relationship to the characters presented on stage can shift. Wallace, too, wants us to understand, to associate, and to make sense by dismembering language and reconstituting it in our own minds and bodies. Baley describes this drive in Wallace's work as a "longing to witness, to see possibilities of another reality, a utopia in the midst of chaos" (240). Tony Kushner, who directed a production of the play at Long Wharf Theatre in New Haven, Connecticut in November of 1994, four months after its premiere in London at the Bush Theatre, provides another articulation on the back cover of Wallace's anthologized works. "Naomi Wallace commits the unpardonable sin of being partisan, and, the darkness and harshness of her work notwithstanding, outrageously optimistic. She seems to believe that the world can change. She certainly writes as if she intends to set it on fire."[23]

Multilingual "utopian performatives" in *Homebody/Kabul*

Tony Kushner's gestation of the social-political and interest in the Middle East extends beyond one play.[24] Among Kushner's plays *Homebody/Kabul* can be seen as an articulation of the inter-dynamics of deterritorialization and reterritorialization in a world still reeling from 9/11 and still in conflict. *Homebody/Kabul* was, in fact, written before the events of 9/11 and performed as a reading in London (1997) at the New York Theatre Workshop (December 2001). The play went through a series of consequential revisions, including the publication of two versions (2002, 2004) that significantly alter the tone of the play and change elements of one of the main characters.[25] In the play, the Afghani character Mahala voices a composite language made of French, Pashtun, and the Dewey decimal system. Kushner, whose intrigue with multilingualism as a form can be traced to his *Angels in America* (of which a key example is the American nurse's lapses into Hebrew), takes the multilingual female character a step further in *Homebody/Kabul*. Distinctive is Kushner's methodical attempt to use other languages not as pastiche but very deliberately, as interwoven text whose meaning is crucial to the play as a whole. For this reason, he provides transliteration of all of his text, where Wallace had indicated that the text is to be spoken in Vietnamese or Arabic. Kushner also offers full translations in the text copy of the play.

In *Hombebody/Kabul*, Kushner makes symbolic use of an exiled female character, but in his theatrical articulation, the character, Mahala, a transnational figure, reflects the two-sided nature of the deterritorializing/reterritorializing process. The exchange takes place literally in that a Western, English woman voyages to Taliban-ruled Afghanistan and disappears there, her absence complicated because we are never sure if she chose to disappear or was killed. That degree of uncertainty seems to be Kushner's way of challenging his audience's gut-level orientalist response to the usual trigger of a white, Western woman overtaken by the foreign and dangerous unknown. The exchange is two-sided because the mirror opposite of this migration occurs when Mahala, an Afghan female character, relocates to London where she begins to root herself anew. In fact, Homebody's daughter Priscilla and her husband Milton figuratively adopt Mahala, thereby replacing their missing mother and wife by a Middle-Eastern surrogate.[26] In this way, the play literally realizes the continuum between the deterritorialization and reterritorialization process, since for each woman the act of exile implies embedding herself in a new nexus. As Homebody says: "So lost; and also so familiar. The home (she makes the gesture) away from home. *Recognizable* ..." (2004: 27). More poignantly, for each woman, it is unclear whether she was not always occluded and deterritorialized from her "home" to begin with. The agoraphobic Homebody was already traumatized living in London and, as a professional and an intellectual, Mahala was disenfranchised by the Taliban in her homeland.

The two women are symbolically connected in other ways as well, notably in their penchant for unusual usage of language. Mahala is a trained librarian, herself invested in words whereas Homebody's logorrhea is evident in her use of obscure words, "I love [...] this guidebook. Its foxed unfingered pages. Forgotten words: 'Quizilbash,'"(2004: 27). In fact, Priscilla wryly comments about herself and her mother: "Daughter of a dictionary, me" (2004: 65). Priscilla says this regarding her mother Homebody, but the same may be said of her adopted mother, Mahala. On another level, both are explorers of the past through language – Homebody at first in her pursuit of an imaginary voyage to Afghanistan through a guidebook, and Mahala in her librarian's curiosity to uncover texts. Furthermore, both employ a kind of multilingualism, evident either in the dusty words Homebody interlaces with everyday speech or in Mahala's much more overt combination of English, French, Dari, and Arabic. In that regard, of both it can be said, as Priscilla says of Homebody, "she [...] demanded interpretation."

Mahala's multilingualism becomes increasingly central to Kushner's dramatic strategy in staging the Middle East. As M. Scott Phillips writes:

> Kushner plays upon the theme of language, which can be both a means toward understanding and an insurmountable barrier to meaningful human interaction. The most obvious device is Kushner's use of Dari and Arabic, translated for readers, but largely undecipherable in performance [...][27]

In fact, there are two multilingual models within the play that are embodied in Khwaja and in Mahala. Khwaja Aziz Mondanabosh, the Tajik poet who serves as Priscilla's guide and protector in Kabul, writes and speaks using Esperanto, an invented linguistic amalgam reflecting the utopian vision of its creator, the Polish Jew L. L. Zamenhoff in the late nineteenth-century. So, for example, Khwaja's question to Priscilla: "Çu vi parolas Esperanto? (Do you speak Esperanto?)" (2004: 47). Khwaja's naïve address displays Esperanto while serving to make Phillips's point about the impotence of Esperanto, given that the question remains unanswered. Instead of using Esperanto, Mahala communicates through her own amalgamation of languages in the ad hoc, code-switching common to multilingual speakers:

> The Quran these cannot read! Illiterates and child murderers, Nettoyeurs ethniques. Suray char, seporahyay noh (*Arabic: surah four, chapter nine*): "Let people fear the day when they leave small children behind them unprovided." (*In Dari, to Khwaja and Zai Garshi*) Wah too khodraw mard may donee? [and you call yourselves men?]"
>
> (2004: 87)

Mahala's use of Dari, Arabic, and French keeps the languages distinct and ensures that an audience member who speaks any one of these languages may be able to pick up that portion of her text. Though both characters are polyglot, each suggests a different model of multilingual communication, reflecting the politics of nineteenth-century Internationalism onto the 1990s idea of hybridity. Internationalism aims at world peace through cooperation among nations and the use of a universal second language, Esperanto, to be used in diplomacy, travel, and public relations. The utopian spirit inherent to Internationalism is embedded within the word "Esperanto", which literally means "one who hopes". The idea to create an invented, neutral language to be shared and used among peoples is nonetheless based on Western, Indo-European languages. If Internationalism and hybridity appear to be the same solution to multiculturalism and multilingualism, they are not. Internationalism and Esperanto evolved from a European context while hybridity and cosmopolitanism, at least in theory, suggest a more global world perspective. However, the claim to a more global perspective has recently been challenged by Pheng Cheah who critiques Homi Bhabha's ideas of hybridity as elitist and naïve in their suggestion that the privileges of hybridity and cosmopolitanism are shared by all global dwellers. Cheah argues that Bhabha's notion of hybridity as correlative with globalization ignores the rise of nationalism in parts of the "post-colonial South", instead focusing on metropolitan centers to which postcolonial, global dwellers arrive: "My point here is that Bhabha's picture of contemporary globalization is virulently postnational because he pays scant attention to those postcolonials for whom postnationalism through mobility is not an alternative" (93). In the play, Mahala's identity suggests a Cosmopolitan pluralism in her reflection of knowledge of both Western and Eastern traditions, her linguistic competence in a variety of languages and her eventual travels to different contexts. The consequences of each paradigm in the play are allegorical – Esperanto is ineffective, and Kushner is forced to abandon it as a theatrical device beyond a mere line, as opposed to the multilingual code-switching which is the main way in which the play unfolds, partnered with the monolingual use of English only. Symbolically too, there is the suggestion in the play that Khwaja may not actually survive, whereas Mahala survives and makes herself a new home in England, partially due to her nomadic linguistic capacity to reterritorialize. Theatrically, this is significant too, because Khwaja's Esperanto reflects on earlier dramatic attempts to create a kind of theatre version of Esperanto, especially the experiment undertaken by Tom Stoppard in his play *Dogg's Hamlet* (1971).[28]

Mahala's interlingualism is quite different from a utopian use of Esperanto because it can significantly alienate audience members who do not speak either of the languages she draws on, especially since her text is only partially translated into English by herself or Khwaja. This creates an intentional alienation in the audience which itself is political. Arguably, segments of the audience who speak Dari would respond to parts of the text spoken in that language (laugh, sigh, agree with Mahala), leaving monolingual audience members in the dark. This brings to mind Priscilla's observation regarding her mother, "she [...] demanded interpretation" and suggests that by extension, Mahala as a personification of Afghani women is not simply comprehensible but actually requires her audience to work a bit too. In fact, Mahala switches codes but rarely self-translates, while the function of the translator is reserved for the male character, Khwaja. In this way, Kushner reconfigures the historically gendered representation of the translator as female. The deliberate use of multilingualism through Mahala suggests a phenomenon that has recently been commented on by Marvin Carlson in two publications about multilingualism in theatre. As Carlson suggests, the use of many languages within a single play has been increasingly explored by theatre practitioners.[29] Mahala's language and her multilingualism is significant not only for creating babble on stage and in that sense disorienting the audience. Multilingualism can be a utopian performative in itself, a creation of a space that democratizes languages, making each "one of many". But also, as I have suggested, multilingualism opens up to audience members who themselves speak a variety of languages.

Mahala's command of so many languages makes her susceptible to the binarism inherent in deterritorialization and reterritorialization. She is culturally rooted in Islam (marked by her proficiency in Arabic,) but she does not define herself in the extreme version of Islam espoused by the Taliban. She is rooted in the grounds of Afghanistan and therefore speaks Pashto and Dari equally, even though they reflect different cultural streams within Afghanistan. And she speaks in French, the language of colonization as well as diplomacy. Although she is restricted in her ability to use English when she is first introduced, by the end of the play she has mastered that language, symbolic of reterritorialization, as well. In her ability to nomadically traverse the globe, Mahala is a theatrical embodiment of a transnational linguistic ideal, albeit a somewhat utopian one. But at the same time, her journey – linguistic and otherwise – suggests the difficulties inherent in transnationalism and in espousing hybridity as an ideal. The coincidental encounter with the Ceilings, which secures her passage out of Afghanistan, signals the one-way nature of hybridity that Pheng Cheah reminds us of. In her more idealistic presence, the same can be said about Mahala as Afghanistan: "Energies, languages traverse a passing-through place, a, an ... intersection" (2004: 127). Milton's description of linguistic intersection can also be understood as a definition of the state of deterritorialization which is itself, like a network, always in flux. Mahala's experience similarly rehearses nomadic passage and cultural collusion. For Mahala the move to England does not necessarily constitute a new identity of an English-woman, but a vehicle for survival. She, in fact, exists in the interstice in the process of deterritorialization and reterritorialization. Unlike the characters in Wallace's play, she is in the first generation of this reterritorialization process and her vehemence about the West, articulated in Afghanistan, is mitigated in her adoption by England. The ambivalences expressed by Remzi do not yet surface, for this expatriate still too enchanted by her new environs and dazed by her global traversal.

By beginning the journey to Afghanistan in the West, through an orientalizing guide book, Kushner invokes previous colonialist visions of Afghanistan. His dramaturgy suggests that in order to take new steps we must first retrace the steps of previous journeys, always mediated through the Western gaze. By book-ending the narrative – that began with Homebody – with Mahala, Kushner is attempting to disrupt the inevitability of this gaze. Mahala's multilingualism enacts the most visceral disruption Kushner can evoke. Unlike Wallace's introductions of other languages – in Vietnamese lullabies and in the tentative language acquisition scene between Remzi and Craver, Kushner thrusts the multi-lingualism of his play toward his audience in disquieting ways. The text of many of the characters, and especially Mahala's, is first uttered in violent sequence, loudly, in a near shout. Her words in French and Dari are presented as assaults at the audience who, most likely, remain baffled by them. Language, Kushner suggests, is a dangerous terrain. True bridges – cultural and linguistic – must be forged acknowledging this violence as a site of unmaking and making.

Conclusion

Mahala, like her counterparts in Hartman's *Gum* and Wallace's *In the Heart of America,* is a female protagonist used by Kushner as a dramatic surrogate for the exploration of cultural interchange. Despite the divergences among the playwrights' strategies, all make use of female figures as a device in their explorations of the cultures and conflicts of the Middle East and the Arab world. Processes of territorialization are rehearsed in all three plays, facilitated by the use of these female characters that are particularly susceptible to the interrelated processes of deterritorialization and reterritorialization. However, whereas this binarism remains true of Hartman's *Gum*, which presents the characters through a mono-lingual, orientalizing lens, the other two plays attempt to explore cultural collusion in terms that reflect both on problems and on possibilities of the notion of hybridity as an alternative to the binarism.

Wallace and Kushner's exploration of hybridity is premised in the multilingual make up of their texts. The multilingualism which is increasingly pronounced in Kushner's play, exemplifies a possibility of cultural hybridity by grafting together more than one language within a single expression or within a single communication context. Characters such as Kushner's Mahala code-switch exhaustively, cascading among languages and colluding cultures that are otherwise distinctive. Because multilingualism enables the writers to represent characters in hybridic states, Wallace and Kushner use it to suggest the interstices between the states of de- and reterritorialization without forcing their characters into one state or the other. In the dramas and within the performance space, hybridic identities suggest that transnationalism comes at a cost and is not only a multicultural ideal. For example, characters such as Remzi reflect on the pain and loss inherent in the notion of hyphen-ated identities. Mahala suffers because she embodies the internally riven nature of late twentieth-century Afghanistan. Furthermore, the audience is implicated in these hybridic dilemmas when the performance language is purposefully made only partly comprehensible. The writers very deliberately use language as a way to paradoxically occlude members of the audience from certain expressions, enforcing through this multilingual dramaturgy the stakes and politics of language. Last but not least, hybridized language or multilingualism enables not only the representation of a multilingual reality, but a shift in the positionality of the writer in relation to his or her subject. By incorporating different languages within the text, and in creating an internally hybridic text, the writers implicate themselves more directly within the language of the cultures they are trying to depict. Kushner and Wallace mediate their acts of staging by shifting away from a perspective that strictly reinforces the gaze towards the Other from a safe distance.

Notes

1. Deleuze and Guattari: 10.
2. See the anthology *Performing Hybridity*. In that collection Celeste Olalquiaga's "From Pastiche to Macaroni", presents a description of one person's individualized "cityspeak" as an exemplar of hybridity (Joseph and Fink: 171–6). See also *Unthinking Eurocentrism: Multiculturalism and the Media*, ed. Ella Shohat and Robert Stam. See Homi Bhabha, *The Location of Culture*, New York: Routledge, 1994. Recently, Pheng Cheah in his work *Inhuman Conditions on Cosmopolitanism and Human Rights* critiques theories of hybridity, referring to Bhabha's theories as "closet idealism" (90).
3. Benhabib: 185.
4. See Susan Buck-Morss, *Thinking Past Terror: Islamism and Critical Theory on the Left*.
5. This important aspect of theatre has recently resulted in a number of works. For examples, see Marvin Carlson, "Speaking in Tongues: Multiple Languages on the Modern Stage" (2001). In his book *Speaking in Tongues: Language at Play in the Theatre* (2006), Marvin Carlson also offers a sustained, historical account of the distinctiveness of theatrical uses of multilingualism. See also Erith Jaffe-Berg, "Babel, Babble and Multilingualism in Tony Kushner's Homebody/Kabul" (2007).
6. In the words of theatre critic Alisa Solomon, "the theatre is a place where the public practices and sharpens their critical attitude" (2006: 393).
7. Between representation and "put on" there is a range of possibilities that occur when the theatre confronts the Middle East as a subject and the plays I will refer to reflect this range of: staging, intervening, simulating, revising, and rehearsing.
8. This is also true of other playwrights, notably Yussef El Guindi, whose work I do not study here. El Guindi, writing as an Arab-American of Egyptian decent, wrote *Acts of Desire*, two one-acts staged together in November of 2005 at the Los Angeles Fountain Theatre. In those two one-acts El Guindi adapted stories

of the Egyptian writer Salwa Bakr. The stories and the plays present female characters at the heart of the drama. For a discussion of these and others of El Guindi's work, see the recent article by Misha Berson, "Yussef El Guindi: Are We Being Followed?" The use of the female character to signify the state is seen in a variety of Egyptian works, including the novels of Nobel laureate Naguib Mahfouz, and the plays of Farid Kamal. Two important Canadian plays written and performed in the 1990s and dealing with the Middle East are Guillermo Verdecchia's *A Line in the Sand* (1997) and Jason Sherman's *Reading Hebron* (1996). Both these plays use male figures as main characters, a curious contrast to the frequency in which female characters appear in the US-based plays. Separately, I have looked at a broader selection drawn from the influential work of Betty Shamieh who has become an important Arab-American voice that contrasts to some degree with the perspectives expressed by her non-Arab counterparts. I have presented my analysis of Betty Shamieh's play *The Black Eyed* at the Comparative Drama Conference, LA 2008. A publication based on that presentation as well as others of her plays, including *Roar* and *Chocolate in Heat* is forthcoming in an anthology, *Occupying the Stage*, ed. Masu'd Hamdan and Hala Kh. Nassar.

9. *Webster's New Collegiate Dictionary*: 1457.

10. For the two definitions, see the term "Arab" in *Webster's New Collegiate Dictionary*: 56.

11. Susan Ossman,*Places We Share: Migration, Subjectivity and Global Mobility*: 5. In this segment of her introduction, Ossman is referring to the ways in which the region is often configured.

12. The scholarly contestation of the terminology used is evident in the ways in which the recently formed research group on "Performance and Arab Worlds: Arab Migrations" describes their focus of study in the website of ASTR (the American Society for Theatre Research). "This on-going research group looks at performance by or about Arabs, whether that work originates within the traditionally defined Arab World, within the Arab Diaspora, or outside self-identified Arab communities. Since the formation and representation of Arab identities is central to this working session, it also examines performances that take up broader issues or concerns widely associated with Arab identity (whether accurately or not), such as Islam, the Middle East, "third-world" feminisms, terrorism, militancy, the civil society movement, and religious fundamentalisms": http://www.astr.org/.

13. Colonial configurations of women often pitted them ambivalently, as catalysts in the process of colonization, due to women's roles as translators of native languages, and betrayers of their culture. Post-colonial theatre revisits this role of woman translator/betrayer by introducing the possibility of silence within the scheme of colonization. Thus, a play such as Brian Friel's *Translations* (1984), concerned with the process of English colonization of Ireland, presents a female character who speaks in Gaelic and initially rejects the process of studying English. Similarly, Marianne Ackermann's play *L'Affaire Tartuffe*, investigating English struggles in Quebec, presents a female character whose resistance to colonization is marked by her silence. The "silent" witness or the woman who speaks in a language unknowable by the colonizer is a kind of counterpart to the Malinché, the mythic version of the historical figure Malintzín Tenepal, the Aztec woman who translated for the Spanish

conquistador Cortes and aided him in the process of taking over Aztec lands and conquering Mexico. For more on this figure, see Yvonne Yarbo-Bejarano, "Female Subject in Chicano Theatre".

14. Initially the play was workshopped in Connecticut, as a presentation for the Playwriting Program at the Yale School of Drama (1996). The play was premiered in Baltimore at Center Stage with Tim Vasen directing (1999) and had a run at the Magic Theatre in San Francisco (1999) directed by Jean Randich before premiering in New York by the Women's Project and Productions Theater where it was directed by Loretta Greco. The reviews are from the New York production which is listed in the play's introductory notes as the last production before the play was published by Theatre Communications Group in 2003.

15. In quoting from Hartman I have tried to maintain the spacing she provides in her text, since the text is written visually in a way which suggests the pauses and breaks an actor would make in performing the words.

16. Edward Said, *Orientalism*.

17. David Bogoslaw, "Eschewing *Gum*".

18. For more on this, see Shannon Baley's insightful article "Death and Desire, Apocalypse and Utopia".

19. A university production is slated for the play in the University of Hawaii and at the University of California, Riverside and the LA-based Son of Semele Ensemble holds a reading of the play in preparation for a staging in their season.

20. Here Ella Shohat writes about her and Robert Stram's strategy in *Unthinking Eurocentrism*.

21. Dolan's publication of *Utopia in Performance: Finding Hope at the Theater* has also returned to this idea of the Utopian Performative in greater detail.

22. Baley discusses negative Reviewers of Wallace's productions in the United States as opposed to the United Kingdom (246–7). However, Wallace's work received stage readings in LA's Son of Semele Ensemble, and a production of *In the Heart of America* in the 2006/7 year at the University of Hawaii.

23. Kushner on the back cover of Wallace's *In the Heart of America and Other Plays*.

24. In fact, he, Wallace, and Betty Shamieh traveled to Israel and the Palestinian territories together, as part of a group. Their travel experience is reported in *American Theatre* July/August of 2003. In addition, Kushner co-authored a book with Alisa Solomon culling different responses to the Israeli-Palestinian conflict. See *Wrestling with Zion*.

25. For a detailed discussion of the two versions and their different implications, see my article "Babel, Babble and Multilingualism".

26. Symbolism is rife in the names Kushner selects: Priscilla (in pursuit of her mother and as of yet unknowingly, of herself), Milton (English poet and author of *Paradise Lost*), Homebody (who becomes "at home" no matter where she is, due to her name), and Mahala (whose name may suggest in Arabic either tenderness or be related to *mahal,* meaning town, another designation of place).

27. M. Scott Phillips, "The Failure of History: Kushner's *Homebody/Kabul* and the Apocalyptic Context". Elsewhere, I have dialogued with Phillips's conclusion that Kushner uses multilingualism primarily to underscore its impotence and to reflect an apocalyptic view of reality. See my article in *Text & Presentation*.

28. Tom Stoppard, *Dogg's Hamlet*: 147. I am indebted to Silvija Jestrovic who first made me aware of this play and by extension, the linguistic experiment in it. In this play, Stoppard experiments with teaching the audience a shared language that is only viable for the duration of the performance. A word is first introduced with an obvious reference, for example, the play's use of the commonplace microphone text "testing, testing … one-two-three … "is supplanted by: "Breakfast, breakfast … sun-dock-trog." The experiment involves the possibility that the next time either of the four words *breakfast, sun, dock* or *trog* will be introduced, the audience will refer to their initial context and substitute their new rather than their English language meaning. Though not the same as Esperanto, "Dogg's language" as a performance device similarly plays with the teaching of a new, invented language. "Dogg's language" does not rely on previous linguistic knowledge or the cultural background of its audience, and in that sense is egalitarian.
29. See Carlson's article, "Speaking in Tongues: Multiple Languages on the Modern Stage": 15. This article was followed by a full-length book dedicated to contemporary and historical use of multilingualism in theatre, *Speaking in Tongues: Languages at Play in the Theatre.*

Works cited

Baley, Shannon. "Death and Desire, Apocalypse and Utopia: Feminist Gestus and the Utopian Performative in the Plays of Naomi Wallace", *Modern Drama* 47.2 (Summer 2004): 237–49.

Benhabib, Seyla. *The Claims of Culture: Equality and Diversity in the Global Era.* Princeton, NJ: Princeton University Press, 2002.

Berson, Misha. "Yussef El Guindi: Are We Being Followed?", *American Theatre* (January 2006). 50–53.

Bogoslaw, David. "Eschewing *Gum*" Offoffoff.com The Guide to Alternative New York: http://offoffoff.com/theater/1999/gum.php3. 10/28/1999 (accessed 17 August 2006).

Buck-Morss, Susan. *Thinking Past Terror Islamism and Critical Theory on the Left.* London and New York: Verso, 2003.

Carlson, Marvin. *Speaking in Tongues: Languages at Play in the Theatre.* Ann Arbor: University of Michigan Press, 2006.

———. "Speaking in Tongues: Multiple Languages on the Modern Stage", *Text & Presentation* 22 (2001): 1–16.

Cheah, Pheng. *Inhuman Conditions on Cosmopolitanism and Human Rights.* Cambridge, MA, and London: Harvard University Press, 2006.

Deleuze, Giles and Félix Guattari. *A Thousand Plateaus: Capitalism & Schizophrenia.* Minneapolis: University of Minnesota Press, 1987.

Dolan, Jill. *Utopia in Performance: Finding Hope at the Theater.* Ann Arbor: University of Michigan Press, 2005.

Hartman, Karen. *Gum.* New York: Theatre Communications Group, 2003.

Jaffe-Berg, Erith. "Babel, Babble and Multilingualism in Tony Kushner's *Homebody/Kabul*", *Text & Presentation* 2007 (2008): 77–92.

Joseph, May and Jennifer Natalya Fink, eds. *Performing Hybridity.* Minneapolis: University of Minnesota Press, 1999.

Kushner, Tony. *Homebody/Kabul*. Revised version. New York: Theatre Communications Group, 2004.

———. *Homebody/Kabul*. New York: Theatre Communications Group, 2002.

Kushner, Tony and Alisa Solomon. *Wrestling with Zion: Progressive Jewish-American Responses to the Israeli-Palestinian Conflict*. New York: Grove Press, 2003.

London, Todd. "Introduction". In Karen Hartman, *Gum, The Mother of Modern Censorship*, pp. xi–xiv.

Ossman, Susan. *Places We Share: Migration, Subjectivity and Global Mobility*. Lanham, MD: Lexington Books, 2007.

Phillips, M. Scott. "The Failure of History: Kushner's *Homebody/Kabul* and the Apocalyptic Context", *Modern Drama* 47.1 (Spring 2004): 1–20.

Said, Edward. *Orientalism*. New York: Pantheon Books, 1978.

Shohat, Ella and Robert Stam, eds. *Unthinking Eurocentrism: Multiculturalism and the Media*. London: Routledge, 1994.

Solomon, Alisa. "Artists in Perspective, In their Own Words: Alisa Solomon". In *The World of Theatre: Tradition and Innovation*. Ed. Mira Felner and Claudia Orenstein. Boston and New York: Pearson Editions, 2006, pp. 393–4.

———. "Heady Intentions: Salomé; Gum; The Clearing", in *The Village Voice* online: http://www.villagevoice.com/theater/9942,solomon,9259,11.html (accessed 8 August 2006, p. 2).

Stoppard,Tom. *Dogg's Hamlet* (1971). In *The Real Inspector Hound and Other Plays*. New York: Grove Press, 1993, pp. 139–74.

Wallace, Naomi. *In the Heart of America and Other Plays*. New York: Theatre Communications Group, 2001.

Webster's New Collegiate Dictionary. Springfield, MA: G. & C. Merriam, 1981.

Ybaro-Bejarano, Yvonne. "Female Subject in Chicano Theatre". In *Performing Feminisms: Feminist Critical Theory and Theatre*. Ed. Sue-Ellen Case. Baltimore, MD, and London: The Johns Hopkins University Press, 1990), pp. 131–49.

9
Current Trends in Arab-American Performance

Dalia Basiouny and Marvin Carlson
City University of New York

The history of the American nation is more deeply involved with the dynamics of immigration and exile than that of any other major modern nation. Founded by European exiles, it was profoundly altered by the waves of newcomers that arrived on its shores between 1850 and 1930. The effect of this new exile community was especially strongly felt in the major cities, to the extent that historian Alan Brinkley reports that in 1890 between 80 and 90 percent of the population of New York, Chicago, Milwaukee, and Detroit were immigrants. In contrast, London, the largest industrial city in Europe, was 94 percent native.[1] Since large urban centers are traditionally the sites of theatrical activity, it is hardly surprising that these same cities saw a flourishing of theatre among their exile communities during the late nineteenth century, helping the new immigrants to adjust to their changed circumstances and often at the same time providing a connection to their roots and traditions.

The first major immigration to the United States from the Arab world began in the 1880s, when many other immigrant communities, often with flourishing theatres in exile, were already established in cities like New York, Chicago, and Milwaukee. Here one could find substantial offerings in Yiddish, German, Swedish, Italian, French, Chinese, Polish, Hungarian, and Latvian, to name only some of the most prominent. The pioneer Arabic immigrants, mainly Syrian, Lebanese, and Palestinians fleeing from the economic and political hardships of the late Ottoman Empire, were mostly men who began as peddlers and gradually became small shopkeepers, too few and too scattered to really form ethnic communities.

That development occurred around the turn of the century when Arab women immigrants began to arrive and distinct communities, largely

Syrian, formed in cities like New York, Boston, and Chicago. Within these communities, as in other and earlier immigrant communities, theatre was developed. The pattern of these early theatre offerings closely followed that of other exile theatres in America. Most of the early examples of such theatre were performed in the home language, here Arabic, and most sought to connect the community to its roots in the homeland by presenting plays about Arabic history and culture. Later, Arab-Americans presented farces about living in the new country, using comedy to explore the cultural challenges facing the immigrants. Most of these plays were amateur community-based performances, a tradition that continued all through the twentieth century.

During the past few years, however, both the cultural situation of the Arab-American community and the theatre written and performed by Arab-Americans have changed dramatically. After 9/11 and the American responses to it, Arabs were no longer invisible. They were thrust into 'negative' visibility through the consistent portrayal in the mainstream media of Arabs, Muslims, and Middle Easterners as the enemy. In response to 9/11, the current wars in Iraq, Palestine, and Afghanistan, and their repercussions locally and globally, Arab-American artists started to form groups and networks to support each other, work together, and create platforms for their work to be seen both by fellow Arab Americans and by a more general public. Thus a very different role was created for Arab-American theatre. Plays were now developed to explore and express the hybrid identities of this community in these new and tension-filled circumstances, and also to present to non-Arab audiences a more accurate picture of this community and of the tensions in its various homelands than was available in the often biased and uninformed mainstream media.

This chapter will present an overview of this new Arab-American theatre and performance, presenting a brief introduction to the major figures and most significant works in terms of cultural and identity exploration, and indicating how and why the theatre has become such a significant part of the cultural self-expression of this community in recent years. One of the most interesting and perhaps surprising features of the current flowering of Arab-American theatre and performance is that a great majority of the artists involved are women. There are male performers, and a few male writers, but the dominant voice is a female one. Thus, even on this most basic level, current Arab-American theatre and performance is working to present a more accurate picture of Arab-American culture by contradicting the standard Western stereotype, according to which Arab women are widely if not universally oppressed and not allowed any voice or outlet for expression within Arabic culture. In fact, within the Arab world there are many important women authors, although they are most commonly writers of novels. Nehad Selaiha, a woman who is the best known and most respected theatre critic in Egypt and indeed in the Arab world, has suggested that this is probably due to the fact that creating theatre involves a more public life than the normal housewife can manage.[2] It is thus highly significant that Arab-American women are finding a strong voice in the diaspora.

The focus of this chapter will thus be upon the women artists who at present form the most important and visible part of the Arab-American performance community. Before discussing their contributions, however, and in order to provide a more complete picture, we will provide a brief overview of the contributions of current Arab-American male performers and authors. Perhaps the most prolific of these is the Egyptian-American playwright Yussef El Guindi, who has written a number of radio plays and adapted some short stories into plays. He served as the literary manager of Golden Thread Productions in Seattle, an organization dedicated to theatre that explores Middle East cultures and identities as represented throughout the world. His best-known play, *Back of the Throat* (2006), dealing with the disastrous effects of racial profiling, has had successful runs in several major cities in the United States.

A few words also should be devoted to the work of the Nibras Group, a group of six Arab-American artists, four women, including the artistic director Ms Chehlaoui, and two men, who created their own version of a docudrama based on interviews for their production *Sajjil*, a project begun just a few weeks before 9/11 but taking on a new urgency after that. In their quest for a clearer sense of identity, the group interviewed Americans and Arab-Americans seeking responses to the question, "What does it mean to be Arab?" The play was first presented at the International Fringe Festival in New York in 2002, and various versions of this play were offered during the following years in New York and elsewhere representing Arab-Americans and other Americans attempting to discover the associations of this cultural construct.

The most extensive representation of the Arab-American male artists' work has been offered by the Arab-American Comedy Festival, started in 2003 by stand-up comedians Dean Obeidallah and Maysoon Zayed, who began to attract attention in the wake of 9/11. The festival seeks to provide an alternative to the misrepresentations of Arab-Americans so common in contemporary films and on stage. As the festival developed, it attracted established artists like Yussef el Guindi, Aron Kader and

Ronnie Khalil and encouraged new talents like Amer Zahr and Najla Said. Although the emphasis in the festival has remained upon skits and stand-up comedy routines, it has also provided opportunities to show excerpts from full-length plays, both by women dramatists like Betty Shamieh, Kathryn Haddad, and Liena Rizkallah, all of whom will be considered in more detail presently, and also by male dramatists such as Obeidallah with *Now a Word from our Sponsors* (2005). Longer plays by male dramatists often remained in the stand-up tradition, being composed basically of a series of skits. On the other hand, resent work of Arab-American women dramatists has not only been more extensive but also more varied in its approaches and content. To that body of work we will now turn.

Plays by Arab-American women are not purely a post-9/11 phenomenon. These were already appearing in the 1990s, such as Faiza Shereen's *The Country Within* (1991) and Etel Adnan's *Like A Xmas Tree* (1998). In the first years of the twenty-first century theatre by Arab-American women blossomed, especially in New York City, which saw the works of writers and performers Heather Raffo, Betty Shamieh, Leila Buck, Elmaz Abi Nader, Soha Al Jurf, Rania Khalil, Kathryn Haddad, Lena Rizkallah, and Mayson Zayed. The theatre works of these artists vary in style, form, and production values; some are autobiographical solo performances, some stand-up comedy, others are based on interviews, and some are play texts that are published and performed.

The majority of the plays and performances of these artists deal in one way or another with the negotiations of being Arab in America today. This is certainly true of the work of one of the most widely produced of this generation of Arab-American dramatists, Betty Shamieh, all of whose plays have had readings and performances in a number of major cities in the United States. Shamieh's first play, *Chocolate in Heat*, is a series of monologues about growing up Arab in America, performed by two actors, a male and a female (performed by Shamieh herself in the first production, at the New York International Fringe Festival in 2003). The play's six monologues, primarily dealing with the fictional Harvard student Aisha Hagger, whose experiences to some extent echo those of the author, created a mosaic of the expectations, frustrations, successes, and the negotiations of living between two cultures. The production is organized around an FBI report on this "suspicious" Arab-American. Her second play, *Roar*, depicts a Palestinian-American couple who are successful business owners and their teenage daughter's dream of becoming a singer in the United States. Their "normal" life is disturbed by the arrival of the wife's sister, who was forced to leave Kuwait as a result of the 1991 war, and an old flame between the sister and the husband is reignited. Though the play's focus is the love triangle which becomes more complicated when the husband's brother reveals his feelings for the wife, this play brings to the American stage some pivotal moments in the Palestinian struggle, like Black September, offering the American audience a taste of the diasporic condition of Palestinians' lives in their multiple exiles.

Shamieh's most recent work, *The Black Eyed,* was presented as part of the 2007–08 season of the New York Theatre Workshop, one of the leading Off-Broadway theatres. This, somewhat in the style of Caryl Churchill's *Top Girls,* depicts four women from across the ages – the Biblical Delilah, Tamam from the age of the Crusaders, Aiesha, a contemporary Palestinian martyr, and a contemporary female architect from an Arabic background – who meet in the afterlife on a common quest to find martyred friends and lovers whose souls apparently reside in some other part of the afterworld. As they discuss their own struggles and those of the ones they are seeking, they reveal various aspects of the effects of political and sexual oppression that women have suffered in Palestine through the ages. Eventually a Palestinian American architect emerges as the most recent figure to become involved in this ongoing struggle and in fact to die in a plane hijacked by Arab terrorists whose language she, as an American, cannot speak.

Egyptian-American Rania Khalil's short solo performance *Flag Piece* is probably the most unconventional of the recent works by Arab American dramatists, being presented entirely without words. It is a response of an Arab-American woman to the flag displays and patriotic fervor following 9/11. In it, a Muslim-attired woman salutes a small American flag as it flies high over her head, then eventually moves the flag close to her face to cover her eyes, then the flag covers her mouth acting as a veil to silence her. At the end of the piece the pole goes through her face, pushing her lips and deforming her face, with its head forcing one of her eyelids to open. Khalil first performed this piece – during the intense period of flag displaying – in New York in various galleries and centers of performance such as Xanadu, Tribes, Patrias, the Knitting Factory, and the Judson Church, and has continued to perform it at various arts festivals and universities in the United States and abroad. Its graphic presentation of the oppression felt especially by Arab-Americans after 9/11 to demonstrate their commitment to patriotic ideals has proven extremely powerful.

Lebanese-American Rizkallah's *Layla's Sahra* presents the preparations for the wedding of Layla by her Lebanese family, who live in Brooklyn,

Figure 9.1   Sami Metwassi and Waleed Zeitar in Kathryn Haddad's *With Love From Ramallah* (Comedy Festival 2004) directed by Omar Metwally. Photo by Memo Zack.

New York. Layla is the first in her family to marry a non-Arab, and the play presents cultural differences among the members of the two families. *With Love From Ramallah* (Figure 9.1), written by Palestinian-American Kathryn Haddad, discusses the problems of assimilation and the challenges of immigration and occupation as experienced by a pair of separated lovers, one in Minneapolis in the United States while his beloved is in Ramallah, in Palestine.

During the rise of the feminist theatre movement in America, autobiographical solo performances became a particularly popular medium for women theatre and performance artists, particularly for the exploration of the forces that encourage or discourage the formation of identity. Not surprisingly, a number of Arab-American women performers, for whom questions of identity are of particular importance, have followed the first generation of American feminist performance artists in turning to this theatrical form. Among the artists particularly associated with this approach are Soha Al Jurf, Leila Buck, and Elmaz Abi Nader.

Soha Al Jurf is a Palestinian-American playwright and performance artist, born in Nablus, Palestine, and raised in Iowa City. In her late twenties, Al Jurf was struck by the lack of representation of the Muslim, Palestinian-American woman's voice on stage, and as a result, she decided to write her story as a performance piece. During the early stages of writing this piece, which she called *Pressing Beyond In Between* (first presented at the Theaters Against War Festival in New York City in 2003), her aunt was killed in Palestine, and this incident became the central focus of the performance.

Al Jurf performed *Pressing Beyond In Between* in different versions, in festivals, colleges and regional theatres, after which she decided to live in Palestine for one year, to connect with her roots. Upon her return to the United States, she wrote other dramatic pieces, but she also continued to perform and develop *Pressing Beyond In Between*. In its most recent form (2006), the play starts in the near past, then moves backwards to some significant moments of her childhood, visiting her relatives in Palestine at ages 5 and 12, then moves forward to the moment of the aunt's death and what follows it. In *Pressing Beyond In Between* the performer enacts each section of the play as if it is happening in the present moment, then she offers a commentary on it. After enacting segments of her life as they happened (or as she chooses to present them), the writer/performer then offers a commentary on them from her current perspective, shifting from being the main character sharing her autobiographical narrative to being a guide to the audience, helping them to have insights into her world, how her mind worked as a child, how she felt in a particular situation, or how her family reacted to her. Every performance concludes with a talkback session, allowing the audience to ask for more details about either the personal or political dimensions of the piece.

Leila Buck's one woman performance *ISite* has many similarities to *Pressing Beyond In Between*. Buck, who is Lebanese-American, spent part of her childhood in Arab countries, thanks to her American father's diplomatic posts. She wrote the early drafts of *ISite* in 1998, and later expanded the play and started touring with it. Since 9/11, hoping to further better understanding of Arabs, Buck has performed her piece at many festivals, colleges and conferences, mainly in the United States but also in

France, Belgium, Canada, Finland, and China. Like Al Jurf she follows the play with a talkback with the audience, and sometimes uses her performance as part of workshops about diversity and living between two cultures. The talkbacks take place immediately after the performance and are announced in advance. Usually most of the audience remains, and the questions are much more frequently about the performer's views on the current Middle Eastern situation and possible courses of action there than on details of the performance text itself. Buck feels that this suggests a strong need on the part of her audiences to find out more about this part of the world than they can through the conventional media presentations and that Arab-American artists, with a foot in both cultures, can play an important role in responding to this interest and need.

ISite is structured as a journey of the artist into her past, where she visits some of her formative moments as a child and young adult. The play is divided into 16 short scenes, varying in length from a few lines to a few pages. This voyage is clearly indicated by the titles of the first and last scenes; "Take off" and "Touching Ground". The journey starts before the writer/performer is born, since the first line of the performance is "I took my first international flight in the womb." This short first scene ends with the question that sets the play in motion, "But where is home?", and the performance can be seen as an attempt to answer that question, for the artist and for all those with hybrid parents who feel suspended between two cultures.

The final scene returns to this question and to a location of the playwright's childhood, on a beach, where writer/performer comes to recognize the ocean as the unifying element she has been seeking, becoming a metaphor for the performer herself. The expression of this gives an idea of Buck's poetic style:

> Sometimes I feel like the ocean – (She steps into the pool, holding its *sides as she crouches there.*) It's touching so many shores at once that forms the shape of whom I am. [...] We all take our shape from the lands we touch. That's what home is I guess – where you make contact with the earth.[3]

The play ends with the performer carrying her suitcase, indicating her diasporic condition, yet finding a sense of home through her identification with the all-encompassing ocean.

An interesting blend of documentary and autobiographical performance may be seen in Elmaz Abi Nader's play *32 Mohammeds* (2004). Abi Nader is a second generation Lebanese-American writer of poetry, memoirs, fiction, and drama, all concerned with issues of immigration, immigrant communities, and how women's lives are affected by dislocation, loss, and the extreme changes of conditions. She has performed her plays in colleges, art centers, and theatres in the United States and overseas. Her play *Country of My Origin*[4] (1997) is in an autobiographical documentary mode, telling the stories of three generations of Arab women from the same family. Act one recounts the struggles of a Lebanese woman, raising her two daughters on her own, en route to the United States; act two follows one of the daughters, a young Lebanese woman who has spent most of her life in the United States on her way back to Lebanon to marry her cousin, and act three describes the life of the playwright at age 7 while living in a small coal-mining town in Pennsylvania.

While *Country of My Origin* involves family stories, Abi Nader's *32 Mohammeds* is an unusual blending of other peoples' stories with her own story, mixing documentary theatre with autobiographical performance. *32 Mohammeds* traces the writer's journey to the Arab world, where in her first day teaching a class in Helwan University in Cairo, she finds that among her 80 students there are 32 men named Mohammed. This is not surprising, as the name of the prophet Mohammed is the most popular name in countries of Islamic faith. She wonders about the connection between these Mohammeds and others who carry the same name; the prophet Mohammed, Mohammed Ali, Elijah Mohammed, and most centrally various Mohammeds who were killed in the first two months of the Intifada. Thus her autobiographical experience as an Arab-American teaching in Egypt provides an introduction and frame presenting the stories of the Palestinian Mohammeds, whom she relates back to the students in her class.

Although *32 Mohammeds* provides an extreme example of such blending, most autobiographical performance mixes to some extent the life story of the author with other life stories that have an actual or thematic relationship with her own. This not only provides the artist with an emotional grounding for the work, but provides an extra kind of authenticity for audiences, who are often informed of this dimension either directly by the artist in the performance or in talkback or indirectly through publicity or program notes. An important part of current exilic Arab-American performance, however, deals entirely with non-autobiographical material, the life stories of others collected, arranged, and presented, often in the form of a solo performance, by the artist. One of the best known contemporary Arab-American performances, Heather Raffo's *Nine Parts of Desire* (Figure 9.2), is an excellent example of this approach.

Figure 9.2 Heather Raffo in *9 Parts of Desire* directed by Joanna Settle. Photograph by Irene Young.

Raffo began her project by doing research on the Iraqi artist Al Attar, who had been killed by an American air raid in June of 1993, a few months before Raffo visited her father's land. In a manner somewhat similar to the process of the American *Laramie Project*, where the Tectonic Theater Project members investigated the life and death of Matthew Shepard by interviewing people who knew him, and others who knew about his death,[5] Raffo began to collect material about the artist, interviewing a number of women whose stories appear in *Nine Parts of Desire*.

The play's main character, "Lyal", is inspired by the artist Al Attar, while the other eight characters are women activists, artists, doctors, housewives, mothers, teenagers, mourners, and lovers. Unlike the creators of the *Laramie Project*, Raffo does not reproduce her interviews with these figures verbatim, but instead creates a collage of the lives of these women, in which their stories are intertwined to give the audience an insider's look into the lives of these ordinary, yet exceptional Iraqi women. The play was first performed in August 2003, at the Traverse Theatre, Edinburgh. It later moved to the Bush Theatre in London. It was next developed and performed as a reading at the Public Theatre in New York as part of their New Work Now Festival in the Spring of 2004.

Its New York premiere was in October of that year at the Manhattan Ensemble Theater, where it ran for nine sold-out months.

The playwright/performer's position as a researcher in Iraq is unusual because of her exile status: she is both an insider and outsider to the culture. She is related by blood to her father's family members, most of whom live in Iraq. At the same time, she is American-born and raised and does not speak their language. The insider/outsider position allows Raffo access to meet Iraqis in their homes, and be part of the normal daily life of a household, while at the same time giving her the freedom to remain above the details of daily life, registering the cultural contradictions, nuances of existence, and the different styles of speech. *Nine Parts of Desire* is thus not primarily an exploration of the artist's own "in-between-ness" as an Iraqi American, though it is created from the perspective allowed by the double consciousness and double identity created by that in-between-ness, simultaneously inside and outside the society she is presenting. In addition, one character in this play, the American, provides a kind of embedded autobiographical section in this otherwise largely documentary project.

The American is an Iraqi-American young woman living in New York City, who follows the war coverage on television in the hope of getting information about her family, while suffering over the mass graves, the Abu Ghraib prison scandal, and the American public's reaction to the war. In her apartment she repeats, like a prayer, the names of the Iraqis with whom she feels a close kinship. It is clear that this character represents Heather Raffo's own feelings and experiences. Through the words of the American, the playwright makes allusions to her own family history, her frustrations at the war, and uses her cousins' names as a prayer.

Thus within a wide range of dramatic genres, from stand-up routines and solo performance, through documentary theatre to conventional drama, in conventional theatres and through the ongoing work of the Comedy Festival, a generation of talented and dedicated young Arab-American artists are currently making a significant contribution to the American theatre. The majority of these artists, as we have seen, are women, and surely one of the most striking features of contemporary Arab-American performance is the extent to which it is dominated by women, and especially by solo women performers. The tradition they are following is an old one, using the theatre as a means of exploring and expressing the tensions and formations of identity of one of America's many multicultural communities, but their work has a particular importance and urgency at a time when the non-American cultures to which they are intimately connected are the subject of such widespread suspicion and misunderstanding. Their work has a therapeutic and educative dimension for themselves and their community, but it has even more widespread therapeutic and educative work to do in the American culture within which it is created.

Notes

1. Brinkley: 489.
2. Selaiha: 439.
3. From the unpublished manuscript of the play.
4. This play was presented at the Kennedy Center's "Arabesque: Arts of the Modern World" in March 2009, directed by Dalia Basiouny.
5. Matthew Shepard was an openly gay university student beaten and left for dead near Laramie, Wyoming, in 1998, focusing national attention on hate crimes.

Works cited

Al Jurf, Soha. *Pressing Beyond In Between*. Unpublished MS.
Brinkley, Alan. *An Unfinished Nation: A Concise History of the American People*. New York: Knopf, 1993.
Buck, Leila. *Isite*. Unpublished MS.
Nader, Elmaz Abi. *32 Mohammeds*. Unpublished MS.
———. *Country of My Origin*. Unpublished MS.
Raffo, Heather. *9 Parts of Desire*. New York: Dramatists Play Service, 2006.
Selaiha, Nehad. *The Egyptian Theatre: Plays and Playwrights*. Cairo, n.d.
Shemieh, Betty. *The Black Eyed*. Unpublished MS.
———. *Chocolate in Heat*. Unpublished MS.

10

"We know you're not Somalia": Radical Performance and Canadian-American Exile in *Ali & Ali and the aXes of Evil*[1]

Jerry Wasserman
University of British Columbia

"Are you ready Mogadishu? Butt out your cigars and wipe the buckets of sweat from your really black black brows, put your stumps and prostheses together and give a GREAT BIG CLASH OF CIVILIZATIONS WELCOME TO ALI AND ALI!" (Youssef, Verdecchia and Chai: 11–12). The opening lines of *The Adventures of Ali & Ali and the aXes of Evil* by Canadians Marcus Youssef, Guillermo Verdecchia, and Camyar Chai neatly package grotesque orientalist images of third-world abjection and suffering together with the rhetoric of the War on Terror and the clichés of commodified Western pop culture. A brutally funny metatheatrical satire, the play ridicules in equal measure the American response to 9/11 and Canada's own hypocritical embeddedness in the ideology and misadventures of the new American imperium. But the play's setting is not Mogadishu. "We know you're not Somalia", Middle Eastern exiles Ali and Ali admit to the audience. "We know where we are" (12). Where they are is within the "utopian cartographies" of Guillermo Gómez-Peña's Fourth World, "a conceptual place where the indigenous inhabitants of the Americas meet with the deterritorialized peoples, the immigrants, and the exiles" (Gómez-Peña 1996: 6, 245). It is at one and the same time a Canadian theatre, a refugee camp – *"a vaguely tent-like structure [… with] laundry (socks, some underwear) drying on the set"* (Youssef, Verdecchia and Chai: 11) – and that border zone on the margins of American imperial power where Canadian politics and Canadian theatre are always already engaged.

In the production directed by Verdecchia that has played across Canada since 2004 and had its American premiere in Seattle in 2007,

Iranian-Canadian Chai and Egyptian-Canadian Youssef portray Ali Hakim and Ali Ababwa, two stateless, entrepreneurial asylum seekers from war-ravaged Agraba, a fictional Middle Eastern country (home of Disney's Aladdin) resembling both Iraq and Iran. In the original production and published script – many elements of which have been altered or updated for subsequent remounts to reflect local conditions and current events – they put on a cabaret for their Canadian audience in hopes of acquiring official refugee status. Constantly interrupted by the outraged Scottish-Canadian theatre manager who has contracted them to perform "an ethnic family drama that offers you a window into [Canada's] cultural diversity yet resonates with universal themes" (49), Ali and Ali instead perform an outrageous critique of American policies and politicians that includes a shadow play of Donald Rumsfeld (in later productions Barack Obama) masturbating to a fantasy of Hillary Clinton, and a puppet show in which Semi-Colin Powell tells President Dubya, "I ain't no mothafuckin' office boy" (74). The two Alis invade the audience searching for weapons of mass destruction (the infamous aXes of Evil) and Osama bin Laden makes an appearance as a corporate sponsor "for the poor and downtrodden members of Canada's artistic community" (114). At the same time the Alis engage the audience in complex comic challenges to Canadians' smug illusions about their own multiculturalism and geopolitical positioning.

Invoking the historically ambivalent position of Canada and Canadian theatre on the margins of American economic, military, and cultural power, the play enacts a series of hilarious and not-so-funny political lessons, mock-physical confrontations with the audience, and emotional engagements with the plight of real-life refugees and victims of statist violence. Re-embodying the Canadian nation and its national cross-border gaze in brown, diasporic performing bodies, it provides fertile terrain, in Homi Bhabha's familiar formulation, "for elaborating strategies of selfhood – singular or communal – that initiate new signs of identity, and innovative sites of collaboration, and contestation" (1–2). Yan Haiping reformulates Bhabha's privileged liminal space as a "trans-nation": "a material space of alternative temporality, where new alliances and forms of citizenry as flexible social solidarity become tangible" (241). *Ali & Ali* aspires to a version of Yan's performative transnation "where the dialectic between the performer and the spectator is brought forth as a focus for imagining a complex shifting of the socially given positionality of all those present and involved", and "where desires for alternative political community and human solidarity precipitate into choices to join the action to make such community and to actualize such solidarity" (Yan: 242). Optimistic without being naïve, in both its ambitious aim to change the world through theatre and the means it uses to do so, the play offers up a "radical performance [that] can insinuate pathologies of hope" (Kershaw: 26).

The racial profiling that followed in the aftermath of the 9/11 attacks provided the impetus for the play. As men of Middle Eastern origin with suspicious names and appearances, Youssef and Chai felt uncomfortable and sometimes frightened for themselves and their young families. Residents of Vancouver and co-directors of the city's neworld theatre,[2] they were invited by Vancouver's Canadian Broadcasting Corporation (CBC) radio affiliate to provide multicultural Canadian commentaries on their post-9/11 experiences. In response Youssef and Chai wrote a series of five-minute satirical sketches in which they appeared in the comic personae of refugees Ali and Ali. (Ali Hakim is the name of the stage-ethnic peddler in Richard Rodgers and Oscar Hammerstein II's 1943 musical, *Oklahoma!*) After the invasion of Iraq they expanded the skits into a stage play with help from Verdecchia, who at the time was artistic director of Toronto's Cahoots Theatre Projects. The play came together in about a year, co-produced in Vancouver, Toronto, Montreal, Edmonton, Seattle, and a number of smaller west coast communities by neworld and Cahoots, both companies with mandates to reflect their communities' extraordinary cultural diversity.

The politics of the play and its creation owe much to the historically vexed relationship between Canada and the United States as reflected in so many facets of Canadian life and creative arts, including theatre. But they also owe a great deal to the particular border-dwelling, internationalist perspectives of the three individual artists, whose insider/outsider relationship to the North American experience is increasingly typical of a Canadian theatrical community beginning to embrace its own growing diversity. Youssef is the Canadian-born son of an Egyptian father and an American mother; Chai and Verdecchia immigrated to Canada as children from Iran and Argentina respectively. All three are products of Canadian theatre-school training, and all have dedicated a good part of their work in the theatre to exploring their own and Canada's hybrid relationships to the rest of the world, especially the Middle East. *The Adventures of Ali & Ali and the aXes of Evil* emerged out of a web of previous collaborations among the three.

With Verdecchia as director and Youssef and Chai in the cast, they first collaborated in the 1995 production of Verdecchia and Youssef's co-authored *A Line in the Sand* for Vancouver's New Play Centre, a play and production that anticipate much of the rest of their work. Referencing a notorious 1993 incident in which a local boy was tortured and murdered by Canadian soldiers on a UN mission in Somalia, *A Line in the Sand* tells the naturalistic story of a Canadian soldier in Qatar during Operation Desert Storm in 1990. He murders a Palestinian teenager (played by Chai) after they get involved in a homosexual relationship. Act two in the original production (relegated to an appendix in the published text) provides political meta-commentary that explodes the naturalism. Interviewed by an aggressive Vancouver Caucasian actor using his real name, Youssef talks about writing the play and being a self-identified "Arab" in North America. He critiques "the fundamental hypocrisy at the heart of" the Gulf War, didactically providing facts ("Saddam Hussein was a Western ally for many years"), statistics ("150,000 Iraqis were killed and 300,000 wounded. American casualties were 146"), and revelations of Canadian complicity: for example, McGill University's research for Fuel Air Explosives, "a whole new generation of conventional weaponry designed to reproduce the effects of nuclear weapons" (104–05). At the same time the interviewer challenges the increasingly defensive Marcus about his personal credentials and agenda: "you sound to me like a totally assimilated, enculturated young North American. A perfectly average, if somewhat over-privileged, maybe a bit fucked up, but entirely North American. Just where do you get off calling yourself Arab? Preaching to me about the Gulf War?" (119).

This kind of metatheatre works on multiple levels. It provides a forum for direct antiwar agitprop: the Gulf War is "a scam. A pack of lies. A criminal act of monumental proportions" (Verdecchia and Youssef :104). It makes transparent the playwrights' political agenda, self-consciously questions its legitimacy, and anticipates (and thereby helps defuse) the audience's potential antipathy to the political message. The technique also enlists the audience in what Joanne Tompkins, borrowing Bhabha's term, calls the "spectacular resistance" of post-colonial metatheatre: a "dislocation of text and subtext and dominant paradigm [...] the splitting (and multiplication) of the gaze" (Tompkins: 49). Mimicking the kind of aggressive right-wing interview found on CNN or Fox News, it returns the audience to the fictive text with a subversive awareness of the dominant paradigm through which events such as those the play fictionalizes are normatively filtered before they reach us.

The *Ali & Ali* triumvirate's geopolitical engagement emerged again in the late 1990s when Chai wrote and performed *I Am Your Spy* (unpublished),a play about Israeli nuclear scientist Mordechai Vanunu who was imprisoned for revealing the existence of his country's nuclear arsenal. *I Am Your Spy* was dramaturged by Verdecchia, the major impetus behind the combination of aggressive political attack and politically self-conscious self-interrogation that characterizes the work of the trio. Verdecchia first came to public attention in 1990 with *The Noam Chomsky Lectures*, which he co-wrote and performed with Toronto director Daniel Brooks. The play is indeed a lecture, illustrated with slides; the published text concludes with 24 pages of footnotes and a four-page bibliography. Brooks and Verdecchia, playing themselves, present Chomsky's argument that North American media collude with big business and the imperialist policies of their governments to manufacture consent. The opening slide quotes Chomsky's *Necessary Illusions*: "Citizens of the democratic countries should undertake a course of intellectual self-defense to protect themselves from manipulation and control" (Brooks and Verdecchia: 11). Teaching that course, as it were, Brooks and Verdecchia aim to free us from our ideological blinders by first making us aware of them. Comically and sometimes brutally, they illustrate the collusion of business, government, and media in regard to the shaping of North American public opinion about US policies in Central America and the Gulf War, Israel's actions in the Middle East, and Canadian involvement in various international atrocities. "[T]he real Canadian traditions are quiet complicity and hypocritical moral posturing", the play argues. Far from being the nation of peacekeepers that Canadians, reinforced by their mainstream press and politicians, believe themselves to be, "this nation of quiet diplomats, of peacekeepers, is in fact a nation of quiet profiteers, a nation that has enriched itself on the misery and destruction of millions of lives all over the globe" (33).

While revealing concealed political truths and the methods whereby consent is manufactured, Brooks and Verdecchia interrogate their own potential complicity as citizens and artists: "we are concerned with our own collective moral hypocrisy and cowardice, and [...] the movement in theatre towards a greater and greater focus on market forces" (17). Lest this seem like earnest moralizing, their comical pedagogy undercuts any temptation to take themselves too seriously. One of them smacks the Artstick or blows the Whistle of Indignation whenever the other becomes overly didactic. Along with a flow chart illustrating links between major corporations and the media, they produce a sexual flow chart illustrating "corporal mergers" (52) among members of Toronto's theatre community: "not to give people the impression that all we do in the theatre is fuck. We do fuck a lot, there's no question about that, but we do other things. We work in restaurants, ride our bikes, dine with our families ... [W]e are part of a community, and [...] within any community there are shared interests, shared ideas, shared ideologies, shared lives" (54–5). Like the Youssef interview imbedded in *A Line in the Sand*, these devices acknowledge the extent to which all performance and performers are implicated in the dominant cultural formations (Auslander: 61). Aiming to maximize political transparency while strategizing to find a new structure or rhetoric of theatrical resistance, they remind us of what Chomsky acknowledges in *Necessary Illusions*: "To escape the impact of a well-functioning system of propaganda that bars dissent and unwanted fact while fostering lively debate within the permitted bounds is remarkably difficult" (Chomsky: 67).

Many of the same performative and metatheatrical elements – the lecture with slides, the cultural and political criticisms, the personal self-examination, and the attempts to imagine, discover, or effect an alternative to the permissible – also characterize the best known of the plays created by these three, Verdecchia's 1993 solo show, *Fronteras Americanas (American Borders)*. This multiple award-winning, semi-autobiographical performance piece explores Verdecchia's border life as Argentinean-Canadian, or rather Argentinean-North American, since the Canada he experiences is so saturated by US media, pop culture, and ideology. Adapting the border theory of Gómez-Peña and Gloria Anzaldúa, Verdecchia finds that the border is not so much a geographical barrier as a permanent condition of ambiguity that he must embrace with something like Anzaldúa's *mestiza* consciousness (Anzaldúa: 101). Verdecchia's intense feelings of displacement ("I feel not nowhere, not neither" (1993: 51)) lead him to explore the Latino stereotypes constructed by the powerful American entertainment industry: Columbian drug lord, Latin lover, Ricky Ricardo, Antonio Banderas. His metatheatrical strategy of spectacular resistance involves splitting the gaze and reversing it in the comic persona of his cultural commentator, barrio greaser and postmodern pachuco Facundo Morales Secundo, aka Wideload. Among the humorous ethnographic discoveries Wideload shares with the audience is his realization that his "Saxon" friends have their version of Latino dances like the mambo and tango: the Morris Dance. But Wideload also questions whether his own persona sugar-coats the critical pill so effectively "dat it doesn't really matter what I say. Because it's all been kind of funny dis evening" (75). Meanwhile, Verdecchia travels through the United States and back through Chile and Argentina on his journey of self-discovery, only to find that Canada "is where I make the most sense, in this Noah's ark of a nation" where he is "learning to live the border" (73, 77) – which "also means to practice creative appropriation, expropriation, and subversion of dominant cultural forms" (Gómez-Peña 1993: 43).

In its practice of creative appropriation and subversion *The Adventures of Ali & Ali and the aXes of Evil* recapitulates and reframes much of what these three playwrights have done before. It also encapsulates a long history of Canadian political attitudes towards the United States. Since the American Revolution, when the Loyalists headed north to Canada, Anglo-Canadians have defined themselves as not-American. The geopolitical facts of life in North America – a less populated, weaker Canada living alongside the larger, stronger, charismatic American economic and cultural powerhouse – have meant that Canadians must inevitably concede a certain amount of integration and American influence. But that does not mean they have to like it: "To every generation of Canadians, the American presence has been an unavoidable fact of everyday life. Since there was no other external threat to Canadian autonomy and identity save the United States, it was against Americans that Canadians repeatedly pledged to 'stand on guard' in the lyrics of their national anthem" (Thompson and Randall: 4–5). Moreover, Canadians have developed a wry resentment at being identified by much of the rest of the world *as* Americans: "It's a fact [...] that so far as most of the world is concerned, the Americans personally invented everything in the continent, including Canada" (Gwyn: 196). A pervasive, sometimes subtle, sometimes overt anti-Americanism comprises another strand in Canadians' complex, ambivalent historical attitude toward their southern neighbors (see Granatstein: 1996).

Add to those deeply rooted traditions a divergence of fundamental values at the turn of the twenty-first century as the United States moved significantly to the right and Canada moderately to the left (see Adams). Just before 9/11, the pop cultural barometer on both sides of the border registered those tensions: the *South Park* movie's "Blame Canada" theme, given high profile by Robin Williams's high-kicking performance of the song on the 2000 Academy Awards show, faced off against the hugely popular Joe Canada character in the mock-patriotic, mock (but also genuinely) anti-American "I am Canadian" Molson beer ads on Canadian TV.[3] Many American politicians really did blame Canada for harboring the 9/11 terrorists and allowing them to cross the border into the United States, aspersions long since proven untrue.[4] As Canadian humorist Allan Gould intimates, other elements of the ideological divide may have played a role in those accusations:

> True, all nineteen of the terrorists who attacked the World Trade Center and the Pentagon on 9/11 ... were legal residents of the United States. But all Americans know in their pure hearts that, had those evil

men been legal residents of Canada, they would have had no trouble whatsoever in entering the United States had they chosen to during that fateful time. Today they would get caught up in traffic jams of gay marriage parties in Niagara Falls, Ontario, and lose valuable time as Canadian border guards offer to sell them cheap marijuana [...]

(188)

Ali & Ali expresses genuine revulsion towards American foreign policy in the post-9/11 era, filtered through Canada's traditional antithetical politics and cultural positioning, exacerbated by the contemporary atmosphere of cross-border suspicion, and mediated by the personal politics and cultural practices of the playwrights. Right from the pre-show, where internet-constructed video pastiches of George W. Bush and Tony Blair apparently singing "Endless Love" and "Gay Bar" to each other ("I want to take you to a gay bar!") are projected onto the rear wall of the set (Youssef, Verdecchia and Chai: 11), the play reveals its contemporary, media-savvy agitprop consciousness. It assumes a shared awareness with the audience of how media work to commodify and sell political ideas, and how such media strategies can be hijacked and reappropriated to deconstruct and ridicule those same ideas. Early in the play, another video projection introduces "Ali and Ali Security Expert" Dr Mohandes Panir (16). Played by Chai with a thick black moustache and a heavy South Asian accent, he wears a security-guard outfit and sits before a computer screen with a box of Tim Horton's donuts, an icon of contemporary Canadiana (Figure 10.1). He interrupts the action to warn of increased security threats resulting in higher levels on the security-risk scale he has developed. Its categories include Decaf, Double Double (a Tim Hortonism that has entered the Canadian lexicon, meaning coffee with two sugars and two creams), and Boot Cut. "This level of the Mohandes Panir Threat Level Assessment System is now proudly brought to you by the Gap", he announces (17).

Here we see a kind of double double post-colonial mimicry. First, the paranoid discourse of Homeland Security's color-coded threat levels has its authority undermined by the ineptly self-serious, *"almost the same but not white"* Mohandes (Bhabha: 89), re-casting defense-of-the-homeland rhetoric in the lingua franca of corporate-branded designer jeans and coffee,[5] which in turn conjures the military-industrial system exploited so profitably by the Bush administration. This is made explicit later in the play by the actor playing Duncan, the theatre manager, who steps out of character to complain that the playwrights could be doing more with their material, like "exposing the connections of the American elite, you

Figure 10.1   Ali & Ali and the aXes of Evil, (left–right) Marcus Youssef as Ali Ababwa, Camyar Chai (on screen) as Dr Mohandes Panir, Camyar Chai as Ali Hakim. Produced by neworld theatre and Cahoots Theatre, Vancouver East Cultural Centre, February 2004. Photo by Tim Matheson.

know George W. and Arbusto Energy; Dick Cheney and Haliburton Oil; Condoleezza Rice and Chevron [...]" (Youssef, Verdecchia and Chai: 112). Second, when this swarthy, accented Asian-Canadian subaltern speaks, and when he deploys the Dr Mohandes Panir Panopticon (18), "the look of surveillance returns as the displacing gaze of the disciplined, where the observer becomes the observed" (Bhabha: 89). The normative, presumably non-Asian North American audience finds itself on the receiving end of the security apparatus – albeit one controlled by a comical brown man who claims to be "very busy profiling potential terrorist suspects" while *"[b]ehind him, an image of a bikini babe is on his computer screen"* (Youssef, Verdecchia and Chai: 64–5).

In his final appearance Dr Mohandes will claim that weapons of mass destruction, the dreaded aXes of Evil, are hidden in the audience, causing the Alis to take the War on Terror directly to the house. Equipped with *"tiny white cardboard jeeps"* (which in the first production I saw they tied around their waists), "cool helmets", and toy ray guns (96), they invade and offer ultimatums at the same time: "If you do not co-operate fully, we will leave the country and you will have the shit bombed out of you. If you do co-operate fully, we will leave the country and you will have the shit bombed out of you" (97). Ali Ababwa demands that a woman open her purse for inspection. She hesitates. "She's obfuscating. Must have something to hide" (98). In a moment that ironically foreshadows prohibitions that Homeland Security would subsequently impose on air travelers, the search of the purse reveals not the aXes of Evil but a potentially dangerous weapon that must be confiscated nonetheless: a tube of lipstick. "[T]his is certainly a weapon of mass destruction to some poor little bunny who had it shoved up his EYEBALL!" (99). Although the Alis ultimately find nothing to justify their invasion, they remain unrepentant: "We believe people with white skins can govern themselves and we'll just stay here until you learn to do so" (100).

The commodity and media fetishism represented by advertising reappears in another important comic motif. Insisting that they want to "make every effort to communicate with [the audience] in ways to which you are culturally accustomed", entrepreneurial Ali and Ali project Shopping Channel-like video ads for "merchandise and commemorative memorabilia" for sale. They even have a website: "www dot (*ALI HAKIM ululates*) dot com" (25–6). Here the playwrights playfully combine orientalist stereotypes of the wily Arab merchant and the tourist bazaar with notions of cultural difference and the real-life phenomenon of contemporary refugees who attempt to perform intercultural competence to reveal their possession of skills desired by the country of asylum. Such moments in the play reflect Loren Kruger's description of *diaspora* as an evolving or "traveling term", marking "the current pervasive interest in transnational networks that complicate national identifications". Seizing agency and offering up their hybrid mercantile and media skills as performance, Ali and Ali metatheatrically take part in the re-visioning and "reformation of the migrant from the abject figure of the petitioning immigrant required to submit to full assimilation as the price of naturalization [...] to *the mobile actor* able to access multiple loyalties if not always dual citizenship" (Kruger: 260; my emphasis).

But typically, the playwrights immediately shift gears to remind us of the vulnerability and needs of the real people represented by the characters on stage. Ali and Ali are mobile and actors only because they are forced to be, and they are entrepreneurial of necessity.

> *(ALI HAKIM enters the audience and addresses one person in particular.)* Give me twenty dollars and we get pizza. [...] How 'bout you put it on gold card. You get points; I get pizza. What, you ate before the show? Must be nice. (*He returns to stage.*) They think nobody else needs to eat.
>
> (Youssef, Verdecchia and Chai: 27)

From time to time Ali Hakim drops the actor's mask and reveals his suppressed rage – when, for example, they try to telemarket commemorative miniatures of the Agrabanian General Strike of 1968 (53). In a history lesson about an Agraba that sounds a lot like Iran, we learn that the strike helped to overthrow the ruling oligarchy, giving rise to a brief, exhilarating period of democracy and freedom until a CIA-supported coup by fundamentalists put in place the Theocratic State of Agraba. (The fundamentalists are not Shia or Sunni but Sammi – a fanatical sect whose members worship Sammy Davis, Jr., poke out their left eyes, and tap dance in the throes of religious ecstasy (60)). Getting no offers for his product, Ali Ababwa desperately haggles his asking price down to a few dollars per figurine with a promise that a portion of every purchase will go to Agraba's Fire Department. Ali Hakim interrupts angrily:

> Stop. That's enough, all this bullshit. There's no fire department in Agraba. Provisional Authority disbanded fire department. For being part of old regime. [...] Cheap bastards. You Canadians – you can't buy me a slice of pizza? How much did you make selling weapons to Americans, huh? Who armed the fundamentalists!
>
> (54)

Reminders of the realities of exile and the hard facts of contemporary *realpolitik* are never far beneath the comic surface or the complicit wink to the media-savvy audience or the optimistic suggestions of new syncretic forms of theatre or polity.

This is clearest in two of the play's cleverest segments, both extensions of the Alis' understanding of the North American mania for commodification and media convergence. The first is a lengthy movie pitch aimed at a famous Canadian supposedly in the audience, Ian Hanomansing (they call him Ian Handsomemanthing), the good-looking, popular, dark-brown-skinned host of the national news on CBC television – or CBCNN, as the Alis call it, suggesting again the unacknowledged mainstream Canadian convergence with American political perspective and ideology. "We are very great admirers of yours, Successful Brown Person, and have a proposition for you!" (28). The proposition is that Ian star in their movie about a brave soldier in the invading army who sacrifices himself to save a soccer jersey for a young Arab boy (named Ali) who has lost his arms and legs in a blast from an "anti-personnel land mine that has been left behind by your boys – good boys!" (37).[6] Their mimicry of the romantic/heroic style of the Hollywood myth- and propaganda-making machinery – "think *Black Hawk Down* meets *Singing in the Rain*" (35) – is hilariously accurate, and offers ample opportunity for comment on the unfunny realities of the post-9/11 invasion of Iraq:

> ALI ABABWA: They do not want revenge.
> ALI HAKIM: No. They want justice.
> ALI ABABWA: They want to liberate people of small dusty country that had absolutely nothing to do with the unspeakable crime we saw a few minutes ago in the movie.
> ALI HAKIM: They have no quarrel with PEOPLE of small dusty country.
> ALI ABABWA: No.
> ALI HAKIM: Therefore, they kill by the dozens.
> ALI ABABWA: The hundreds.
> ALI HAKIM: The thousands. Tanks crush houses.
> ALI ABABWA: Dusty brainwashed people rush to defend their city.
> ALI HAKIM: Some of them are burned alive. Or mangled by machine-gun fire. [...]
>
> (33–4)

As actors, Youssef and Chai's own stage embodiment of those brown people from dusty countries lends added poignancy to these reminders of the reality behind the comedy.

The second instance comes just before the end of the play when Ali and Ali introduce their "very first corporate sponsor" – Osama bin Laden (Figure 10.2). Osama recognizes, "It is not enough to blow up big buildings once every ten years. We must win the hearts and minds of the infidel" (113–14). So he offers his support: a suitcase full of what Ali and Ali think is money but turns out to be explosives (that go off). In return the Alis offer to help Osama and Al Qaeda with their image problems:

> ALI HAKIM: Many groups have them.
> ALI ABABWA: Monsanto, for example.
> ALI HAKIM: Pfizer.
> ALI ABABWA: Shell.
> ALI HAKIM: Dow Chemical.
> ALI ABABWA: Or GE. Making and selling all those weapons to Israel, Kuwait and Egypt. How many people do they kill?
> ALI HAKIM: Or Lockheed Martin, maker of F-16. How many people do they kill?
> ALI ABABWA: Or Raytheon. Maker of wide variety of missile. How many people do they kill?

ALI HAKIM: Or Ronald Reagan. Or Madeleine Albright and Bill Clinton. How many people did they kill? Or Henry Kissinger.

ALI ABABWA: How many people did he kill?

ALI HAKIM: Like you a very rich man and also wanted in several countries.

ALI ABABWA: Just as these shady individuals and organizations utilize the tools of public relations to minimize the consequences of their crimes, so too can you and your organization, Mr. Osama.

(116–17)

They propose a re-branding of Al Qaeda as Al Qaeda 2.0 – or better yet, AQ2. And a name change to suggest a kinder, gentler Osama: "How about [...] Osama bin [...] Oprah" (120). It's all just public relations. "Sure, my client drove some big planes into some tall buildings but who here hasn't made mistakes? Like U.S.A. – getting into bed with Shah of Iran, with Saddam Hussein, with Taliban. These are mistakes anyone can make" (119).

In scenes like this *Ali & Ali* deploys its transnational agitprop arsenal to speak the unspeakable, a strategy foreshadowed early in the play by Ali Hakim's retelling a joke he first told in Mogadishu in the presence of

Figure 10.2   Ali & Ali and the aXes of Evil, (left–right) Marcus Youssef as Ali Ababwa, Tom Butler as Osama bin Laden, Camyar Chai as Ali Hakim. Produced by neworld theatre and Cahoots Theatre, Vancouver East Cultural Centre, February 2004. Photo by Tim Matheson.

"Mr. Biggest Warlord". The joke concerns a warlord ("black man [with] small penis") "taking a piss" in the desert, when he notices beside him a small white man with a large penis also taking a piss. In the joke the warlord's penis envy allows the white man to outwit him – and bugger him. The Alis get away with their lives because the warlord in their Mogadishu audience likes the joke (14–15).

The Adventures of Ali & Ali and the aXes of Evil has as its subtitle, *A Divertimento for Warlords*. The playwrights and their characters understand that we in their Canadian audience "are not Somalia". They take the piss out of Western warlords, American and Canadian warlords, the men who wish to prove they have big penises and screw the undeveloped world; and Youssef et al. get away with it because we like their jokes. They also didactically remind us of the realities masked by our dominant political consensus. The play dares to draw analogies between demonic Al Qaeda and Osama on the one side, and mainstream American corporate giants, Secretaries of State, and even Presidents on the other. It accuses the Americans of state terrorism and war crimes. In 1989 Chomsky argued that in American political discourse this would be unthinkable: "the phrase 'U.S. terrorism' is an oxymoron, on a par with 'thunderous silence' or 'U.S. aggression'" (114). Although Bush and his policies in the Middle East have had many outspoken critics, and have gained many more since this play was written, Chomsky's assertion has remained largely true even post-Michael Moore (and is likely to remain true even in the Obama era). Most such criticisms are still contained within what Chomsky calls "the bounds of the expressible" (45). The play, then, manifests "radical performance" in Baz Kershaw's sense, invoking "not just freedom *from* oppression, repression, exploitation – the resistant sense of the radical – but also freedom *to reach beyond* existing systems of formalized power, freedom to create currently unimaginable forms of association and action – the transgressive or transcendent sense of the radical" (Kershaw: 18; his emphasis).[7]

But even these transgressions feel satirically soft-core compared to the play's direct frontal assault on American political leadership and its absurd/obscene foreign policy strategies in the scenes in which Bush himself and his inner circle are mimicked. In the play's longest sequence after the movie pitch, "The Classical Puppet Theatre of Agraba", the actors voice the characters of Dubya, Cheney, "Rummy" Rumsfeld, and "Semi-Colin" Powell (and in later versions "Condi" Rice, whom Dubya calls Candy), all represented by stick puppets with photocopied faces. The actors manipulate the puppets against a background photo of the Oval Office, and the puppet show is projected onto the screen by a live camera.

(You can watch it on YouTube.) This is classic agitprop, utilizing puppets and projections as Piscator did in the 1920s when he developed the form (Goorney and MacColl: xlii), and representing ruling class characters as (literally) flat stereotypes within a broad comedy of manners.

Depicting a meeting about the occupation of Iraq, the scene is politically direct, intentionally outrageous, and exceedingly obscene. At first it sounds no different from the White House tapes of the Nixon era:

> SEMI-COLIN: Mr. President, the media are having a field day with the prison abuse –
> RUMMY: Fuck 'em. Keeps their mind off the really nasty shit we're doing.
>
> (Youssef, Verdecchia and Chai: 68)

But then Rummy and Cheney begin expressing their appreciation of Rush Limbaugh (changed in the most recent remount to Bill O'Reilly):

> CHENEY: I'd like to shake his hand.
> RUMMY: I'd give him a pat on the back.
> CHENEY: I'd like to pinch his ass.
> RUMMY: Put a clamp on his balls.
> CHENEY: Let him suck my dick.
> RUMMY: While Semi gives it to his old lady from behind.
> CHENEY: And we watch!
> DUBYA: Oh, just like those frat parties we used to go to.
>
> (70)

Dubya is presented as a moron who claims that he speaks to God ("Laura and I give thanks to Him for clearing up my hemorrhoids") and God to him: "He told me that the coming apocalypse in the Middle East will herald the beginning of the Second Coming. [...] And Jesus is gonna sleep over in the Lincoln Bedroom" (71–2). But the satirical portrait of Bush is much the gentlest. When Rummy proposes that one of the ways to "spread freedom" is to "put more black guys in jail", he turns to Powell and says, "No offence, Leroy."

> DUBYA: Why would he take offence? Semi's not black.
> SEMI-COLIN: Mr. President uh, I'm uh African-American.
> DUBYA: You see?
>
> (72–3)

The boundaries of satirical decorum are maintained in this sequence, which would not feel out of place on *Saturday Night Live*. But the line gets crossed again when Semi-Colin finally has enough and lets his minstrel mask slip for a moment – only to reveal another kind of blackface: "Sheeeit, what up, dog? Sho, stick it to de negro. I ain't no mothafuckin' office boy. I'm de mothafuckin' secretary of the mothafuckin' state. [...] And Rumsfeld, you mothafuckin' cracker, any more lip from you and I'll fuck you up, mothafucka. (*beat*) I mean, I'll get my people on it, sir. Right away" (74). The line is even more radically crossed a few minutes later. When the Alis offer to placate the theatre manager by doing impressions, a voiceover announces "the Secretary of Defence for the United States of America", and *ALI HAKIM appears in shadow on rear (tent) wall as DONALD RUMSFELD masturbating*:

DONALD RUMSFELD: Who's in power now, Hillary?!!!!!

(84)[8]

Although the person of the American President is no longer as immune from nasty political satire as he may once have been in the United States, and his cronies are certainly fair game, these scenes overstep the usual acceptable boundaries of obscenity, racism, and sexual impropriety assumed to govern the relationship among the political attacker or theatrical satirist, the satirical/political target, and the audience. Even Chai and Youssef have felt the need to offer unsolicited justifications for the radical nature of their portrayals. I have heard them suggest in interviews that they felt able to present their racially stereotyped Colin Powell only because they themselves are actors of color. And they have argued that the Rumsfeld masturbation scene is far less obscene than the statement by once Secretary of State Madeleine Albright – this appears as an informative footnote in the *Ali* script – "who, when asked how she felt about the half a million Iraqi children dying as a result of U.S.-imposed sanctions (after the First War on Iraq), answered, 'It's a tough choice but we think it's worth it'" (117 n.14).

These shock tactics are aimed at pushing the envelope of Canadians' vaunted tolerance, a point of national pride and one of the qualities by which the nation defines itself. As theatre manager Duncan complains in a moment of frustration with the Alis' antics, "Ye've got to respect your audience. Ye understan' that? RESPEC'. It's part of our culture. [...] You people. We give ye this opportunity and ye just push our tolerance till it snaps" (86–7). Breaking through the audience's normal levels of liberal tolerance is exactly the playwrights' intention. Their theatrical disrespect aims to force audience members – whom the Alis call "the good people of Real Life Canada" (19) – outside their cultural comfort zone, and remind us that tolerance can also mean toleration of the intolerable: apathetic acceptance of what is purported to be or, indeed, of what is, including poverty, hunger, war, torture, and statelessness.

In order to explode Canadians' illusions and self-delusions, the playwrights challenge the way Canadian theatre itself tends to reinforce them. The play's neo-agitprop confronts many of the same issues addressed by radical companies of the 1930s. The 1936 manifesto of Manchester's Theatre Union insisted, "The theatre must face up to the problems of its time: it cannot ignore the poverty and human suffering which increases every day. [... B]y intensifying our efforts to get at the essence of reality, we are also attempting to solve our own theatrical problems both technical and ideological" (Goorney and MacColl: ix). Facing up to contemporary problems and exposing the realities hidden by the powerful machinery of the political, business, and media establishments also means grappling with one's own strategies and those of the theatrical status quo. The Workers' Theatre of the 1930s spent much time arguing over the comparative virtues of naturalism and agitprop, usually coming down on the side of the latter because the former "is suitable for showing things as they appear on the surface, but does not lend itself to disclosing the reality which lies beneath" (qtd in Samuel, MacColl and Cosgrove: 101). *Ali & Ali* aims one of its most effective satirical barbs directly at Canadian theatrical multicultural naturalism, the kind of "ethnic family drama" that Duncan praises because it offers "a window into our nation's cultural diversity yet resonates with universal themes" (Youssef, Verdecchia and Chai: 49).

Pretending to bow to the theatre manager's demands, Ali and Ali present three versions of the same stereotypical Canadian "ethnic" play. In each, a culturally assimilated Canadian son confronts his stubbornly traditionalist father – the first Chinese, the second Russian, the third Native Canadian. Embarrassed by his father's Old World habits, the son explodes with the anger and frustration of being torn between modernity and tradition: "Can't you see that I am drowning in a tidal wave of Old World, neo-Stalinist, patrio-masculinist repression?" (80). Eventually, the fathers concede, fathers and sons fall into each others' arms, the son cries "I'm Canadian, dammit. I'm Canadian", the father comforts him ("We're all Canadian"), then accidentally kills the son ("*PROJECTION: Blood spatter in the shape of a maple leaf*"), and ends by cursing, "Damn you, Canadian Dream!" (51–2, 81).[9]

The ridiculous scenario with its sentimentalized ending mirrors the Alis' movie pitch. In the same way as the conventions of Hollywood film

Figure 10.3   Ali & Ali and the aXes of Evil, Marcus Youssef as Ali Ababwa, Tom Butler as Tom/Tim, Camyar Chai as Ali Hakim. Produced by neworld theatre and Cahoots Theatre, Vancouver East Cultural Centre, February 2004. Photo by Tim Matheson. Note the cultural cross-dressing: the Alis' hybrid garb of cheesy Vegas-style tux and turban, silver jacket and camouflage shirt, and their Caucasian assistant's stereotypical genie outfit.

obscure the political realities of battlefield Iraq, the superficial trappings of such multicultural theatrics mask the realities of the Canadian experience of ethnic Otherness. "[O]ur mandate [is] to represent, accommodate, dignify, and empower cultural communities through theatrical productions of high artistic quality", insists Duncan (47). But this kind of bureaucratic affirmation of cultural diversity rings hollow in the face of the concrete personal and political realities of exile and diaspora as Ali and Ali experience them. The generic sameness of the dramatic scenario, with its interchangeable parts, mocks the ideal of "universal themes" intrinsic to naturalism and dear to Duncan's heart: "Look, this is not the place, and I'm sure you (*audience*) agree with me, NAE the place for your local, petty, feudal grievances, yer decontextualized finger pointing. The theatre is where we explore the timeless verities of the human condition" (76). Like Youssef's interviewer in *A Line in the Sand*, Duncan challenges the very premise of the play and the legitimacy of political theatre itself. This is another wake-up call for the generalized Canadian or "United Statesian" audience (as the Alis called it in the Seattle production), a pointed reminder that we have indeed learned to *agree* that a certain idea of theatre is normative and that anything beyond its boundaries is illegitimate. For agitprop theatre like this, in fact, "[s]uch aesthetic criteria as subtlety, durability and universality are irrelevant" (Endres: xvi).

Ironic though it may be, the cry "Damn you, Canadian Dream!" echoes through the final scenes of the play which return us, bluntly, to what Edward Said calls "the unhealable rift" and insurmountable sadness of exile (Said: 173) and the concrete conditions of statelessness. Ali Hakim goes to sleep hungry, pessimistic that he will ever be reunited with his pregnant wife who languishes without papers in a Maltese detention centre – off stage, invisible, "unmarked" in Peggy Phelan's term, and unremarked by the audience, the surrogate for those who have power to "legitimize" lives like hers and the Alis'. The play has challenged Canada's dream of its geopolitical innocence, its clean hands and generosity, its multicultural exceptionalism and moral superiority to the materialist, imperialist United States. But in the first production and published script, another kind of Canadian dream emerges out of the experience of the play as the Alis suddenly awaken to *"see the audience and realize they were dreaming"* (Youssef, Verdecchia and Chai: 124). Their dream is of a budding utopia:

> ALI HAKIM: I had the most
> ALI ABABWA: beautiful dream.
> ALI HAKIM: I was at my sister's house.
> ALI ABABWA: back in Agraba.
> ALI HAKIM: Only the whole world was Agraba.
> ALI ABABWA: And everyone was there. You
> *They "see" these people in the audience; they tell their dream to the house.*
> ALI HAKIM: Ana
> ALI ABABWA: Souad was alive.
> ALI HAKIM: Spring had come.
> ALI ABABWA: The snow melted
> ALI HAKIM: and the village overflowed
> ALI ABABWA: with children.
> ALI HAKIM: Our words had grown taller than our swords.
> ALI ABABWA: The battlefields were green with grass.
> ALI HAKIM: And everyone had meaningful work.

Ali Hakim has the final words of the play:

> I think perhaps it was the future.

(124–6)

I have never clearly understood this ending, which the playwrights have changed a number of times since the first production and cut from the most recent remount. In one sense it seems nothing but the exile's perpetual dream of return, a romantic fantasy of spontaneous healing and transnational brotherhood and sisterhood. In one of the play's first scenes the Alis mock exactly such a notion, parodying transnational singalongs like "We Are the World" and "Do They Know It's Christmas?" in their "World Dreaming Together Song":

> From the towers of Calcutta
> To the sewers of U.S.A.
> To all the men and women
> And yes, even the gay
> From the old man who lost his nutter
> To the child allergic to peanut butter
> [...]
> Do they know it's dreaming together time right now?
> (*Overcome with emotion, they embrace*)
>
> (24)

But maybe, by the end, the play's "radical performance" has, in Kershaw's terms, "insinuate[d] pathologies of hope" (26). Maybe it has brought together, in just the right combination, what Jill Dolan describes as "the material conditions of theatre production and reception that evoke the sense that it's even possible to imagine a utopia" – the condition she calls the utopian performative (455). Maybe the Alis can imagine Agraba reborn and green again by seeing it *in* and *through* the (transformed) audience; by projecting it across the transnational Fourth-World space of exile and possibility – the refugee camp/theatre/borderland – cleared, like a minefield, by their agitprop deconstruction of the lies and limitations of the dominant American paradigm and its Canadian clones.[10]

Notes

1. An earlier incarnation of this chapter was published under the title "Bombing (on) the Border: *Ali and Ali and the aXes of Evil* as Transnational Agitprop", *Modern Drama* 51 (Spring 2008): 126–44. My thanks to *Modern Drama* for permission to publish this revised version here.
2. neworld theatre was established in 1992 in Vancouver by Camyar Chai and some of his classmates at the University of British Columbia, with a mandate to create "new plays that reflect the multiple facets of Vancouver's diverse populations", a mandate reflected in its current artistic directorship of Chai,

Youssef, and Adrienne Wong (http://www.neworldtheatre.com/company-mandate.html).

3. See Wikipedia entries: "Blame Canada" (http://en.wikipedia.org/wiki/Blame _Canada) and "Joe Canada" (http://en.wikipedia.org/wiki/Joe_Canada).

4. See, for example, Struck "Canada Fights Myth It Was 9/11 Conduit.", and Alberts, "U.S. Senator Revives 9/11 Myth about Canada".

5. *Starbucks* immediately comes to mind but the *Tim Horton's* references implicate the Canadian audience in a double doubly ironic way, since the company, although named after a legendary Canadian hockey player and omnipresent in Canada, is mostly American-owned.

6. There is rich ambiguity in the idea of this Canadian icon starring in a movie transparently about the American invasion of Iraq. Notwithstanding Canada's then-Prime Minister Jean Chretien's refusal to join the so-called Coalition of the Willing in the Iraq invasion, the idea that Ian and "[his] boys" are part of the occupying army suggests at least a residual Canadian ideological allegiance to American foreign policy. Many Canadians were vehemently in favor of sending Canadian troops at the time, and Chretien did send soldiers to Afghanistan, a gesture widely understood in Canada as a sop to the United States. Or this may be a comment on the frequency with which American icons are played by Canadian actors in Hollywood films – from Raymond Massey as Abe Lincoln to Bruce Greenwood as JFK (in *Thirteen Days*) to, more recently, Adam Beach and Barry Pepper raising the flag at Iwo Jima in Clint Eastwood's *Flags of Our Fathers*.

7. In the May 2007 issue of *Theatre Survey*, James M. Harding worries "that 9/11 has effected a de facto retreat from the central assertion of Kershaw's book [...] I would suggest that 9/11 has pushed the discourse of our discipline [of theatre scholarship] back toward a conventional, indeed reactionary, understanding of the interrelation of politics, theatre, and performance" (20). I argue that *Ali & Ali* revitalizes radically discursive political performance in a way that both Kershaw and Harding should find reassuring.

8. With Rumsfeld no longer Secretary of Defense as of November 2006, the playwrights changed this sequence for the 2007 remount so that the masturbator was then Democratic primary candidate Barack Obama screaming, "Debate this, Hillary!!!" Their updates have included references to Dick Cheney's accidental shooting of his friend, the latest conflict in Lebanon, Jerry Falwell's death, and the New Orleans flood. In response to the controversy around the satirical Danish cartoons of Mohammed, they added an outrageous video clip in which Chai as a near-naked Jesus, dressed only in a diaper, runs down a city street and is demolished by a bus. For the Seattle production, in addition to general substitutions of "United Statesian" for "Canadian", they replaced the CBC's Ian Hanomansing with CNN correspondent Sanjay Gupta. The Seattle reviews suggest that American audiences and critics in the northwest were as receptive and appreciative of the show as Canadians have been. See Adcock "Diabolically funny, 'Ali & Ali' takes aim at Bush & Co.", and Berson "'Ali and Ali' is political satire with an extra bite". My thanks to Camyar Chai for supplying information about script changes.

9. The primary model for this parodic play is David French's realist domestic drama *Leaving Home*, first produced in 1972. In French's scenario a family of Newfoundlanders who have immigrated to Toronto is torn between the

parents, who still consider Newfoundland "home", and their fully assimilated Central Canadian sons. At the end of the play the father and eldest son have a confrontation not unlike the parodies in *Ali & Ali*, although without the bloodshed. Critically and commercially one of the most successful Canadian plays of its era, *Leaving Home* was also criticized as early as 1974 by Newfoundland playwright Michael Cook for its "appeal to the well-heeled, hungry for ethnic entertainment that stirs the mud of their tragically empty souls, only to let it settle back in sentiment" (qtd in Johnson: 36). An equally canonical Canadian play, though not realist, George Ryga's *The Ecstasy of Rita Joe* (1967) features a traditionalist Native Canadian father and his eponymous daughter who wants to assimilate (and actually is killed, but not at her father's hand). Other Canadian "ethnics" have since played a similar theatrical card. See, for example, Chinese-Canadian Marty Chan's *Mom, Dad, I'm Living with a White Girl*. Another Canadian metatheatrical in-joke counterpoints this sequence: a monologue by the Alis' white helper, whom they call Tim but who insists his name is Tom, and who doubles as the theatre manager, Duncan. In the original production and published script Tim/Tom was played by veteran Canadian actor Tom Butler. In this monologue he gets to show excerpts from his actual audition reel (scenes from *The X-Files* and a movie with Meryl Streep), laments the Canadian TV and film industry's vulnerability to the whims of American producers, and talks about his early experience as a stage actor "in the original TWP days" (Youssef, Verdecchia and Chai: 110–11). TWP is Toronto Workshop Productions, established in 1959 by director George Luscombe, who modeled it after Joan Littlewood's Theatre Workshop in East London. Canada's first post-war alternative theatre company, TWP had a strong leftist political bent, was grounded in collective creation, and became known for plays about American politics (e.g., *Chicago '70*) and the disenfranchised in Canada (*Ten Lost Years*) – not unlike the *Ali & Ali* collective itself. See Carson, *Harlequin in Hogtown*.

10. The play took on new relevance with the coming to power in 2005 of a Conservative minority government in Canada that embraced the foreign policy positions of George W. Bush and even adopted his rhetoric. The Canadian troops in Afghanistan became combat troops, and as the casualties mounted and critics demanded that the troops be brought home, Prime Minister Stephen Harper responded with this Bushism: "There will be some who want to cut and run, but cutting and running is not my way and it's not the Canadian way." See his speech of 13 March 2006 ("Canada").

Works cited

Adams, Michael. *Fire and Ice: The United States, Canada, and the Myth of Converging Values*. Toronto: Penguin Canada, 2004.

Adcock, Joe. "Diabolically funny, 'Ali & Ali' takes aim at Bush & Co", *Seattle Post-Intelligencer*, 17 May 2007.

Alberts, Sheldon. "U.S. Senator Revives 9/11 Myth about Canada", *Ottawa Citizen*, 20 December 2005.

Anzaldúa, Gloria. *Borderlands/La Frontera: The New Mestiza*, 2nd edn. San Francisco: Aunt Lute Books, 1999.

Auslander, Philip. *From Acting to Performance: Essays in Modernism and Postmodernism*. London: Routledge, 1997.

Berson, Misha. "'Ali and Ali' is political satire with an extra bite", *Seattle Times*, 18 May 2007.

Bhabha, Homi K. *The Location of Culture*. London: Routledge, 1994.

Brooks, Daniel and Verdecchia. Guillermo. *The Noam Chomsky Lectures*. Toronto: Coach House, 1991.

"Canada committed to Afghan mission, Harper tells troops", 13 March 2006: www.cbc.ca/world/story/2006/03/13/harper_afghanistan060313.html.

Carson, Neil. *Harlequin in Hogtown: George Luscombe and Toronto Workshop Productions*. Toronto: University of Toronto Press, 1995.

Chan, Marty. *Mom, Dad, I'm Living with a White Girl*. Toronto: Playwrights Canada Press, 1999.

Chomsky, Noam. *Necessary Illusions: Thought Control in Democratic Societies*. Toronto: CBC Enterprises, 1989.

Dolan, Jill. "Performance, Utopia, and the 'Utopian Performative'", *Theatre Journal* 53.3 (2001): 455–79.

Endres, Robin. *Introduction to Eight Men Speak and Other Plays from the Canadian Workers' Theatre*. Ed. Richard Wright and Robin Endres. Toronto: New Hogtown Press, 1976, pp. xi–xxxvi.

French, David. *Leaving Home*. Don Mills, Ont.: General Publishing, 1972.

Gómez-Peña, Guillermo. *The New World Border*. San Francisco: City Lights, 1996.

———-. *Warrior for Gringostroika*. Saint Paul, MN: Graywolf Press, 1993.

Goorney, Howard and MacColl, Ewan, eds. *Agit-prop to Theatre Workshop: Political Playscripts 1930–50*. Manchester: Manchester University Press, 1986.

Gould, Allan. *Anne of Green Gables vs. G.I. Joe: Friendly Fire Between Canada and the U.S.* Toronto: ECW Press, 2003.

Granatstein, J. L. *Yankee Go Home? Canadians and Anti-Americanism*. Toronto: HarperCollins, 1996.

Gwyn, Richard. *The 49th Paradox: Canada in North America*. Toronto: McClelland and Stewart, 1985.

Harding, James M. "Counterbalancing the Pendulum Effect: Politics and the Discourse of Post-9/11 Theatre", *Theatre Survey* 48 (May 2007): 19–25.

Johnson, Chris. "Is That Us? Ray Lawler's *Summer of the Seventeenth Doll* and David French's *Leaving Home*", *Canadian Drama/L'Art dramatique canadien* 6 (Spring 1980): 30–42.

Kershaw, Baz. *The Radical in Performance: Between Brecht and Baudrillard*. London: Routledge, 1999.

Kruger, Loren. "Introduction: Diaspora, Performance, and National Affiliations in North America", *Theatre Research International* 28.3 (2003): 259–66.

Phelan, Peggy. *Unmarked: The Politics of Performance*. New York: Routledge, 1993.

Ryga, George. *The Ecstasy of Rita Joe*. Vancouver: Talonbooks, 1970.

Said, Edward. *Reflections on Exile and Other Essays*. Cambridge, MA: Harvard University Press, 2000.

Samuel, Raphael, MacColl, Ewan and Cosgrove, Stuart. *Theatres of the Left, 1880–1935: Workers' Theatre Movements in Britain and America*. London: Routledge & Kegan Paul, 1985.

South Park: *Bigger, Longer & Uncut*. Animated feature film. Written and produced by Trey Parker and Matt Stone. Paramount, 1999.

Struck, Doug. "Canada Fights Myth It Was 9/11 Conduit", *Washington Post*, 9 April 2005.

Thompson, John Herd and Randall, Stephen J. *Canada and the United States: Ambivalent Allies*, 2nd edn. Athens: University of Georgia Press, 1994.

Tompkins, Joanne. " 'Spectacular Resistance': Metatheatre in Post-Colonial Drama", *Modern Drama* 38 (Spring 1995): 42–51.

Verdecchia, Guillermo. *Fronteras Americanas (American Borders)*. Toronto: Coach House, 1993.

Verdecchia, Guillermo and Youssef, Marcus. *A Line in the Sand*. Vancouver: Talonbooks, 1997.

Yan, Haiping. "Other Transnationals: An Introductory Essay", *Modern Drama* 48 (Summer 2005): 225–48.

Youssef, Marcus, Verdecchia, Guillermo and Chai, Camyar. *The Adventures of Ali & Ali and the aXes of Evil*. Vancouver: Talonbooks, 2005.

11
Exiles and the City: Krzysztof Wodiczko's New York Interventions of Making the Familiar Strange[1]

Silvija Jestrovic
University of Warwick

> *Between the speechless pain and despair of the actual stranger, and the repressed fear of one's own strangeness [...], lies the real frontier to be challenged. Can art operate as a revelation, expressive and interrogative passage to such a frontier? Can it be an inspiration or a provocation to and an opening act for a new form of communication, a new form of non-xenophobic community? Can it provide an iconic object, a symbolic environment, an interface, with which to create or design such reconstructive psychocultural project?*
>
> Wodiczko, "Open Transmission": 90–1

So asks Krzysztof Wodiczko, the artist whose diverse projects have in many instances explored the encounter of the stranger, the immigrant, the marginal, and the homeless on the one hand, and the North American metropolis on the other.

Wodiczko, who graduated from the Academy of Fine Arts in Warsaw, emigrated from Poland in 1977, first to Canada and then to the United States. Settling in New York in 1983, he became known for his public art, particularly his projections onto buildings and monuments that have engaged politically with the urban landscape and its structures. For instance, among his best known works is the projection of a human hand onto the AT&T building in New York in 1984 in response to Ronald Reagan's re-election, displacing a gesture of American political ritual onto an 'overt symbol of corporate power' (Kaye: 35). Wodiczko's work has been showcased at numerous international festivals and exhibitions, including his major solo show at the Galerie Lelong in New York in 2005. Wodiczko runs the Research Interrogative Design Group at the Massachusetts Institute of Technology, where he continues to develop a series of tools for urban interventions as well as various portable communication instruments, some of which have been central to his projects *Xenology* and *Homeless Vehicles*.

In this chapter I will refer often to these two projects, as well as his *Homeless Projection: Proposal for a New City* project, arguing that they tackle different aspects of the exilic experience (in a broad sense of the term) – immigration as a form of physical exile, and homelessness as marginalization within and as an instance of internal exile. In both cases Wodiczko explores the exilic situation as a way of rethinking the encounters between strangers and a means of proposing new communicational practices through performative interventions. The performers are "authentic subjects". *Alien Staff* engages genuine immigrants from different backgrounds, including the artist himself who performed in some of the various versions of the project. Likewise, homeless people of New York were key collaborators on the *Homeless Vehicle* project. For Wodiczko, the authenticity of the performing subject is very important, as a proof that the *Xenology* project is run by true *xenologists* – foregrounding the immigrants and the homeless people as experts on displacement.

The exilic experience profoundly marks Wodiczko's work, but a strong sense of space and place as political categories truly shapes his projects. Wodiczko describes himself in the following way:

> One could look at my artistic biography and conclude that I am a nomad. Even were I to see myself this way, I would emphasize that, contrary to popular opinion, nomads are not detached from their terrain, but in fact try continuously to affix themselves to it, and must know the characteristics of the terrain well in order to be able to do so. In many instances, they know it better than native residents. After saying this, I must admit that I may indeed be a nomad, since the meaning of each of my projects is strongly grounded in its specific terrain, which in each case I have attempted to approach with the attitude of usefulness, and to leave with a judgmental contribution. This survival tactic is similar to the one used by all those who are displaced and who assume the tricky mission and function of a magician, critic, and soothsayer.
>
> (1999: xi)

Enhanced in various ways by means of technology, Wodiczko's projects are urban and site-specific, exploring the idea of the city as a place to probe the limits and possibilities of democracy. In the *Xenology*[2] project, as in the case of *Homeless Vehicles*, Wodiczko utilizes the idea of the city as a meeting place and performance as a means of disrupting the everyday life and aesthetic of the place to foster a democratic process of inclusion. Similarly to the philosopher Georgio Agamben, for Wodiczko democracy is measured by its capacity to accept and accommodate strangers.

Like the Situationists interventions, Wodiczko's projects aim to disrupt the routine perception of everyday life in the city and are, thus, highly context specific.[3] The case studies that will be explored here are strongly embedded in New York City and the ambiguities of America as a social, political, and cultural site. Wodiczko's work on homelessness, including both his projections (*Homeless Projections*) and his vehicles (*Homeless Vehicles*), is related to the issues of the urban development of New York. These projects, often pointing to the link between luxury housing and gentrification of certain areas such as the Washington Square Park in the 1980s, on the one side, and the growing problem of homelessness, on the other, laid bare the strategy of the city planners to merely remove the homeless people from view. The *Alien Staff* project, a part of the*Xenology* series, took place in a number of North American and European cities, but it was deliberately altered for its performance in New York. The "alien staff" is a multi-purpose walking stick of futuristic design, enhanced with a camera. The first model of the alien staff was created and performed in Barcelona in 1993, but as Wodiczko confessed, it had to be adapted when transferred to New York:

> This version, with the vertically oriented screen of the "xenoscopo" (the top or crook section of the Alien Staff) for a closer view of the owners face, is made of stainless steel to look more powerful and respectable in the New York context.
>
> (1999: 105)

This new version has been created not only to improve the prop and to enhance its performative and its critical potential, but also to ensure its visibility in the city of "spectacle"[4] and confront its culture of disengagement, which the sociologist Richard Sennett has openly lamented:

> New York should be the ideal city of exposure [...] a city of difference par excellence [...] collecting its population from all over the world [...] By walking in New York one is immersed in [...] differences [...] but precisely because the scenes are disengaged they seem unlikely

to offer themselves as significant encounters [...] The leather fetishist and the spice merchant are protected by disengagement [...] social classes, who mix but do not socialize.

(128)

The alien staff, like other high-tech objects of the *Xenology* project, highlights the Otherness of the person who holds it, but also prompts curiosity as a first step towards the possibility for a "significant encounter" between strangers. Wodiczko's projects explore the difference, make the habitual spectacle of multicultural divergence provocative, and show the face of the Other in an unpredictable way. They defamiliarize and make visible a performance inherent in the everyday life of the immigrant and the homeless in their encounters with the social environment. Hence the aesthetic and political strategy of making the familiar strange emerges as the key feature of Wodiczko's projects.

The two most famous concepts of making the familiar strange that were formulated in the modernist context – by the Russian Formalist scholar Viktor Shklovsky, who in 1917 coined the term *ostranenie* (estrangement) to name the art of making the well-known seen as if for the first time, and a few years later by Bertolt Brecht – are based on exilic aspects. Both Shklovsky and Brecht had first-hand experience of exile – the former spent a few difficult years in Berlin after the October Revolution, while the latter fled from Nazi Germany, first to Finland, then to the United States. Although both authors had written about estrangement as an artistic and ethical strategy before their actual experience of exile, their own exile further shaped their views and their writings on estrangement. At the heart of the concept is the perspective of the stranger not only to a particular place, but also to him- or herself. This enables the stranger to see the world around him/her differently and to defamiliarize his/her own story. The other component of the concept, that exilic dimensions and experiences can only enhance, is the strategy of uprooting – of deliberately showing something or someone outside their habitual context to subvert stock response and to *de-automatize* (Shklovsky) our perception. Thus, the concept of making the familiar strange relies on adopting an immigrant perspective, of seeing the world from the margin, from the border, from a place of political, cultural, and linguistic in-between-ness.

Wodiczko's projects use strategies close to *Verfremdung* and *ostranenie*, by displacing the modernist devices of theatrical estrangement into a performance context of site-specificity, technology, and contemporary exile. I will explore three distinct, yet related aspects of defamiliarization strategies embodied and, of course, modified in Wodiczko's estrangement of New York's urban and social landscape:

1. *Acting Beside the Role* as a device used in the *Alien Staff* project to disrupt the predictable inter-subjective exchanges in encounters among strangers.
2. *Contrast and juxtaposition* employed in *Homeless Vehicles* and *Projections* to estrange and upset the relationship between person and architectural environment.
3. *Perspectival estrangement* that enables a view of the iconic American metropolis from the margin.

Acting beside the role: estrangement as a tactic of impression management

Wodiczko's projects echo various dimensions of estrangement not only in the way they employ *Verfremdung/ ostranenie* strategies as performance devices, but also because they highlight the direct relationship between the aesthetic of estrangement and immigrant experience. The props Wodiczko has invented, such as the *Alien Staff* walking stick, are both an embodiment of exilic metaphors and a practical device that prompts communication and eventually, de-objectifies the Other. At the top of the walking stick there is a video monitor and a loudspeaker, the video shows the speaking face of the performer who tells a story of his/her past. The bottom part of the stick is a container where various relics of the immigrant's past are stored, such as rejected visa applications, immigration and legal documents, apartment keys, old photographs, and various identity cards acquired by the owner. The prop is designed to counteract the automatism of the perception, which Shklovsky has diagnosed as deadening – it "devours works, clothes, furniture, one's wife, and the fear of war" (12). One cannot carry the walking stick without feeling self-conscious. Likewise, one cannot look at or communicate in a usual, disinterested way with a person bearing these objects, which is often the case with other random, quotidian encounters between strangers. These odd objects in familiar surroundings assert and expose the stranger, but they also destabilize the gaze of the beholder.

However, the strategies of estrangement shape Wodiczko's projects further through ways in which his technological props are operated. The *Alien Staff* project, for instance, is based on a *Verfremdung* strategy very close to Brecht's notion of acting beside the role, where the performer does not merge with the character, but steps in and out of the role, commenting on it and maintaining critical distance. As in the case with Brechtian *Verfremdung* in acting, in *Alien Staff* too, the distance between the signifier and the signified is fully revealed. Part of this semiotics stems from the everyday performance of exilic identity. The immigrant is the one forced to retell his/her story, facing over and over again the same questions from the hosts: Where are you from? What made you come here? How was it living under oppression? Most of these questions reiterate preconceptions more than they prompt a meaningful exchange and encounter. Wodiczko's prop opens the possibility for the exilic story to be told dialectically in an interactive process, where the listener's stock responses are subverted. The performer is invited to actively relate to his/her pre-recorded story, to comment on it, to complete it, or to challenge it – even to make it different, if he/she wishes so, in every new encounter with random strangers. Wodiczko writes that "through prerecorded video broadcast and live narration, these accounts of the immigrant past are recalled in the face of the immigrant present and become an art of critical history and a critical vision of the future" (1999: 105). While in the case of Brecht's practice of acting beside the role, the split is between the performer and the character, in the performance of *Alien Staff*, the split is between different versions of one singular identity.

Brecht's *Verfremdung* involves laying bare the actor's devices to emphasize that the character played is in fact a different entity – a stranger to the performer. In *Alien Staff*, the strategy of acting beside the role reveals the stranger in the past identities of the performer whom he/she approaches with critical distance. This goes back to Freud, who, according to Julia Kristeva, "teaches us how to detect foreignness in ourselves" (191), to remind us that the familiar is always "potentially tainted with strangenes." (183). The function of the alien staff is to divert the focus of the beholder from the stranger to the strange object. The strangeness of the object would take the gaze away from the stranger, thus de-objectifying the person and opening communication channels between the host and the stranger. Through this intermediate object, Wodiczko hopes, people on both sides of this performative interlocution will come to terms with their own strangeness.

The high-tech prop becomes an extension of the performer's body,[5] a mnemonic device, and a way of empowering strangers to navigate through uncanny landscapes. Moreover, the alien staff determines the social *gestus* of this street performance. In the context of Brecht's practice and theory, *gestus* is both a gesture and the gist of the character. In other words, the alien staff in the hands of an immigrant walking the streets of New York is the main catalyst for the action and its social commentary.

"Gestus is in my own vision" (96), writes Roland Barthes, stressing that the notion is less about the action, and more about the attitude of the one performing. In Brecht's theatre, *gestus* is a strategy of leading the spectator and controlling the reception process – of securing the right interpretation of the performative gesture. Similarly, Wodiczko's estrangement devices are also the performer's means of controlling the reception – of shaping the gaze of the beholder, rather than allowing reception to be shaped through it.

In a way, Wodiczko's alien staff is the immigrant's prop for "impression management". "Impression management" – the key term in Erving Goffman's seminal book *The Presence of Self in Everyday Life* – describes the way in which an individual guides and controls the ideas that others form of him. Goffman, however, talks about impression management as a strategy of social performance, through which one avoids faux pas, embarrassments, and misunderstandings. The success of impression management depends on knowing and following the codes, on playing out scenarios of social conduct with skill and versatility. In other words, the success of impression management depends on the capacity of the subject to meet the expectations of other participants in the scenario. Wodiczko's *Alien Staff* is the opposite of this kind of social performance, since the strategies of impression management in this case are based on estrangement devices such as acting beside the role and *gestus*. The key to impression management in *Alien Staff* is not to meet expectations, but to subvert them in order to disable stock responses in the communication process.

However, this kind of impression management is often not possible, or at least not practical, in the exilic quotidian. Within the legal system, as in performance art, the exile is required to select, condense, and pitch his/her experience so that it comes across as convincing and valid. It is not only a matter of *being* an asylum seeker, a refugee or an immigrant, but also of *performing* accordingly in order not to be rendered bogus. Impression management as a strategy of meeting the expectations on the other end of the interlocution, of performing the scenario competently, could be a determining factor in the process of legalizing one's immigrant status or landing a job. In that sense, Wodiczko's project takes the immigrant performer out of his/her everyday social and communicational patterns. The alien staff becomes the instrument that empowers the performer to temporarily subvert the scenario of the exilic quotidian.

In this exilic context, "impression management" is also about translating one's individual story from one socio-cultural context to the other – about sharing experiences among strangers that hitherto could

Figure 11.1   Alien Staff, 1992–95 © Krzysztof Wodiczko. Courtesy Galerie Lelong, New York.

not be shared. "Impression management" is a performance, but it is inherently also a desire to communicate. Wodiczko talks about one of the participants in the *Alien Staff,* Polish immigrant Jadwiga Przybylak, whose usage of the alien staff turned into a kind of "impression management" that has secured her better communication in her new environment:

> When Jadwiga took the Alien Staff to the New York Institute of Technology, she decided bravely to present herself as an immigrant and not as a professor. And most of her students are Long Island children of immigrants. Somehow, electrified or hypnotized by her presence with this Alien Staff, they suddenly felt the desire to see their parents. They recognized something similar between her and their parents, something they never really understood.
>
> The students completely changed their normal seating positions in relation to her. They created a different space in the classroom. And she thinks that they respected her afterwards much more.

> (1998: 147)

Walking around with the alien staff (Figure 11.1) as an impression management strategy is a way of finding a language for sharing disrupted immigrant narratives, while attempting to prevent the romanticizing of exile and the exoticizing of the Other. The alienation and Othering of the self, manifested in cultural stereotypes, is but a loss of control over the gaze of the beholder – a kind of impression management gridlock.

Counteracting invisibility: strategies of contrast and juxtaposition

> Why are you afraid of living in the park, children? Our park it's the best park in the city. The only ideal location, if you plan to stay in Manhattan, of course.
>
> (Glowacki: 106)

In the play *Hunting Cockroaches*, mentioned in the introduction to this volume, Janusz Glowacki's Polish immigrants, jobless and confined in their cockroach infested apartment in New York's infamous Alphabet city, encounter a homeless man from their neighborhood only to realize that they share the same predicament. However, Glowacki is not alone in drawing parallels between the experiences of exile and homelessness. Theorist Rosalyn Deutsche uses the term refugee to describe the position of the homeless in New York:

> Since, under capitalism, land and housing are commodities to be exploited for profit, the marginalization of large number of workers engendered a loss of housing for the poor as New York devoted more space for profit-maximizing real-estate development – high-rent office towers, luxury condominiums, corporate headquarters – that also provided the physical conditions to meet the needs of the new economy. Today's homeless, therefore, are refugees from evictions, secondary and exclusionary displacement – the conversion of their neighborhoods into areas they can no longer afford.
>
> (54)

Wodiczko's work treats the issue of homelessness as a form of internal exile and it is deeply imbedded in very specific socio-political problems of urban planning and gentrification. This form of exile emerges by way of denying the homeless inhabitants of New York the right to the city. As Deutsche suggests, Wodiczko's work might be read "as a symbolic declaration of new rights – for homeless people" (42).

While in *Alien Staff* defamiliarization strategies politicized the encounters between strangers on an inter-subjective level, the projects about homelessness make the familiar tourist images and vistas of New York strange by foregrounding, in an almost Brechtian fashion, the contrasts and contradictions of the urban environment. In his notes on *Dulle Griet*, the painting of the Elder Brueghel, Brecht writes about contrast as an estrangement device:

> In the war painting *Dulle Griet* it isn't the war's atmosphere of terror that inspires the artist to paint the instigator, the Fury of War, as help-less and handicapped, and to give her the features of a servant. The terror that he creates in this way is something deeper. Whenever an Alpine peak is set down in a Flemish landscape or old Asiatic costumes confront modern European ones, then the one denounces the other and sets off its oddness, while at the same time we get the landscape as such, people all over the place. Such pictures don't just give off an atmosphere but a variety of atmospheres. Even though Brueghel man-ages to balance his contrasts he never merges them into one another, nor does he practice the separation of comic and tragic; his tragedy contains a comic element and his comedy a tragic one.
>
> (157)

In Wodiczko's projects, too, a "variety of atmospheres" reveals the city as a socio-political palimpsest (*Homeless Projections*) and as a heterotopic space (*Homeless Vehicles*), while the comic element, emerging through estrangement devices of contrast and juxtaposition oscillates between the uncanny strangeness of the grotesque and the sharpness of political satire.

The *Homeless Projection: A Proposal for the City of New York* came to being as a direct reaction to the gentrification and "cleansing" of the Union Square Park in the 1980s. The park and the surrounding area under-went significant changes and restorations when a powerful New York real-estate company, Zackendorf, bought a near-by city block occupied by an abandoned department store. The company intended to develop a luxury complex of residential and commercial properties, which went hand-in-hand with the city's plan to restore the park. The restoration of the park included significant changes in its physical appearance includ-ing reducing the walkways from six to two, removing some of the trees and walls, getting rid of secluded spots – in short, the park was made more accessible for surveillance. Due to this redevelopment, the park, as well as the abandoned buildings in the neighborhood, were no longer habitable for its homeless residents. The city and its big businesses joined forces to make the neighborhood appealing and comfortable for high-income residents of the city. In his comments to *The Homeless Projection* project Wodiczko proposes to read architecture critically – not as a set of permanent structure but as a social system:

> Mimicking and embodying a corporate moral detachment, today's "architecture" reveals its inherent cynicism through its ruthless expansionism. What has been defined as architecture is really, then, a merciless real-estate system, embodied in a continuous and frightening mass-scale event, the most disturbingly public and central operations of which are economic, physical eviction, and the exodus of the poorest groups of city inhabitants from the buildings' interiors to the outside.
>
> (1999: 55)

The monuments in Union Square feature the statues of historical figures both domestic and foreign that shaped America as a democratic state, including the statue of Abraham Lincoln, the Lafayette monument, and the well-known statue of George Washington. These monuments celebrate the late eighteenth-century revolution and the individual freedoms – "the rights of men" – guaranteed under the Constitution.

In *The Homeless Projection: A Proposal for the City of New York*, Wodiczko superimposed the images of homelessness and trivial objects, such as a shopping cart, wheelchair, a bottle of Windex, on the park's neoclassical monuments. An image of an open palm, as if begging, is projected onto the Mother and Child Fountain, George Washington rides on his mighty horse with a can of Windex and a cloth in his hand, the dignified Abraham Lincoln statue is now supported by crutches (Figure 11.2), and so on. As in the paintings of the Elder Breughel that Brecht describes, Wodiczko's contrasting imagery is never amalgamated; rather, it functions in a similar way to yet another defamiliarization technique – Sergei Eisenstein's montage of attractions, which is not about a sum-total of contrasting images, but a specific kind of representation of the theme through montage sequences. Yet unlike Eisenstein's montage, where the juxtapositions establish meaning through metaphors, Wodiczko's montage of attraction is metonymic in its reliance on iconic and gestic imagery. In this way, as Deutsche comments, the statues, "in their altered state, are forced to acknowledge their own contradictions and repressions" (42).

The Homeless Projection evokes both the comic and the disturbing dimensions of grotesque estrangement, which is further reinforced in

Figure 11.2   Homeless Projections: A Proposal for Union Square, 1986 ©Krzysztof Wodiczko. Courtesy Galerie Lelong, New York.

Wodiczko's proposal for a new type of city monument – the homeless:

> The surface of *the homeless* – over- or underdressed, unwashed, cracked from permanent outdoor exposure, and posing in their frozen, "classic" gesture – weather and resemble the official monuments of the city. The *homeless* appear more dramatic than even the most colossal and expressive urban sculptures, memorials, or public buildings, however, for there is nothing more disruptive and astonishing in a monument than a sign of life. To the observer the slightest sign of life in the homeless is a living sign of the possibility of the death of the homeless from homelessness.
>
> (1999: 55)

Freud uses the term uncanny (*unheimlich*) to describe the grotesque as a category of estrangement which leads back to what is known as familiar. The term *unheimlich* is an aporia since the word home (*Heim*) is hidden in it. *Unheimlich* – derived from *Heimlich* (hidden, secluded) – also means uprooted. The grotesque uproots (decontextualizes) the familiar from its customary context, often exposing that which is hidden or repressed. As in Molière's *Don Juan*, through Wodiczko's projections, the statues come to life and the live body turns into a statue, producing the effect of uncanny strangeness.

Robert Musil wrote: "The most striking feature of the monuments is that you do not notice them. There is nothing in the world as invisible as a monument" (quoted in Tompkins, 44). Wodiczko's project not only makes the Union Squire monuments and their symbolism visible again, but also reveals the socio-political contradictions that they represent. In other words, he ensures that the monuments are not only seen, but that they are seen anew and that their meaning is not fixed – that what the monuments stand for is never taken for granted. In his writing on the site-specific art of Wodiczko, Nick Kaye points out:

> Inscribing on the monument that which it hides or silences, Wodiczko unveils the complexity of its architectural, ideological or political subtexts, complicating a reading of the city's signs.
>
> (34)

The projections, by introducing a foreign element into the structure, defamiliarize the monuments – erected in celebration of democracy and the "rights of man" – to reveal those whose rights have been ignored and denied in the name of historic preservation and urban development.

Wodiczko's *Homeless Vehicle* project is also about new ways of seeing a familiar social reality, yet the strategies of contrasts and juxtapositions are not inherent qualities of the work; rather, they unfold in the performance process – in the act of homeless people walking the streets of New York. A photo from the *Homeless Vehicle* project captures a nicely dressed woman and a homeless man – pushing Wodiczko's futuristically designed homeless vehicle – as they walk on the Fifth Avenue, passing Trump Tower. The *homeless vehicle* is the technologically enhanced shopping cart that stores all the homeless person's belongings and can be extended into a narrow sleeping compartment. The vehicle is created in collaboration with the homeless and it is, in the first place, an ironic commentary on social programs aimed to assist homeless people. The constellation of the figures in the photo – including both human bodies and objects – makes us acutely aware of the enormous contrast between

Figure 11.3   Homeless Vehicle, 1988–89 © Krzysztof Wodiczko. Courtesy Galerie Lelong, New York.

the realm of capitalist excess that the shiny façade of the Trump Tower represents, the world of security and upper middle-class comfort that seems to be where the figure of the woman belongs, and the minimalism of bare-bones existence on the social margin, where everything that a person owns fits in one shopping cart (albeit of somewhat improved design). Should the shopping cart be an ordinary one, this street scene would not elicit much attention, since the stark social contrast and the highly problematic urban reality that it reveals would have been absorbed by the everyday spectacle of the city. It would have been nothing but a common New York street scene of habitualized social contradictions. By turning a shopping cart into a "homeless vehicle" Wodiczko has framed the scene and made the invisible visible again. Through this performative action, the well-known city avenue and its landmark building, known even to those who have never been in New York, becomes a heterotopia. Michel Foucault points out that the heterotopia has "the power of juxtaposing in a single real place different spaces and locations that are incompatible with each other (354). The image of the homeless man pushing a strange-looking shopping cart (Figure 11.3), like the *Homeless Projections* on neoclassical monuments of the Union Square park, invokes into the centre of the city a consciousness of the margin, of "other" places hidden from the view, forcing us to look closer into an everyday environment that we had previously taken for granted.

America: the view from above and the look from below

There seem to be two kinds of 'America' in Wodiczko's discourse and practice that are best described under his own headings as the "city of the victors" and the "city of the vanquished". In his essay "Designing for the City of Strangers", Wodiczko draws from Benjamin's concept of the history of the victors, when he writes the following:

> I recognize this kind of history as a foundation or cement that stabilizes the continuity of the "legitimate" and the "familiar" city. The history of the victors, the official presence of the official past, constitutes the *official* city. [...] Such a history (as represented in textbooks, national literature, films, and public monuments) cherishes a notion of progress that, according to Benjamin, is inevitably linked to a legacy of destruction.
>
> (1999: 4)

The other side of the coin – the "city of the vanquished" – not only subverts the selective memory of the victors, reminding them of the catastrophes that paved the way to triumph, but has the potential to confront the history of the victors, revealing a scenario for an alternative narrative. The immigrant and the homeless emerge as central figures to stage this intervention and to assert the tradition of the vanquished. Wodiczko, who finds that the stranger functions as a contemporary version of a prophet or messenger in healing the city, writes the following:

> With the official account of the population of refugees soon to reach 40,000,000, the United Nations has called the last quarter-century the "Migration Era." The influx of immigrants to the United States has now reached the historic levels of the nineteenth-century immigration wave. By the year 2010, foreign-born residents and citizens will probably outnumber U.S.-born inhabitants in most American cities. By then, these cities will undoubtedly be the sites of the greatest challenges and hopes for democracy in the United States.
>
> Historically, the city has always been a hope for the displaced. And today, as it was in the past, our cities are worth nothing and will be condemned to destruction if they cannot open themselves to strangers.
>
> (1999: 6)

Wodiczko's notions of the "city of the victors" and the "city of the van-quished" highlight the contrasts inherent in the urban landscape of the metropolis. This is often epitomized in the architectural configuration of the place symbolically represented through the contrast between the castle and the marketplace, which reveals the structures of power and the potential sites of subversion. In the iconography of a contemporary North American metropolis this configuration is embodied, on the one side, in the images of skyscrapers – the ivory towers of capitalism – that offer a view from above, from the heights of the power structure. On the other, is the bustling street, where everything is seen and experienced from ground level and where both the 'victors' and the 'vanquished' maneuver and occasionally must brush shoulders.

Benjamin and Brecht both engaged with these contrasting view-points – the perspective from above and the view from below – but they interpreted them somewhat differently. In Wodiczko's notion of the "city of the victors" and the "city of the vanquished" there are traces of Benjamin's contemplations and elements of Brecht's strategies. Benjamin problematizes the view from above – which is visual – as opposed to the view from the street – which is tactile – when he writes in "One-Way Street":

> The airplane passenger sees only how the road pushes through the landscape, how it unfolds according to the same laws as the terrain surrounding it. Only he who walks the road on foot learns of the power it commands, and of how, from the very scenery [...] it calls forth distances, belvederes, clearings, prospects at each of its turns like a commander deploying soldiers at a front.
>
> (1999: 50)

Wodiczko's 'performers' are immigrants and homeless people who uti-lize the art of walking the city as a strategy of confronting the colonial gaze that has been cast upon them. Wodiczko's projects such as *Alien Staff* and the *Homeless Vehicle* exploit the view from the street and the tactile nature of walking to subvert symbolic distances in the architec-tural layout of power and to offer a new insight into the socio-political contradictions of the urban landscape. Yet Benjamin makes it clear that it is not a particular perspective he favors, but ways in which a certain perspective invokes estrangement between person and his/her surrounding.

However, the notion of estrangement that Wodiczko is after is more epistemological and focused on a political goal than that described by Benjamin. In that sense, the view from below and the look from above as estrangement perspectives come close to Brecht's approach as a means not only of new ways of seeing, but also as a way of politically contextualizing the figure who performs the viewing. The look from below sees the world from the margins of the power structure; while the look from above is not necessarily the view from the penthouse of the Trump Tower, rather it is the perspective of intellectual independence regardless of the onlooker's position in the social hierarchy.[6] This approach allows for transgressions, and Wodiczko's gadgets to aid the strangers and the displaced are aimed exactly at such transgressions, which he finds necessary for the building of community:

> The community can only be legitimate when it questions its own legitimacy. This is certainly true in a co-called community of city inhabitants. New York as a community has to question itself immediately. "We New Yorkers." The homeless people can define what they mean by being New Yorkers, and this does not correspond to the others.
>
> (Wodiczko 1998: 146)

The act of walking with the *alien staff* or pushing the *homeless vehicle* is not only an assertion of a hitherto socially marginal presence and view, but also a statement, an intervention, a gesture and a social *gestus* of intellectual independence.

In Wodiczko's approach to America there is a mixture of radical critique and irony, on the one side, and a belief that artistic practices could foster a better social arrangement, on the other. Thus, America appears as a performance space where the possibilities of a new community can be exercised:

> The city operates as a monumental stage and a script in the theatre of our way of life, perpetuating our preconceived and outdated notions of identity and community, preserving the way we relate to each other, the way we perceive others and ourselves. [...] Media art, performance art, performative design: they must interfere with these everyday aesthetics if they wish to contribute ethically to a democratic process.
>
> (2000: 88)

The city here emerges as a Thirdspace possibility that Edward Soja, taking his cue from both Foucault and Henri Lefebvre, defines as a "strategic meeting place for fostering collective political action against all forms of human oppression" (22), and also as a "distinctive way of looking at, interpreting, and acting to change the spatiality of human life". (21) *Thirdspace* is an open and inclusive space of action and intervention.

Wodiczko described a moment when the immigrants in one of the *Alien Staff* happenings encountered other immigrants, and got so much into conversation that they ended up in a café. The walking sticks were left to lean against the wall, as the immigrants exchanged stories, tips, strategies, legal and job advice. Out of this random encounter a network, a community of immigrants started to emerge. The *Thirdspace* is also a site where a utopian performative takes place. Jill Dolan describes her concept of the utopian performative as a "fleeting contact with a utopia" (165). Dolan's utopian performative is heterotopic in nature – not perfect, but realizable – and it comes with an expiration date. In Wodiczko's urban interventions the utopian performative emerges within the city as a Thirdspace strongly linked to fostering new communal relations. Thus the notion of utopian performative goes beyond its emotional affect, even beyond its political resonances, turning into a spatial and social practice of everyday life and becoming an interventionist strategy.

Wodiczko's 'America' oscillates between two common visions of the place. On the one hand, 'America' emerges as a problem place – a *geopathology* that "unfolds as an incessant dialogue between belonging and exile, home and homelessness." (Chaudhuri: 15). On the other hand, it is a site of possibility and intervention. This is, however, not so different from more traditionally experiential and imaginary takes on the exilic 'America'. Yet it diverts from others in its emphasis on the city not as an object, but as "an environment formed by the interaction and integration of different practices" (Ledrut: 122) – a paradoxical megalopolis that swallows but also has the potential to sustain strangers. Wodiczko's exilic 'America' is not so much about a nation or a state, it operates on a rather smaller scale – a street, a neighborhood, a site where critical intervention through performance is still possible.

Notes

1. The research for this chapter was in part enabled by an AHRC small research grant. The author would also like to thank Lisa Fitzpatrick, Milija Gluhovic, and Yana Meerzon for their input and feedback on this chapter.
2. Wodiczko describes his neologism *Xenology* as the science of strangers and describes it in the following way: "By xenology I mean a field of knowledge which also connects with the fields of experience. The field of historical intuition or present intuition. I want to propose an existential knowledge combined with live practice. A struggle of displacement" (1998: 142).
3. The Situationists (1957–72), who emerged in France as an avant-garde movement, had their roots in surrealism, but gradually became radically political in

their critique of Western bourgeois society. Wodiczko's work has some aspects in common with the Situationists – from the somewhat surreal effect his hi-tech gadgets and projections make on the habitualized environment to his overt political commitment. More specifically, Wodiczko's projects like *Alien Staff* and *Homeless Vehicles* embody to some extent one of the main concepts of the Situationists – Guy Debord's notion of *dérive* which Michel de Certeau describes as "a calculated action determined by the absence of a proper locus" (36–7).

4. I am again alluding here to the Situationists and Guy Debord's seminal book *The Society of Spectacle*. Debord was not denying that the city of power and capital was seductive, even fascinating, yet he also insisted that "the spectacle was merely a manufactured wonderment, a hype that concealed real processes of exploitation" (Sadler: 17)

5. In his exploration of otherness and encounters among strangers, Wodiczko has been using various versions of technological gadgets attached to the body that have served both as metaphors and as estrangement devices.

6. Darko Suvin recognizes two basic perspectives in Brecht's epic dramaturgy: the view from below, which sees the world from the margins of the power structure; and the look from above, which is the position of intellectual and ethical independence:

> The view from below is the anarchistic, humorous "Schweyk look" of plebeian tradition; it is inherent in the stance, which Brecht's (and Hašek's) Good Soldier assumes in facing the world. Its richness streams from a constant juxtaposition of the official and the real, the sentimental and the naïve, the ideological and the practical. Figures like Azdak are obvious protagonists of this comic look. The view from above, on the other hand, is the rationalist "Diderot look" of intellectual tradition; it is inherent in the stance, which the author of *Jacques the Fatalist* (or *Candide*, or of *The Persian Letters*) assumes in facing the world. It critically illuminates the most intimate structures of bourgeois life and art.
>
> (124)

Works cited

Barthes, Roland. "Diderot, Brecht, Eisenstein". In *The Responsibility of Forms: Critical Essays on Music, Art and Representation*. Trans. R. Howard, Berkley: University of California Press, 1985, pp. 89–9.

Benjamin, Walter. *One-Way Street*. Trans. E. Jephcott and K. Shorter. London: Verso, 1979.

Brecht, Bertolt. *Brecht On Theatre: The Development of an Aesthetic*. Ed. and trans. John Willett. London: Methuen Drama, 1990.

Certeau, Michel de. *The Practice of Everyday Life*. Trans. Steven Rendell. Berkeley: University of California Press, 1984.

Chaudhuri, Una. *Staging Place: The Geography of Modern Drama*. Ann Arbor: University of Michigan Press, 1997.

Deutsche, Rosalyn. *Evictions: Art and Spatial Politics*. Cambridge, MA: MIT Press, 1996.

Dolan, Jill. "Utopia in Performance", *Theatre Research International* 31 (2004): 163–73.

Foucault, Michel. "Of Other Spaces: Utopias and Heterotopias". In *Rethinking Architecture: A Reader in Cultural Theory*. Ed. Neil Leach. London: Routledge, 1997, pp. 350–6.

Freud, Sigmund. "The Uncanny". In *The Standard Edition of the Complete Psychological Works of Sigmund Freud*, vol. XVII. Trans. James Strachey. London: The Hogarth Press and The Institute of Psycho-Analysis, 1955, pp. 217–57.

Glowacki, Janusz. *Hunting Cockroaches and Other Plays*. Evanstone, IL: Northwestern University Press, 1990.

Goffman, Erving. *The Presentation of Self in Everyday Life*. London: Penguin, 1990.

Kaye, Nick. *Site-Specific Art: Performance, Place and Documentation*. London: Routledge, 2000.

Kristeva, Julia. *Strangers to Ourselves*. Trans. Leon S. Roudiez. New York: Columbia University Press, 1991.

Ledrut, Raymond. "Speech and the Silence of the City". In *The City and the Sign: An Introduction to Urban Semiotics*. Ed. M. Gottdeiner and Alexandros Ph. Lagopoulos. New York: Columbia University Press, 1986, p. 122.

Sadler, Simon. *The Situationist City*. Cambridge, MA: The MIT Press, 2001.

Sennett, Richard. *Conscience of the Eye: The Design and Social Life of Cities*. New York: Norton, 1990.

Shklovsky, Viktor. "Isskustvo kak priëm" ("Art as Device"). In *Texte Der Russischen Formalisten*. Ed. J. Striedter. München: Wilhem Fink Verlag, 1969, pp. 2–36.

Soja, Edward. "Thirdspace: Expanding the Scope of the Geographical Imagination". In *Architecturally Speaking: Practices of Art, Architecture and the Everyday*. Ed. Alan Read. London: Routledge, 2000, pp. 13–31.

Suvin, Darko. *To Brecht and Beyond: Soundings in Modern Dramaturgy*. New Jersey: Barnes & Noble, 1984.

Tompkins, Joanne. *Unsettling Space*. Basingstoke and New York, Palgrave, 2006.

Wodiczko, Kryzstof. "Open Transmission". In *Architecturally Speaking: Practices of Art, Architecture and the Everyday*. Ed. Alan Read. London: Routledge, 2000, pp. 87–109.

———. *Critical Vehicles: Writings, Projects, Interviews*. Cambridge, MA: The MIT Press, 1999.

———. "The Science of Strangers". In *Open City: Alphabet City*, no. 6. Toronto: House of Anansi Press, 1998, pp. 134–48.

Index